THE FILTH

D1241955

THE FILTH

The Explosive Inside Story of Scotland Yard's Top Undercover Cop

DUNCAN MacLAUGHLIN

WITH WILLIAM HALL

MAINSTREAM
PUBLISHING

EDINBURGH AND LONDON

For Ashley, Sara and Anna

Reprinted 2007

First published in Great Britain in 2002 by
MAINSTREAM PUBLISHING COMPANY (EDINBURGH) LTD
7 Albany Street
Edinburgh EH1 3UG

ISBN 9781840186697

Reprinted 2003, 2004, 2005, 2006

A catalogue record for this book is available from the British Library

Printed and bound in Great Britain by
Cox & Wyman Ltd, Reading

Oxford English Dictionary definition:

Filth - *n*: disgusting dirt, stagnant pools of filth. Obscene and offensive language or printed material. Corrupt behaviour; decadence. - Used as a term of abuse for a person or people one greatly despises: Nazi filth. *n* (as a plural noun) (the filth) Brit. informal, derogatory the police.

Police/Underworld definition:

Filth – The Criminal Investigation Department, a Detective.

CONTENTS

ACKNOWLEDGEMENTS

I would like to thank Stephanie De-Sykes and Valery MacDonald, who realised there was a story to tell and introduced me to the literary agent Andrew Lownie, whose faith in the project never wavered.

In particular my appreciation goes to William Hall, without whose experience and professionalism in collating the vast amount of material and assisting me in its writing, this book would not have been possible. He showed me the way from base camp to summit.

Special thanks go to Jill and Alex for their continuous love, support and patience during the preparation of my story.

And finally to Cindy, my American enigma. For being there.

FOREWORD

The appetite for adventure. What makes one person seek out excitement and danger while others are content to sit back and let the world roll on by with only a passing nod, until maybe one day events take a hand and they are dragged unwillingly into that other world of violence and crime? I wondered about this from time to time, and still do after a lifetime of mixing with the good guys and the bad guys on opposite sides of the street, the lawmakers and the lawbreakers. The men and women who ensure you sleep safely in your beds at night, and those others who would rather disturb it, the shadowy, unpleasant figures that walk on the dark side of the street.

I never set out on a crusade against crime. It just looks that way. I was never squeaky clean either, and make no pretence otherwise. All I wanted was to be a detective, nick villains and put them away for a long time. I did this with some success, earning myself a number of gratifyingly impressive awards in the process. But mingling with the criminal fraternity, becoming one of them as an undercover cop, handling both sides of the coin, you can't help but become a little tarnished yourself. I know I couldn't.

So, no excuses and no apologies. Take me as I am. And if this book lifts the lid on a side of the police force that may not seem as acceptable as it should, well – that's the way it was, and that's the way, I suspect, it still is today. Most of the coppers I worked with at street level are ace guys, and we'd risk our right arms and sometimes our lives for each other. You'll always get a few rotten apples in the basket. Some are more rotten than others. But most coppers – well, like me, let's just say they're a bit bruised.

Duncan MacLaughlin

PART ONE

ONE

EARLY DAYS

Maybe I got it from my father. Not my real one, because I never knew who he was. But the Action Man father who was a true hero, won the George Medal for it and was an abiding influence on my life from the moment I came into his.

Actually, I came into the world as a Celt and ended up a Cockney. This may sound illogical, as Mr Spock would say, but that's the way it happened. I was born on 23 March 1960 in the London Hospital in the East End, within the sound of Bow Bells, which makes me a true Cockney by birth. But my natural mother, Anastasia Kelly, already had children back home in Ireland. And abortion being a bit of a taboo subject in the Emerald Isle, she came over to Britain so that I could be delivered – and farmed out. Within eight weeks of my first yell I had a new mum, Margaret MacLaughlin, who together with her husband Rick was later to adopt me.

So instead of County Waterford my first home turned out to be in Rochester, Kent, close to the Chatham Naval Dockyard where my new dad was serving in the medical branch of the Royal Navy.

My first real memory was being taken up to London at the age of two to collect baby Amanda from an adoption agency. She was a tiny dark-haired bundle dressed all in white, and we brought her home in the battered old family car with a mixture of curiosity and pride. I had a little sister! In truth, though I never told anyone, I really wanted a cat.

My father came from distinguished military stock, even if the lineage was rather tenuous and had associations with the wrong side of the blanket. The family tree includes Lord Lovat of Fraser – the man who formed the Commandos in World War Two – and his cousin David Stirling, who founded the SAS. So you could say there was fighting blood in the family.

My father was expected to enrol at Royal Military Academy Sandhurst and follow the family tradition. But he stunned everyone by running away from home in his teens to join the Navy as a rating. He ended up a Chief Petty Officer.

Dad actually looked uncannily like that elegant actor Peter Lawford, who you may remember stomping up and down the beaches of Normandy in the epic 1962 movie *The Longest Day*, the one they always show on TV around D-Day. Lawford was fitted out in a white submariner's polo-necked sweater, green beret and stalking stick, and accompanied by his piper, all very natty. His role? Why, Lord Lovat! I always thought that stalking stick was a nice touch.

Years later, the media would hail my father as a hero when he was awarded the George Medal for gallantry after tangling with the IRA in a particularly nasty skirmish. Several historical books on the Marines would talk about his selflessness and courage, and you can find them on library shelves today. For me, his 'Number Two Son' as he always called me, I can add the footnote that my dad was the most honest and compassionate man I ever knew.

There's no doubt that the oxygen of adventure he breathed filled my young nostrils too. Dad was a rebel by nature – maybe that's where I acquired the same attitude – and swiftly became bored with shore hospitals. Instead he opted for something more challenging. After an early stint working with submariners, he volunteered for the Commandos and spent the rest of his career attached to the Marines.

It isn't generally known, but the Marines depend on volunteers from certain of the professions to swell their ranks. Doctors, dentists, teachers – even padres from all faiths – can be found wearing the coveted green beret on ceremonial occasions, the headgear which marks a man out as a Commando rather than a Royal Marine. And they have had to earn that precious headgear the hard way at the Commando Training Centre in Lympstone, Devon, home of the Royal Marines.

These guys, often into their thirties and despite the generation gap, are put through the mill just like the tough eager-beaver youngsters desperate to join the ranks of the elite. The 'mill' meaning the longest military training course in the world, a full twelve months of it: handling the most up-to-date weapons, map reading, yomping over hostile MOD countryside (okay, the term hadn't been invented then, but forced marches across a rainswept Dartmoor require the same stamina), jumping in and out of helicopters, abseiling down cliff faces, assault and survival techniques, all the way through to hand-to-hand combat.

So, as Dad remarked one day, if you don't like the sermon, it might be wise to keep your thoughts about the parson to yourself. 'You never know where that dog collar's been!' he said pointedly.

There was never any lack of volunteers. Someone worked out that in one period of ten years more than 50,000 men applied to join the Royal Marines. Some 4,250 were accepted for training. Around 2,500 of those managed to win themselves the Green Beret. My dad was one of them. He enlisted, won his spurs in 1965 at the ripe old age of 33, passed with flying colours and almost immediately found himself shipped off to the Far East with 42 Commando, where his tour was interrupted in 1967 by his unit being deployed to Aden to cover the British withdrawal.

This wasn't Dad's first trip to that part of the world. On a spring morning in 1963 he had picked us up one by one, given us all a hug, kissed Mum goodbye and set off down the garden path. With a final wave at the gate, he was gone. We didn't see him again for eighteen months.

We heard snippets of news from time to time. He was on board HMS *Messina*, giving support to the British troops on shore, including 45 Commando, the unit he was later to join. In Aden, 45 Commando found themselves exchanging unpleasantries with dissident tribesmen holding their piece of ground in the bare hills and boulder-strewn *wadis* of southern Arabia. Ostensibly they were there to combat the terrorists who were conducting a guerrilla war in the State of Aden, subversives employing the usual tactics of snipers, minefields and bomb outrages. Privately, the general feeling was that we were there to keep the locals from each other's throats while the politicians sorted it out. Either way, it wasn't a place to take your summer holidays with a deckchair and a knotted handkerchief.

In 1967, back amongst the sand and scrub as a paramedic with 42 Commando, my father found himself in the bizarre position of being on call to tend injured troops by day, while keeping his trigger finger busy during patrols through hostile territory at night.

42 Commando were based in the Radfan, a 400-square-mile wasteland of scrub and desert where every drop of water was precious, and as one military memo warned our troops: 'Every tribesman has been brought up from boyhood with a rifle in his hands, and knows how to use it.'

That was okay, because our boys did too.

Mum, held up well. Three kids kept her busy. My brother Ian, four years older than me, was my parents' natural child, born before Mum and Dad found out they had conflicting blood groups, in medical jargon – the 'rhesus factor', and were advised not to have any more offspring. That's when I came on the scene. Dad always labelled us affectionately 'Number One Son and Number Two Son', naval jargon he had learned below decks, no doubt.

Finally Dad came home from Aden, bronzed and fit, with stories he would tell much later when we were old enough, which kept Ian and me enthralled. They gave us a glimmer of what went on in the controversial 'withdrawal from Empire' that in 1967 finally closed the door on that godforsaken territory on the Yemen border.

Commandos had been on 'operational tours' there for seven years, and I don't think you'll find a single man who was sorry to leave. The conflict had been a cat-and-mouse game of patrols and ambushes, watching your back on dark nights, avoiding the snipers and the landmines. The mines laid by the bad guys, as I found out later, were of British origin (Mark V and Mark VII anti-tank mines), thus adding insult to often-serious injury. 'You know what they say about being caught between a rock and a hard place,' my father observed once. 'Well, I think that shithole is where they invented the phrase.' When you hear that in one seven-week tour 305 night patrols were carried out by a single unit, you'll get some idea of the pressure they were all under.

My father's experiences in the desert instilled in him an intense dislike of Arabs in general, and the Yemen in particular. After all, he mainly saw them through his rifle sights when he wasn't wearing a stethoscope, dividing his time as he did between healing duties in the sick bay and potentially lethal night-time patrols, while politicians tried to work out a face-saving withdrawal from a futile battleground. 'They were the enemy. Communist terrorists. Or tribesmen fighting their own factions as well as us, the common foe. If they caught you, son, that was it. They'd behead you – just like that,' he told us.

Other kids get fireside fairy tales. Ian and me, we were brought up in the real world. Dad talked a lot about the real world as we grew up, and taught us a lot about it too. 'Those oily sods had never heard of the Geneva Convention. But at least when the Whitehall pen-pushers finally ordered us to pull out we gave the bastards something to remember us by. You wouldn't believe the high jinks we got up to.'

Dad went on to explain some of the 'high jinks' with which they did their best to rewrite the Hippocratic oath. 'Nothing was left for the Arabs to get their greasy hands on. We were ordered to burn everything in the hospital. Anything we couldn't put a match to, our engineers sabotaged.

I only wish I could have stayed around to see the results.'

Like what?

'When the rebels broke into our quarters after we pulled out, all hell broke loose. If they went to the loo, the moment they sat down and put pressure on the seat – *boom*! And it wasn't a fart going off. As we used to say, more than the shit hit the fan! The dentist's chair was another beauty; the patient would swivel himself clockwise into position, no problem. But when the chair went the other way, his dental problems were over. No more toothache. No surgery, either.

'As part of the evacuation we were told to throw sheets and pillows out of the windows for a bonfire in the grounds. For the looters, that meant open season – and they'd scurry out of the bushes to grab whatever they could lay their hands on. More than one bootneck [marine] filled a pillowcase with sand and slung it out of the window three floors up . . . to flatten an Arab into the dust! Splat! Three floors is a long way too.'

Dad finally came marching home after his first skirmish with an enemy on foreign soil, eighteen months older and a whole lot wiser. It wouldn't be his last posting abroad. But it had turned him into a cynic – or maybe just a realist. His message to Ian and me was brief and to the point: 'Never trust politicians.'

My father's next posting was to a different killing ground: the Far East. The Vietnam war, once described as 'a bright shining lie', had been dragging on since 1961, when the first US 'advisers' went in, and by now people had long since woken up to the size of the can of worms that had been opened.

All Dad knew was that he was heading for the Far East – and this time we would be going with him.

TWO

LOTUS LAND

Well, not quite all the way. The Ho Chi Minh Trail was hardly a place for a family outing. We flew out to Singapore and stayed based there while Dad, still attached to 42 Commando, went about his own business further down the line. First stop, Malaysia. There he was seconded to the Americans and Aussies as a paramedic, to take care of them in field hospitals and out on manoeuvres while they were undergoing intensive jungle training before going back to the real thing in 'Nam.

'These guys weren't kids, but hardened troops sent back from the field. Our job was to sharpen their skills in tracking and concealment,' Dad recalled later. There was an edge to his tongue. 'When they first came to us it was no wonder they were losing so many men, especially the Yanks. They were the worst jungle fighters I ever saw. When it came to stalking, or making a covert approach, a boy scout could pick up their trail – just follow the Coke cans and sweet wrappers in between the cigarette stubs!'

After a few months of dealing with snake bites, insect stings and venomous spiders, dispensing medicine for diarrhoea and other tropical ailments, and patching up cuts and scratches before they turned septic, it was my father's turn to take the hard road into the real war. There he'd be facing live bullets – the full metal jacket, as the Yanks put it – and, as he told me later, he had to be prepared for some drastic field surgery. 'One of the best antiseptics for an open wound is to piss on it,' he said. That's something they don't teach you in biology at school.

As for Mum and us kids, we were housed along with other military families close to the Royal Marine Camp at Sembawang. Our home was a pleasant, airy two-storey building set in its own grounds, with wire mesh across the doors and windows, and mosquito netting over the beds.

I was only six, but it was like lotus land. The hot humid days went on for ever. I went to sleep to the musical croaking of crickets, a sound I'd never heard before. Huge fronded trees, exotic flowers and lush vegetation outside the windows made a magical playground where we could let our imaginations run riot and invent our own war games.

The favourite combat zones for me and my two best friends Royce and David, sons of neighbouring military families, were the 'monsoon drains', V-shaped concrete trenches three feet deep that would turn into raging torrents during the monsoon season and remain bone dry for the rest of the year. In the dry season we used them for trench warfare, while home-made go-carts made them an exhilarating race track, a concrete Cresta Run, whizzing under bridges where the drains went past houses (*'Don't lift your head!'*) and ending more often than not with one of us crawling out with grazed elbows and knees after coming to grief on a bend.

One hazard you'd never find slithering around on the Cresta were the snakes and terrapins that inhabited the drains. You could stumble on anything from a sleepy python to small, brightly coloured snakes whose names I never knew but whose deceptive hues disguised their lethal nature. Once I brought home a large black worm I'd retrieved from a trench. I showed it in triumph to Dad, who was home on one of his rare visits – only to have him snatch it out of my hand, fling it to the floor and stamp it into pulp. 'You bloody idiot,' he stormed. 'That's a bootlace snake. You're lucky you're not dead!' Dad had a way of making his point.

Another spot of mischief was to catch one of the nameless insects that would evade the mesh netting over the windows, crawl into the house and make our lives a misery. Some of them could give you a nasty sting, so we weren't too concerned about what happened to them. After a chase through the rooms, jumping on sofas and tumbling over chairs, we'd manage to trap our quarry in a tumbler with a piece of card over the rim, listening to the hollow buzz of its rage and panic. Then we'd locate one of the spider's webs we could always rely on festooning a corner of the front porch, and with one swift shake *sping* the frantic insect to its doom.

Sometimes the waiting spider would squat in its lair, partially hidden by a leaf or branch, its beady eye fixed on its quarry for up to an hour without moving. Other times it would scuttle down the web as if someone had prodded it with a live wire to leap on its prey and truss it up like a Christmas parcel, leaving it there for the rest of the day. What must it be like, I sometimes caught myself fantasising, watching that hairy monster approaching you for its dinner? Probably the victim had a heart attack and died of fright. I know I would. Well, that's nature for you. Cruel – and kids can be, too.

Out there in the tropics it was *hot*. For light relief our pet monkey Pickles provided daily entertainment. She was a fun-loving little character who was a natural comic and would scamper over the furniture, and rush through the rooms like a miniature whirlwind. Her particular joy was to ride piggy-back on our patient cross-breed terrier Suna, or spend time sitting on my lap dabbing the sweat off my face and arms with one solicitous paw.

Oddly enough the local Chinese were terrified of her, for no good reason that I could understand. But I was glad of that, because it meant I slept better at night. One of the problems in our 'Brit enclave' was petty crime, particularly localised burglary. All the private houses were fitted with ornate railings over the windows as a deterrent, but that didn't stop the more inventive intruder, who would strip down to a thong, smear his body with grease and slither through like a contortionist to cut the wire netting. Amazing!

Growing up in this privileged environment, the best times were splashing around in the camp swimming pool with my friends. For a start, I learned to swim. I spent every spare minute in that pool – and two years later I was able to show off the Bronze Medal for Survival, and several certificates for distance swimming and endurance as well.

School had its own diversions. We were next door to a camp which housed a batallion of Gurkhas. Once a week, beyond the unfenced edge of the playing field, we witnessed an execution. It was a change from kicking a soccer ball around, and always took place in the lunch break, so that after the ritual slaughter we could go back to our lessons with something to talk about that was never on any school curriculum.

A shrill whistle from one of the kids keeping watch at the far end of the field was the signal for a mad rush. We charged across the coarse grass in time to watch a small brown-skinned man in Gurkha uniform march out from behind the huts. In one hand he led a goat by a rope. In the other he carried a two-handed *kukri*, which was twice the size of the legendary Gurkha weapon, the one they never unsheath without shedding blood. That's a bit of a myth, by the way. Here's another. If these brave little chaps do take out their *kukri* for other than hostile reasons, it has been unkindly suggested that they discreetly nick their thumb when putting it back to show a drop or two of the red stuff! If they did that, as a Gurkha major pointed out to me much later, there'd be an awful lot of four-fingered saluting in the ranks.

The little man strode over to a stained white post under some trees, tethered the beast with a few quick loops, and stepped back. Then he raised the gleaming blade with both hands.

It was all very quick. The sound across the dry afternoon air was like someone slicing a watermelon. Blood gushed from its neck. Then the animal's head was bouncing on the ground, its eyes bulging and staring with shock. But the memory that remains with me, and probably with all of us, is the way the poor headless beast stood motionless as if propped on stilts for what seemed an eternity, but was really probably less than a second, before toppling into the blood-stained dust.

There was no ceremony. No onlookers lined up to pay their last respects, face Mecca or offer up a prayer. No last rites or 'Last Post'. Just a poor old goat lying on the ground. If this was a ritual sacrifice, we must have missed something. The big one apparently occurs at the religious festival of *Dashera*, an annual event which takes place every autumn and is their equivalent of our Christmas. Then the sacrifice can be a buffalo, and the *kukri* is garlanded with flowers and blessed with the animal's blood. That I never saw.

But for now, no such formality. The little man wiped the blade on a piece of cloth, untied the rope, and nonchalantly dragged the carcass away by its back legs, into a hut and out of sight.

The rest of us went back to our lessons.

THREE

THE BORSTAL BOYS

For those who were lucky enough to live it, the '60s have been hailed as the greatest decade in history, especially in so-called swinging London. Think of the headlines and the Beatles, the Great Train Robbery and a little matter of England winning the World Cup spring to mind. Perhaps I should have been fifteen years older.

The other side of the coin included the Vietnam War, of course, escalating alarmingly. Most old soldiers I've met never talk much about the really bad times they went through in whichever conflict they fought – and I mean the *really* bad times, whether it was being gassed in the trenches in World War One, or seeing all kinds of horrors in World War Two. That same coin included Britain's Far East War, being fought at the same time as Vietnam, namely the conflict between Indonesia and Borneo in which we took the latter's side. This was where my father ended up.

Dad, I suspect, was no different. His experiences in Borneo remained largely a closed book, and I never pressed him. Maybe he did a few things, maybe not. Perhaps the Official Secrets Act got in the way. He did once drop a hint of one mission, something about paddling ashore from a submarine with sixteen men from the Special Boat Service to 'probe and penetrate' Indonesian territory up the coast. That was it, whatever it was. And since he was as adept with a rifle as with a syringe, Dad could have been involved in anything.

Years later he did mention an early encounter he had with the former Lib-Dem leader Paddy Ashdown. It was on one SBS 'excursion' – and, sad to relate, Dad didn't think very highly of him. 'Pompous idiot,' he summed up scathingly, and that was that. Apparently the now ennobled hard man of politics, as I suspect he likes to be thought of, had liked to be called 'Sir' by his men. Now, in the SBS there's a traditional informality that goes hand-in-flipper with the camaraderie essential to men flung close together in dangerous waters – as I would find out later when I worked with them on a big cocaine bust. The SBS call sign, incidentally, is 'Tadpole', and their motto is 'Not by strength, by guile' – and make sure you don't spell it 'gill'. It's Christian names all round with those guys – but not, apparently, with Paddy.

After two blissful years my Far East childhood came to an end, along with my father's posting, and it was time to head back to Britain. Thankfully, it was spring, and the days were getting lighter and longer.

The cultural shock was traumatic but bearable, as I tried to adjust to surroundings which had suddenly become foreign. At least I was the only kid at my new school with a tan. At Delce Junior School in Rochester I proved myself a strictly average pupil with a leaning to English and geography.

The summer of 1969 also saw my first meeting with the criminal classes. Our house, I discovered, was only half a mile from a village which wrote its name in history with the unfortunate name of Borstal, a name that after a century is still linked in the public mind with young delinquents. I'm talking about the Borstal Boys, youthful criminals from the ages of fifteen to twenty-one serving time for 'anti-social behaviour' of varying degrees.

First introduced as far back as 1901, borstal institutions around the country were officially known from 1983 as 'youth custody centres' and were later replaced with the politically correct title of 'young offender institutions'. Call them what you like, the name was different but the game was the same.

To my pal Peter and myself, two nine year olds ripe for fun and mischief, all we saw were groups of young men in blue overalls toiling in the fields in working parties of a dozen or so, the ones with yellow stripes down the side of their trousers being known escapers. We'd watch them digging away as we cycled past on the way to the village shop, and close up the prisoners didn't look so dangerous. Most of them seemed too young to shave, anyway.

Over the long summer holidays we gradually got talking to them. Leaning on our bikes, we'd impart the latest news across the ditches from the great big world outside to the open fields where they worked. There was no TV, no newspapers – and if the truth be known, most of them couldn't read anyway.

They would always be in the mood for a chat to alleviate the boredom of pulling up potatoes and turnips. So we told them about Neil

Armstrong taking his giant leap for mankind on the moon, Concorde's maiden flight, and – the news that seemed to interest them most – the Kray twins being jailed for life at the Old Bailey. Eventually a warder in a peaked cap and uniform would stride up and order us away brusquely – 'Clear off, you kids' – but not before we'd struck up a brief and passing friendship, even if we never knew their names.

To us they were just a bunch of lively older boys hungry to hear the latest news. Of course we knew they must have done something wrong to be stuck out there amid the spuds and weeds, before being marched back into the drab building that dominated the Kentish countryside like a fortress. But they never talked about it, and we didn't ask. Instead they did the asking – on a day when the screw was looking in the other direction.

'Oi, kids! If I give you the money, can you get us some fags?' one of them hissed.

Sure we could. In those days it was no problem. With a glance at the warder's back, the young con slipped a ten bob note under a stone, gave us a conspiratorial wink and went back to the potato patch. 'And keep a tanner for yourselves.'

When the coast was clear, Peter and I retrieved the cash, hared off down the road to the village shop to ask Mr Larkin for cigarettes 'for my Dad' – and presto! Half an hour later the dead letter box harboured ten Woodbines, and some small change. We cycled off sixpence richer, and the Borstal Boys had suddenly found themselves a new source of supply.

This mutually beneficial state of affairs went on for the whole of the school holidays, and as word spread the money under the stone grew by the week. Soon we were distributing the contraband under different stones, and we were the most popular kids on the block! Mr Larkin shook his head at the state of Dad's lungs, but he never queried the orders.

It all came to a head shortly before the holidays ended. As we cycled down to the village shop with a fat bundle of notes in the saddlebag, Pete suddenly said, 'Hey, I've got an idea. We're not going to see that lot after next week, are we?'

'I suppose not . . .'

'Well, then. What if we don't go for the cigarettes?'

'What do you mean?'

'Scarper with the cash. They're only thieves, after all.'

'Yeah, I suppose so.' I hadn't thought of it that way, but it made sense. 'How much have we got in there?'

We pulled up by a hedge and Peter unbuckled the saddlebag. 'Fourteen . . . fifteen . . . *sixteen* pounds!' It was more money than we'd ever seen in our lives. We shared it out, hands trembling with a mixture of trepidation and excitement.

'What if they catch us?'

'They won't,' said Peter. 'Don't worry about it.'

'Well . . . okay, then – '

That night, with eight pounds in ten-bob notes stashed away in my *Blue Peter* annual, I wasn't too sure. But we were the Daddies now. I spent my ill-gotten gains on a series of Airfix kits, but not all at once, so that no one, not even my brother, suspected. Even at that age I was learning. Peter put his own stash towards a spanking new Chopper bike, the kids' equivalent of a Harley. A few months later he was dead – run over in the Maidstone Road, a notorious black spot.

Maybe there's a moral in there somewhere.

FOUR

SNIPER ALLEY

A month later I was able to forget any threat from the Borstal Boys. We were on the move again, this time only as far as Devon to be with Dad who by now had joined 45 Commando, at that time training to be Britain's Arctic watchdogs guarding the Norwegian–Russian border.

45 Commando had been formed in 1943, its emblem dark green with a red dagger in the centre and the numbers four and five on either side. During years of action across the globe – based abroad for the first twenty years – they had built up a reputation for flexibility, able to move an entire unit anywhere, anytime, at next-to-nothing notice. In a matter of hours, for instance, they could switch from ceremonial duties to full operational action. Witness the time 45 Commando received the honorary freedom of the city of Plymouth, marching stoutly down to the Hoe in pouring rain with colours flying and bayonets fixed. Days later the lads found themselves sweltering in the Bermuda sunshine. Their task: to protect the locals from possible violence during a Black Power conference – causing its leader, a certain Mr Roosevelt Brown, to complain disingenuously, though with some truth, that the Governor had 'brought in a hundred trained killers'.

But Dad's first foray with 45 Commando was to a colder climate. 'Exercise Polar Express' in the Tromso area of northern Norway reflected Britain's commitment to defend the northern flank of NATO. Now that *was* the Cold War, and my father would be quoted in an *Illustrated London News* article as saying, 'Up there it's ninety per cent survival, ten per cent warfare.' They would be known as the Snow Commandos, and their brass monkey stint lasted from December to February, the three coldest months of the year. In the end it became an annual fixture. 'I just hope nothing drops off,' I overheard Dad say to Mum with an impish wink as he kissed her goodbye on the doorstep before heading off to

Scotland and some rigorous mountain survival training. I was too young then to know what he meant.

But less than a year later, on a summer's evening in 1970 when I was watching TV with Mum and the family, I wasn't too young to realise that something terrible had happened to my father.

The estate where we had been accommodated was part of the naval establishment at Plymouth, five miles from the historic barracks at Stonehouse that dated back to 1783. The plumbing had certainly improved since then, largely thanks to a £1 million refurbishment, and our terraced house with its small garden was bright, modern and homely.

Being a military quarters, everybody knew everybody else like one big family. In fact some of us had been in Singapore together – you could tell us apart from the rest because we could use chopsticks, even at that tender age. And at school I was no longer the only one with a tan. So when Dad was shot by the IRA the shock of it was all the more intense. The ripples spread through the tight-knit community in a wave of disbelief. I'd been having a kickabout with the other lads in the local park. Mum had called us in for tea. Now I settled down with Ian and Amanda in front of the television to watch the evening news.

Richard Baker's good-natured features filled the screen. The newscaster was saying something about Ireland. 'A naval doctor has been shot during the course of rioting in Northern Ireland': that was the headline. Mum suddenly sat up very still, her hand to her mouth. We looked at her. Dad was in Northern Ireland, on a three-month tour of duty with 45 Commando.

45 Commando had had their first taste of the Troubles as far back as the mid-'50s, but at that time it proved only a brief flirtation with the coming storm. The unit became 'Spearhead Battalion' at a single day's notice, flew out to Belfast, showed their faces on the streets, knuckled a few boisterous drunks at closing time and were pulled out soon after when things calmed down again.

The words 'peace keeping', now part of everyday military life, were virtually unknown at that time and there were other conflicts on the global stage that required 45 Commando's presence.

It was fifteen years later, in 1970, when things had deteriorated a lot further, that the troops were back in action on the streets of Belfast, and not enjoying it any too much. They were given precious little leave or free time to explore the pubs of Belfast, and had to watch their backs every moment they stepped out into a street, even dressed in civvies. Besides which, as one observer pointed out, up to then 45 Commando had rarely had to handle genuine riots, though they had faced angry crowds in Cyprus and Malta. Northern Ireland was different. The warring factions spoke the same language. These were our own people, whatever their professed faith. And the whole mess being fought out in the name of religion seemed so downright pigheaded that it would have been farcical if it weren't so ugly.

In the summer of that year my father found himself caught up in one of the incessant parades in the 'Marching Season', with a Protestant procession due to head down the infamous Crumlin Road and the Ardoyne 'Citizen's Defence Committee' pledged to stop them. The procession, he told me later, numbered eight bands, 'all of the buggers playing the noisiest and most provocative marching music they could lay their hands on'.

With 400 Commandos sandwiched between 3,000 Protestants and 2,000 Catholics, trying to keep the baying mobs from each other's throats, the odds weren't brilliant for handshakes all round and a pint of Guinness in the pub afterwards. The air was filled with stones, bottles, rivets and marbles from catapults, and shards of broken glass were flung like frisbees. Petrol bombs were a comparatively new menace, and it was only a month since the first grim caution from the army that 'anyone throwing a petrol bomb after a warning is liable to be shot dead in the street'.

In the middle of it all the IRA snipers opened up. Shots rang out from rooftops, upper windows and doorways. Within minutes the streets were littered with writhing bodies and one man, a civilian, lay dead on the pavement. The soldiers returned fire and a full-scale gun battle ensued. A pall of smoke drifted across the street. People ran.

At the end of the day the Irish would count five dead and two hundred wounded. Dad, a Petty Officer on 45 Commando's medical staff, tore through the streets at the wheel of his ambulance to reach the carnage. He leaped out, grabbed one wounded victim, dragged him into the rear and raced off for the nearest hospital, the Royal Victoria, in a hail of bullets with all lights blazing and the siren wailing. Then he headed back into Sniper Alley. The blood wagon was painted with Red Cross markings, but that seemed to act as a red rag. What kind of a sick person shoots at ambulances? The vehicle was starting to look like a colander. Still Dad ignored the snipers. He drove into the street – and that's when the bullet got him.

The shot came from an upper window. It went clean through his right cheek, shattering his jaw and lodging in the back of his throat. Strange things happen in the heat of battle. Dad told me later he didn't feel the pain, even though the bullet splintered into pieces and slivers of shrapnel would remain in his neck until the day he died. At that point my father was thirty-eight years old, and it didn't look as if he'd make it to forty. But pausing only to stuff a piece of bandage into the bleeding hole in the side of his face, he leaped out, grabbed the nearest victim, shoved him in the back of the ambulance and took off like a bat out of hell for the hospital. This time they kept him there.

The citation in the *London Gazette* says it all. Dated 8 March 1971, it reads:

> On 27 June 1970 a company of 45 Commando Royal Marines was sent to deal with a gun battle between rival factions in the Crumlin Road area of Belfast. Petty Officer Frederick MacLaughlin accompanied them as medical assistant. After taking a wounded civilian to hospital, the ambulance he drove came under fire while returning to the scene of action. Petty Officer MacLaughlin was hit in the cheek. He refused help, and while bandaging the wound himself heard that another civilian had been wounded. Completely disregarding his own injury, MacLaughlin drove through the line of fire to the wounded man, and accompanied him to hospital. There the Petty Officer saw that the patient was cared for before consenting to be examined himself.
>
> It was found that a bullet had entered Petty Officer MacLaughlin's right cheek, smashed his jaw and lodged in his throat. He was immediately given an emergency operation.
>
> By his example of bravery and complete disregard for his own safety, Petty Officer MacLaughlin showed outstanding courage while evacuating the civilian casualties. His selfless conduct was an example to all who saw him.

Is that a hero, or what?

FIVE

MEDAL FOR A HERO

You can see a copy of the citation for yourselves today if you visit the Naval Hospital at HMS Hasler, the training establishment at Gosport. It is in a big frame in the entrance, along with a photo and a replica of his George Medal, so you can't miss it. We're immensely proud of it, of course, and I only wish Dad could have seen it. They put it up to commemorate him after he eventually died on 27 June 1993 – by sad coincidence, the date of my youngest daughter Anna's third birthday – exactly twenty-three years to the day since he'd been shot.

In fact my father had come closer to death that day in 1970 than the citation made out. When he finally came home months later, after a lengthy convalescence, the details of his near-miraculous escape emerged. He recalled: 'I saw a gun barrel protrude from an upper window, aimed straight at me, and I had a clear glimpse of his face, the man who was trying to kill me.

'I hit the pedal and kept low. But not low enough. He tracked me along the road, firing all the time, and the bullets were thudding into the seat. He was a great shot – I'll give him that! It was fantastic grouping. Then I felt a hefty kick on my jaw, though I had no idea I was hurt so badly. That's why I was able to help a poor guy who was lying in the street in agony and get him into the ambulance.'

Back in Plymouth watching the TV, we knew none of this. I couldn't help noticing Mum's worried frown, but there were no names and few details of the actual incident.

The first confirmation was a ring at the doorbell before the news had finished, and there on the step stood a man in civilian clothes.

'Mrs MacLaughlin?'

Mum's reaction was immediate.

'It's Rick, isn't it?'

She recognised the Welfare Officer from social evenings in the Sergeants' Mess.

'I'm afraid so. He's been injured, but it's not serious.'

'I've got to get out there! Can you arrange transportation?'

'That may not be so easy, Mrs MacLaughlin. It's just too dangerous, and I'm afraid they won't authorise it.'

Mum's jaw tightened in determination.

Friends rallied round, and a loan from a local bank manager got her the flight. Within days, she had farmed us out to willing neighbours and was on her way to Belfast, where by now Dad had been moved to Dundonald Hospital for major surgery. All alone, she made her way to the hospital, getting her first proof of the Welfare Officer's warning at the airport. 'Dundonald Hospital? Sorry, love, we're not going anywhere near there. The streets just aren't safe.'

But someone was willing. Dad, it seemed, was something of a *cause célèbre* – he was the first British soldier to be critically wounded in the unrest, and up to then no British serviceman had been killed. By the taxi rank, a cab driver saw the lone woman standing helplessly with her luggage, overheard her accent, and made an educated guess. 'Are you the doctor's wife?' When Mum nodded, he said 'Get in, I'll take you. No charge!'

Dad was in intensive care. They gave her a room close by where she could sleep and she spent hours at his bedside clinging to his hand. His jaw was wired together so he lived on soup – after he was discharged from hospital he never touched another drop for the rest of his days – and lost a lot of weight. If you looked at an X-ray of the back of his skull, it was more like a scrapyard, seeing the bits of metal embedded in it.

At the hospital, Mum heard more details of how she had nearly lost him. Apparently they left Dad for dead in a corridor at the Royal Victoria while they looked for a doctor to confirm it amid the chaos of casualties being rushed through. A passing orderly saw him on the trolley and noticed one arm dangling down towards the floor. He picked up the hand to lay it by the body as a mark of respect – and felt a faint pulse. That rang a few bells, as medics came racing from everywhere. Next thing, Dad was being transferred to Dundonald for specialist treatment.

Initially they said Dad wouldn't live. Then they diagnosed that he would be paralysed from the neck down. Then it became from the chest down. Then the waist down. Finally he got up and walked – and he would do another five tours of Ireland, revisit the Arctic Circle, and top up his suntan in the Mediterranean on various military exercises.

But he'd been lucky, 'Bloody lucky, son,' he admitted to me later. On the very same day that Dad was brought in, the most eminent surgeons from both sides of the border – top Johnnies in their respective fields – had gathered for a conference in Dundonald Hospital.

Neurology, urology, opthalmology, periodontology (useful for Dad, as it's to do with gums), gynaecology (not so useful) – you name it, they were there. In short, the best of the best were available, for one day only. When word reached them that a medical man, 'one of their own', was under the same roof, it was down pens and up scalpels. They couldn't wait to scrub up and head for the theatre.

Dad's indomitable spirit, as well as his physical fitness, pulled him through. But over the years, that one fraction-of-a-second incident would take its toll, with the shrapnel at the top of his spine causing him to pay a fearful price, and finally the ultimate one. He was in constant pain, though few outside the family saw it.

Doctors convinced him an operation could result in paralysis, but for me it was heart-rending to watch Dad's body gradually give up the struggle. People never realise the damage one bullet can do, and the effects don't all happen at once. Bit by bit his liver, kidneys and pancreas all started to shut down.

Finally came that morning in June twenty-three years later as I sat by his bedside in Ninewells Hospital, Dundee, holding his hand as he took his last breath. Instinctively I looked at my watch – I was a detective constable by then, and on automatic pilot in police mode. Eleven a.m. 'Goodbye, Dad!' I said, closing his eyes for him.

The IRA could claim another scalp, and Mum could only claim a war widow's pension.

Weeks after the shooting, a size eleven boot kicked in a door in the New Lodge district of Belfast, a man was dragged shouting into the street by a group of RUC officers and Marines, a gun was found, forensic evidence showed it matched bullets found embedded in the ambulance and the man was charged with attempted murder.

In the days leading up to the trial, RUC investigators had a word with Dad. 'Gilding the lily,' Dad called it, explaining to me later what they had wanted. There was some uncertainty over the make of the gun. They asked him to swear that the gun he had glimpsed was the same type as the one they picked up. My father refused. 'Son, I couldn't be sure, and I wasn't going to lie,' he said. 'Would you?'

By now I'd been a detective for some years, and seen a lot of the dark side of the street. 'Dad, big boys' games require big boys' rules. I'd have stitched him up so tight he wouldn't know what day it was.'

Dad looked at me challengingly. 'So where's your conscience?'

'It's still there, somewhere. But you tell me which is more important: getting the job done properly at a price, or following the letter of the law?'

The answer, for me, had already been writ in stone. Back then, in the witness box, Dad refused to deviate from his original statement. And on the steps of Belfast Crown Court a man named Kelly walked free, pausing only to laugh out loud as he passed the man he had been accused of trying to kill. The irony for me was that he had the same surname as my birth mother.

A year went by, and at last the MoD recognised Dad's enormous courage. Someone recommended him for a gallantry medal, and there were even murmurs of the George Cross, second only to the Victoria Cross for valour.

But these were early days. Our fellow countrymen across the Irish Sea had not officially declared war on us, and the George Cross (Military division) tended only to be awarded in time of war. It would have meant the government admitting we had an official conflict on our hands.

Instead, Dad got the George Medal, which was no mean recognition. In the pecking order this is one below the George Cross and therefore two below the Victoria Cross. Good enough? I'll say! The whole family put Dad on the pedestal he deserved, and to a ten-year-old kid, Number Two Son, he became a true hundred-carat hero.

As a bonus, the whole family got to see the inside of Buckingham Palace. Proud as punch, we sat on fragile-looking gilt chairs in the magnificent ballroom while the Grenadier Guards played cheery music in the gallery overhead, and watched Dad in his naval uniform march out from the wings to face the Monarch.

The Queen was flanked by two Gurkhas. A click of heels from Dad and a brief bow, and she pinned the silver medal with its red-and-blue ribbon on his chest, shook his hand and said: 'You're a very brave man. How are you now?'

'Recovering well, thank you ma'am.'

'That's good. I'm glad to hear it,' said the Queen.

That medal, the ultimate recognition of my father's courage, would take its place alongside the campaign ribbons, in ironic contrast to the tiny sharp segments of the sniper's shrapnel which even then were slowly killing him.

There and then I vowed: 'I'll be a Commando. Just like my Dad!'

SIX

GROWING UP

Arbroath, 1971, a fishing port on the north-east coast of Scotland famous for its (haddock) smokies and less well-known then for the highest soccer score ever inflicted in the UK (Arbroath 36, Bon Accord, now known as Aberdeen, 0). Historians will tell you that the Declaration of Arbroath, asserting Scotland's independence from England, was issued by the Scottish Parliament in 1320, but that isn't why my mum enjoyed living there so much. She loved the thick mist that rolls in from the North Sea and the continuous mournful sound of the fog horn somewhere out there on the cold grey water, a sound that made a lasting impression on me as my fertile imagination conjured up visions of smugglers rowing their booty ashore on to the sand dunes up the coast.

Mum actually relished that sea mist because it took her back to her own childhood, remembering the bombs that rained down on Chatham, Kent, where she grew up, in the Blitz. 'If there was fog, the German bombers wouldn't come,' she told me, reminiscing about those far-off days. It was as simple as that. No bombers meant no bombs, and a quiet night's sleep.

We had moved north with my father and 45 Commando, who were now occupying a former Fleet Air Arm base nearby. Mum and Dad had spent days house-hunting, then stumbled on an old village school a few miles out of Arbroath, and realised its potential. Over the next weeks they converted it into a wonderful rambling family home, set in an acre of wooded ground, with more rooms than I could count.

As for my father, he stowed his medal away in his socks drawer and left it there. I once heard him tell someone, 'If they'd given me the OBE I'd have sent it back. That one's strictly for footballers and pop singers.' Dad tended to speak his mind. If he sounds a bit churlish, remember that he was still carrying those unwanted bits of metal in the base of his skull, though to the outside world he appeared to be in remarkably good shape. The doctors had actually advised him to chuck it in and take an early pension, but being Dad he ignored them – though on damp days when it played up he was tight-lipped with pain.

By this time 45 Commando was committed to the 'Northern Flank', the Norwegian–Russian border way up in the Arctic Circle. Norway being part of NATO, Russia being Eastern bloc.

Thumbing through my school atlas, I located where he was – an inhospitable sliver of land within spitting distance of the Barents Sea, the area which in the Millennium year would become the dreadful watery grave of the Russian nuclear submarine the *Kursk* and at that time was regarded as the 'point of entry' should the Red Army ever invade.

I was enrolled into St Thomas primary school at the age of eleven. In Scotland children normally don't start secondary school till they're twelve. I was captain of the school soccer team, though I'd given up aspirations of wearing the green hoops of Celtic in favour of the green beret of the Royal Marine Commandos. Away from the sports field, I was what you might call an average scholar. Not thick, but not an Einstein either. The skills I acquired were in other directions, and right on my doorstep. The woods and fields around our home were a magnet for poachers – now *that* seemed just the career move I should be contemplating.

By happy coincidence, Dad had acquired a .410 shotgun. What's more, it was called a 'Poacher's Rifle' because it snapped in half on a hinge and could be slipped down the inside of your trouser leg, concealing it from passers-by, gamekeepers, police and sundry folk trying to mind your business instead of theirs. That gun meant a lot to me.

I was after rabbits and hares, which, following a spot of early negotiation, a local butcher agreed to take from me, provided I skinned and gutted them, for 50p a hare, 30p a rabbit. 'And make sure you leave the tail on the rabbit, young Duncan,' said Mr Cargill in his striped apron, giving me a beady stare. 'A skinned rabbit looks just like a dead cat, and we don't want anyone jumping to the wrong conclusions, do we now?'

I spent hours roaming those woods like a young Davy Crockett, king of the wild Scottish frontier. All that was missing was the beaver hat. Under my dad's tuition I became a better-than-average shot. And (now it can be told) if a game bird came into my sights I wasn't averse to squeezing the trigger, whatever the time of year, to return home in triumph with a grouse or pheasant in the bag for supper.

During those halcyon days I picked up other secrets of the great outdoors, like trapping and snaring. My main source was a character named Jamie, my first informant you might say. He was a small wiry man I spotted occasionally scouting the edge of the woods, and everyone knew what he was doing there. One day when our paths crossed by accident we got talking. Close to, his face was sharp as a fox, with restless, darting eyes that could spot a movement in the undergrowth from fifty feet. 'How do I catch them?' I asked him straight out.

'It's easier than you think, boy. First, you've got to find your rabbit. And that means using your eyes.'

What I should be looking for, my newfound friend expanded, was a 'run'. 'That's the path he takes from his burrow in search of food. No paw prints, just slightly flattened grass is enough to give him away. It won't necessarily be by his hole, but he'll take that run every night, and particularly just before dawn, which is the time he likes to forage.'

After that, it seemed, it was all a matter of technique. Find the right point to set your snare, without disturbing the run. It could be under a fence, or tucked away in thick bracken. The snare consisted of thin wire threaded into a noose, which you attached to a branch or piece of upright fencing. Mr Rabbit hopped through the noose, and his weight as he ran by would snap the wire tight around his neck until he throttled himself. Primitive? Cruel? Yes, both of these – but effective. Think of it next time you pass a butcher.

I learned quickly. Every evening I would lay half-a-dozen traps, returning first thing next morning to check them out. If I didn't, the animal might still be alive, or a fox might get him if it hadn't already. Usually I could rely on finding a couple of rabbits, or the occasional hare, which I'd skin and clean before dropping them in at the butcher's on my way to school.

Sometimes I went out night stalking. After Mum had seen me safe to bed, I'd lie awake counting the minutes until the house was quiet. She went to bed early when Dad was away, and the others were fast asleep too. My shotgun was kept downstairs in a cupboard with Dad's other guns, but the key was in a jar on the sideboard and I had my rucksack packed ready in my room. Torch, Swiss knife, box of cartridges, and that was it. Then I'd slip out the back door and steal off into the night.

Those dark forays were my first real experience of stalking and surveillance – not that I ever saw anything, to be honest, because the night creatures were better at spotting me than I was at spotting them. But I crept gamely through the trees and undergrowth, listening to the night sounds and rustlings, sometimes scaring myself silly imagining what those dark shadows could be hiding. I learned the tricks that moonlight can play, and how easy it is to get lost in the darkness of a wood even when you think you know each path and glade like the back of your hand.

How could I have known that twenty years down the line I would be playing the same game – except that it would be for real, the gun I'd be holding a .38 Smith and Wesson revolver, and the prey I'd be stalking would be human?

On those nightly excursions I seldom pulled the trigger. But in broad daylight I may unwittingly have performed a feat with a gun that could have got me into the *Guinness Book of Records*: as the first person ever to shoot a salmon with a .22 air rifle! My father even witnessed it.

It happened like this. Dad and I were out walking the mud flats of Montrose Basin, looking for geese. This area north of Arbroath is a vast plain of glistening mud and gleaming rivulets running from the headlands at low tide, and a playground for hundreds of birds who arrive around December and spend the winter wandering about in the mud whether the tide is in or out. These geese are known to twitchers as *Anser Brachyrhynchus*, which they can probably spell and pronounce better than me. They've got unusual pink webbed feet and a pink bill, and make a squawking cry best described as 'wink-wink!' or, if they're feeling frisky, 'ung-ung!' All I know is that they've got those strange pink feet and plump grey bodies, and taste very nice for dinner. They breed in the Arctic, and fly south in the winter for warmth, making Montrose Bay their home before flapping off again back to the northern wilds.

It's an extraordinary sight: a shifting, grey-feathered curtain covering the bay, with the geese delicately stepping through the mud or simply standing stock still in the North Sea, which to me was freezing cold but must have been like a warm bath to those hardy birds. They are also the canniest fowls on God's earth, with an inbuilt radar system that detects danger as if reading your mind. One minute they're admiring the scenery like a bunch of tourists, the next they're flapping off to the headland to wait until the coast is clear.

Shooting those wily creatures is perfectly legitimate, providing you've got a licence for your gun and can get close enough. It's a popular sport on that part of the coast, and on this chill winter's day Dad had his 12-bore shotgun at the ready, while Number Two Son had to be content with a .22 air rifle that was part of the MacLaughlin armoury.

We were wrapped up with hats and scarves against the wind, blowing on our fingers, but I could feel the cold seeping through my wellies as we trudged through the ooze, trying to act invisible. If we shot one it would be a small miracle – but there was always the thrill of the chase.

Suddenly, behind us, a splash! We whipped round, raising our guns in unison. Twenty yards away, a silvery blue shape was breaking the surface of the shallows in the channel.

We fired simultaneously. The fish threshed around, and then Dad was wading towards it, flipping it out by the tail.

'Mine!' he said in triumph.

'No, mine!'

'What, with an air gun?'

Back home, Dad gutted a superb fourteen-pound salmon on the kitchen table. 'Hul-lo!' He peered closer. 'What have we got here?' He dug around with a knife – and pulled out a flattened air slug. He grinned at me. 'I guess that's you. Well done, son.'

We ate well that night.

SEVEN

UP THE CREEK

Kids can be little devils, we all know that, and I was no different. It's part of growing up. Anyone watching me closely could spot the seeds stirring inside from an early age. For a start, I drove my Dad's car well below the legal age – just fourteen, and sparky with it.

The old grey Morris Estate Traveller was the kind where you could stuff bales of straw in the back, or maybe take a couple of dogs for a run. It was also uninsured, with no road licence, so neither of us should have been on the road. I was self-taught – which is to say I happily crunched gears and rammed fences with equal abandon, but without anyone ever catching me.

The first Dad knew about my motoring expertise was when I put my face hesitantly round the living-room door one evening when he was watching *The Professionals*. 'Have you got a moment, Dad? I – er – I've got something to show you.' Outside, up the lane, the Morris was embedded in a ditch. My father stared at the crumpled radiator without speaking.

'Sorry, Dad . . .'

Abruptly his face changed. A broad grin came over it. 'Don't worry, Number Two. I knew that bend was too sharp. Now you've proved it.' That was my dad, always full of surprises. After that I drove around the country lanes like a young Graham Hill. It was the shape of things to come. For little devil, read daredevil! Within two years I would become the youngest kid in Europe to perform a parachute jump – a title that chuffed me no end.

Meantime my thirst for adventure was temporarily quenched by the appearance of a canoe, unaccountably acquired by my father. Not just any old canoe, but a Klepper. This is a modern-day descendant of the original two-man Cockleshell Heroes craft immortalised in the famous

1955 film that starred Trevor Howard, and is used primarily by the SBS. These little beauties are collapsible, can be snatched out of a submarine hatch as it surfaces by men already on the deck, reassembled in under two minutes, and stealthily floated away as the sub slides back out of sight beneath the waves, the men of the silent service leaving the men of guile to paddle off on their mission.

Dad ran a canoe club for young marines from a loch at Forfar, teaching the lads the basics of the job. Apart from handling their paddles at different speeds both forward and backwards, they were taught to move in complete silence with hardly a ripple behind them. The climax, of course, was the 'Eskimo roll' – righting the craft in a full 360-degree rollover if you capsized, and hang the ripples if you didn't want to drown.

I was tail-end Charlie to the tough young bootnecks, tagging along behind the convoys in my own small canoe, until one day Dad appeared jauntily carrying a complete Klepper kit under one arm. This was more like it. This was the business! Where did this brilliant piece of nautical engineering spring from? Don't ask me, and I never asked Dad. A fleeting thought that maybe some vital mission had been compromised crossed my mind, but I let it go – '*Shit, anyone seen the canoe!*'

We assembled it on the bank, with me hopping from one foot to the other in excitement. The Klepper was ten feet long, and lay in the grass like a slim pencil. The size was deceptive. It had room to stow a weekend's camping gear, including tent, sleeping bags, rucksacks and billy cans. A spot of near-tearful pleading on my part did the trick, and soon I had the parental permission to stay out all night, provided I took my best pal Stuart along with me. Stuart was the same age as me and in the same form at school, a freckled kid who also shared my sense of adventure.

Those days were pure magic, spent paddling up mysterious waterways and exploring the small islands dotted around the loch, which itself was very large and very deep, and the colour of gunmetal. Eventually we graduated to weekends camping out on the islands, two schoolboys in their element, making fires, listening to the night sounds and the occasional splash from the water, and keeping each other awake with stories we made up of daring exploits in the wilderness.

Fair enough, you could hardly call it sleeping rough. The tent kept the wind out, and the sleeping bags kept us warm. But more importantly for my future, when I was to spend hours lying in ditches covered in leaves and branches on surveillance jobs, it gave me my first real taste of the outdoor life, and I took to it like Davy Crockett himself.

A word about Mum. She had always loved animals, and by now she was making a name for herself in, of all things, the dog-breeding world. We had been forced to leave Suna behind in Singapore, along with the family joke that she had been given her name because 'she'd suna do it on the mat than outside'.

In Scotland, Mum moved on to better things. She established a thriving business, setting up kennels in the old playground behind the house where she could board up to sixty dogs at a time while their loving owners were away. Personally, I hated every day of it, because guess who was given the daily job of cleaning out the kennels during the school holidays? Right first time. I was the original pooper-scooper, and I wasn't happy about it. But family came first, and the extra pocket money became a nice little earner.

Mum had a disarming way of putting it. 'S-h-ONE-t!' she'd say, spelling it out and pointing to the long shed where the beasts were housed. But to this day I still have a lasting aversion to dogs, associating them with shovelling S-h-One-t from dawn till dusk to ensure their nice warm homes were squeaky clean. It's a wonder I never got an allergy.

Mum bred Samoyeds, the pure white 'Siberian huskies' whose fur can actually be spun into yarn and then knitted into garments, normally gloves. She went on to become a judge, and to this day Margaret MacLaughlin remains one of the most respected adjudicators in the dog show world. At any one time we had half a dozen Samoyeds trotting around our small estate, with a basketful of pure-bred pups nestling in a warm outhouse that Dad had converted into what he called his 'breeding wing'. It was impressive enough for Harrod's to take an interest and become one of Mum's chief clients.

When we parted with them the pups headed south, joining the consignment of fresh Arbroath 'smokies' that, for as long as anyone could remember, had been sent down on the overnight train to King's Cross and on to London's swankiest store. Harrod's even sold a couple of Mum's puppies to Peter Ustinov, who promptly christened them Winston and Churchill and took them back to his own, rather larger, estate in Switzerland. I couldn't have wished for them to be in better hands.

EIGHT

IN FOR THE HIGH JUMP

The path that would lead me into the Metropolitan Police actually began on a chilly February day in 1976 when, determined to follow in my father's footsteps, I marched through the doors of the recruiting office of the Royal Marines at an address above a shopping precinct in Dundee.

It was a month short of my sixteenth birthday. I was there to sit the entrance exam that could gain me entry into one of the world's most elite fighting units. A bare room in a bare building. A row of desks and a blackboard. Dad went for a long walk, leaving me with half-a-dozen other hopefuls and two papers to take.

The first was easy, little more than reading, 'riting and 'rithmetic. No problem there. English and geography were still my best subjects. But the second was a shaker, full of puzzles and 'lateral thinking' posers that made my jaw sag – until I studied them more closely, beyond the smoke-screen, to the nitty-gritty. It was the kind of thing that Mensa eggheads do rather well, but they baffled me at first, and churned my brain cells into overdrive. 'If I know what they're getting at, I can solve it,' I told myself, wading through the minefield.

We sat around waiting for the verdicts. One by one we were called in to an office, where a senior non-commissioned officer (NCO) sat at a desk.

'MacLaughlin?' He bent over my papers. 'Ah, not too much in the first one, but you've got through. As for the second –' his eyebrows went up. 'Well, well. One hundred per cent! Congratulations. Do you know, in the four years that we've been open here nobody has ever done that.' He paused. Then: 'You know what this means. I'll have to have a word with your father.'

What about, I wondered? He was still talking. 'With a score like that, you've got to consider a commission.' Dimly I realised that he actually meant I was officer material. Which I didn't like one little bit. It would mean another year at school to take Highers, Scotland's equivalent of A-levels. And I'd had enough of classrooms.

But Dad came back, and after he heard the impressive news he nodded briefly. 'Right,' he said. 'I'll talk to him.' Meaning me. The NCO nodded back, then grinned suddenly across the desk.

'We've had some funny ones, I can tell you. You won't want to embarrass your father, will you, young MacLaughlin? Here, take a look at these.' He pushed over an official-looking report, and gestured at a page. It was from a recent Admiralty officers' selection board. I ran my eye down some of the questions and answers.

'What have you done to prepare yourself for a career in the Royal Marines?'

'I've started work in an abattoir.'

'What attribute do you think you possess which will make you a good Royal Marine officer?'

'I have the ability to speak without thinking.'

'You have a medical tomorrow. Do you have any questions?'

'Yes. Do I wear clean underpants?'

I shook my head in disbelief. 'Come on, Dad. Let's go home.'

Dad spent the drive back trying to convince me. 'I had that same chance once, son, and I blew it. Don't you make the same mistake,' he urged. For once I had no answer. I argued my corner, but deep down I knew he was right. Another year chained to my desk lay ahead.

A brief summary of my life over the next months could read as follows: Finished school term. Passed six O-levels. Went on school trip to Italy. Did parachute jump. Worked on chicken farm in holidays.

Parachute jump? Come again! But canoeing was getting a bit stale. Stuart and I had explored every creek and cranny on the black waters of the loch, camped out on the islands until we could have drawn a map blindfold, and now I was getting restless.

The answer to my prayers came with an advertisement in the local newspaper *The Courier and Advertiser.*

> Join Scotland's growing army of parachute enthusiasts. Learn to paprachute – for only £25.

There was a phone number, of the Scottish Parachute Club, based at Strathallen Airfield near Gleneagles.

'Please, Dad!' Under eighteen, I needed my parents' permission. I was sixteen. 'I'll pay for it myself. I've got the money – I've saved up.' And I had, a tin full of notes gathered from weekend shifts labouring at a local chicken farm – and, yes, armed with a high-powered hose, back in familiar territory, spraying Sh-One-t from the walls of the sheds. None of that namby-pamby collecting eggs stuff. I knew my place, or the farmer did.

Dad thought I was mad, but he went along with it. 'Only an idiot jumps out of a fully functioning aircraft,' he pronounced, with some truth. This was in fact Dad's Achilles heel. My father had ducked, if not dived, out of ever doing a jump, somehow even avoiding a water leap with the SBS into the South China Sea.

But I made the phone call, had the medical, and completed a day's training jumping off benches and rolling onto mats under the watchful eye of 'Biff' Burns, who was himself a legend when it came to jumping out of aircrafts. Portly and bearded, Biff was someone I trusted on the spot. 'Don't worry if you're scared shitless,' he said encouragingly. 'Everyone is their first time. If you lose your bottle, you don't have to jump.'

And believe it or not, that same first evening saw me plummeting from the open door of a Cessna 172 in the direction of Mother Earth from 2,800 feet. They didn't waste time at Strathallen.

The landing spot was on the airfield itself, and as we took off our small team of virgin jumpers couldn't help noticing the air museum, with a dozen historical planes lined up beside the hangars. Avoid that area at all costs!

My turn. The person who had gone before me had been seated on the edge of that doorway, legs dangling in the slipstream – then suddenly cried out, 'I can't do it!'

'Oh yes, you can,' Biff contradicted, and with a reassuring pat on his pupil's back sent another wannabe birdman dropping into space. What was that about losing your bottle?

Me, I wasn't scared shitless – quite. Skid marks on your pants are one thing, but worse would have been the embarrassment of being helped on my way by Biff, and the resulting ribaldry in the clubhouse afterwards.

All the same, a first jump lives with you forever, even if the second one can actually be scarier, because then you know what you're in for.

That first jump, like they all are, was on a static-line, with a thick cord attached to the chute and hooked to the aircraft like an umbilical cord. It automatically pulls the chute open after three seconds – or it should do. There's a second reserve canopy in a green container around your waist which you're supposed to yank open by hand if the main one has a 'mal', i.e. malfunction, but I reckon it would take a very cool head to pull that bright red rip cord in the general panic of somersaulting through the sky on your first drop.

'One thousand'. . . two thousand . . . three thousand . . . *check canopy!*' Strung out in the starfish position as I'd been taught only hours earlier, my shout was whipped away in the wind. There was a sudden jerk on the line. Above me the chute slithered out of its sheath, then billowed into the sky. I looked up at the silk canopy, a transparent umbrella of orange and white stripes against the evening sun, and breathed a prayer of relief.

This may be the time to mention two things. One, my ambition was to jump from 12,000 feet, which is the limit any civilian in this country is allowed to jump and provides a full breathless minute of freefall. The other is that I suffer from vertigo. I'd thought about mentioning it to Biff, but I suspect he would have been less than impressed, and I'd have gone out of that door anyway.

The literature assures you: 'The landing will be equivalent to jumping off a four-foot wall.' I must have misread it. It was more like jumping off a double-decker bus, and when I hit the ground my legs almost came up through my brain. It was close-cropped grass, but at least I had missed the museum pieces, along with their propellers – and for that small mercy my backside and I were duly grateful.

'Well done, son!' A beaming Biff shook my hand. I was gathering my parachute like a pile of washing to dump it in the repacking area. 'How old did you say you were?'

'Sixteen, sir,' I replied. 'And four months.'

'Well, if I'm not mistaken, that makes you the youngest parachutist in Britain, and probably the whole of Europe. Well done again!' He paused. 'Are you coming back tomorrow?'

'Try and stop me!'

I caught a knowing twinkle in his eye. 'You know something, son? You're hooked.'

The problem with tomorrow, and with all the tomorrows that followed when I made more than fifty jumps, was my fear of heights. But I would swallow hard and keep my breakfast down, and somehow managed it. Occasionally, especially in the early days, I failed. Sorry, Mum, more washing for you.

Three jumps later I was doing dummy free-falls. They still insisted on the static line, but now I was pulling a dummy rip-cord handle on my chest to practise. Half a dozen dummies later, I was ready for the real thing.

It wasn't until the '80s that I finally achieved my great ambition, the 12,000 foot AFF (Accelerated Free Fall) floating over Kent with the best view of the hop-pickers anyone could wish for – as well as a glimpse of France across the Channel. I even completed another half-dozen from this height before quitting while I was ahead.

There was just one last occasion when I was called back in May 1992 for a good cause, a police charity jump in Aldershot when I pretended it was the first jump I'd ever made. A minor deception – but it meant cash for the Police Widows and Orphans Fund.

It was always a double-edged sword, a stomach-churning mixture of elation and nausea, whenever I edged towards that doorway with just the open sky beyond. I never told anyone, of course, not even my father. But I was always tempted to pack a spare pair of bicycle clips in my jump bag.

NINE

DECISION TIME

Back to school. I returned to Arbroath Academy after the long summer break to study for my Highers, the most reluctant bookworm on the block. In those days various strangers would put in a surprise appearance in the school lecture hall and take up two hours talking to the senior kids about our future careers, trying to lure us into theirs. A string of architects, solicitors, local government officials, surveyors and the like passed across our glazed vision, and the best reason for being there was to skive off lessons. But occasionally someone lit a fire.

A lieutenant commander from the Royal Navy landed in the school field by helicopter, and, even more excitingly, two Marines abseiled on to the football pitch from 100 feet up. That focused our attention, I can tell you – and the hall was packed to the rafters that afternoon, with even the swots of the upper fifth cramming in to sample the carrot being dangled before us. Afterwards the Action Men allowed us to swarm all over the chopper as it sat on the pitch, like ants over a large insect, which did a whole lot more for the Navy's chances than the earlier chat.

But for me the moment that was to change my young life came another day, when three new visitors appeared on the stage in front of us: a trio in blue from the Metropolitan Police, touring Scotland as part of a recruitment drive on behalf of Britain's finest. They were not shy about tooting their whistle. 'Unquestionably we are regarded as the world's finest police force, an organisation for which every other law enforcement agency feels admiration and inspiration,' declaimed their team leader, a chief inspector with a lot of pips on his shoulder doing a fair imitation of Billy Graham in a police uniform.

I don't know who wrote his speech, but it certainly impressed his audience. We listened in rapt silence as he went through the various ways in which the Met took care of the capital so that Londoners could sleep easy in their beds at night, even if they couldn't always walk safe on the streets.

The man was tall, authoritative, and honest enough to admit the fight against crime would never be won outright. 'But if more lads like you were to swell our ranks, the Yard will have an outside chance of making the world a better place,' he said, or words to that effect.

He finished by using the school projector for a twenty-minute film to show off the various branches of the Metropolitan Police, from a day in the life of a London bobby to mounted horses shrugging off crowds of dustbin-banging yobs and an alsatian bringing down a robber – real cops acting the part of course. There was even a police diver breaking the surface of a lake triumphantly waving a knife that had been used in a murder.

But for me, a light bulb really popped when the film opened the doors on the CID. I had no idea then that the CID are actually known as 'The Filth' within police ranks, and it was not just a caustic jibe emanating from the great unwashed, or the bulb might have dimmed a bit. A mock gun battle pictured the Sweeney taking out a team of bank robbers in a gun battle – Sweeney Todd-Flying Squad, and this time it was not merely the TV title that was one of my favourites. It was only when I actually worked with them that I realised how true to life that series was – even down to the hessian wallpaper at the Yard and where they hid the Scotch in the office. Whoever wrote that series had some first-grade inside information.

Quentin Tarantino might have made a better job of that little epic, because after the staged gun battle the screen went back to static, featuring the Fraud Squad and a lot of accountant-like figures crouched studiously over ledgers. Thanks, but no thanks. The Murder Squad looked slightly more enticing, with a couple of detectives picking up evidence with tweezers and a body lying motionless in the background.

But then: bingo! We had joined the Drugs Squad, and were spying on a couple of long-haired hippies bopping away in a seedy club with mini-skirted chicks draped round their necks. Undercover cops! All this, and they were getting paid, too. Give the man a cigar! There was a stash of white powder in bags in a basement, and doors being kicked in right, left and centre before the ungodly were led away in handcuffs.

That day at Arbroath Academy, the acting wouldn't win any Oscars. But it got my vote. There and then I decided: *That's for me!*

And it was.

It was January 1978. I stepped off the overnight sleeper at King's Cross with a couple of suitcases in my hands and a sense of impending adventure stirring in my veins. Mum had waved me goodbye at Arbroath station, with a packet of ham sandwiches and a flask of coffee to see me through the journey. A packet of Alka-Seltzer would have been better. I hadn't liked to tell her that I had the mother and father of all headaches, having been out on the tiles with my mates the night before and imbibed the best part of a bottle of vodka mixed with Coke. It was my first-ever hangover, if not my last. And certainly the last time I ever touched that particular cocktail.

If you've never been to London you won't have seen the baffling coloured criss-cross lines framed on the station walls that pass for the map of the Underground. Hampton Court Maze, more like. The Metropolitan Police training school at Hendon was about to become my home for the next twelve months, but first I had to get there. The 450 miles from Arbroath were a doddle. The last six miles were a case for Sherlock Holmes.

I'd been told to take the Edgware Line to Colindale station. So, picture the new boy from out of town, aged seventeen, sitting on a platform with his cases for almost half an hour wondering why twenty trains were all going in the wrong direction. A ticket-inspector finally came up and inquired: 'What's the matter, son? Haven't you seen one you liked yet?' You've guessed it, wrong platform. He saw me right, and I was on my way.

I had enrolled in the Metropolitan Police Cadet Corps (MPCC), which today no longer exists. Back then, it was a way of grabbing young men and women below the permissible enlistment age of eighteen and a half to put them on hold until the day they could take the oath to join up for real. Big career decision. Me, I was keen as mustard and determined to go the distance.

I'd got this far with a handful of O-levels and a Higher in my favourite subject, English. So, I'd had no entrance exam, only an interview. For other kids who needed something to show on paper, the test wasn't that hard anyway – basic spelling and arithmetic got you through. You didn't need an IQ of 200-plus to patrol the streets of London. The great thing I would find was that we all had the same *raison d'être* for being there, which gave us a unique camaraderie with no bad apples in the basket . . . yet.

My best mate was to be Phil Brown, a lanky, fair-haired lad from Wiltshire. A couple of months separated us, and we hit it off from day one. Phil shared my outrageous sense of humour, and we would remain pals throughout our training and into the Force itself. There we would become partners on the Crime Squad, as close as Bodie and Doyle, Starsky and Hutch – or, as some wag remarked before we put an arm lock on him, Hale and Pace when the going got tough. In other words, we always saw the funny side of things, however black.

The big difference between us was that I was the kind of guy who would go through a hedge chasing a suspect, whereas Phil, who was a snappy dresser and proud of it, preferred to find a gate and go round it. In appearance we were chalk and cheese, too. I had dark Celtic brooding looks (or so I liked to think), whereas Phil was strictly male model material, boasting the kind of blond features that would once have excited a recruiting officer for the German Youth. The bastard was a wow with the women, with his piercing blue eyes and smooth-talking manner.

I was duly invited to be best man at his wedding but his bride forbade it, mindful of the kind of speech I might make at the reception. I make no comment, except to say that the marriage fell apart with unseemly speed.

It was Phil who later suggested we go to Israel to celebrate my twenty-first birthday, insisting: 'The women are stunning, they've all had military training so their bodies will be in great shape, lean and firm and bronzed. Let's go and shag for England!' We booked a holiday the same day.

But like the best-laid plans, the best-planned lays can come a cropper.

Persuaded by the brochures, my Adonis friend had booked us into a resort seventy miles south of Elat with chalets on the beach ideal for our purpose. Two likely lads on the loose, that was us. The first surprise was to find that Shangri-la was a barren strip of sand in the middle of nowhere, no man's land with a few goats and camels for light relief. No cabaret at night. Not a single girl soldier out on manoeuvres looking for a spot of 'r and r'. The second was to find our accommodation was a honeymoon resort. On our first night as we strode resolutely into the dining-room we stood out like a pair of shirt-lifters in the sudden silence.

'Christ, Duncan,' Phil said apprehensively. 'We must look a pair of spare pricks.'

'Well, that's exactly what we are,' I told him rather curtly. 'And just to make your day – you're not my type!'

We spent the two weeks getting a great tan and avoiding the Arab goat herders. Some coming of age. Thanks, Phil!

Back to Hendon. The main police training complex is a sprawling estate with an oasis of green playing fields and the Northern line from Edgware running alongside its perimeter fence into central London. The far end is for adult police constables under basic training.

My first night in the dormitory with seven other cadets, I spent more hours awake than asleep. That wretched tube line kept me awake, for one thing. I never realised how quiet life had been in the country until I set foot in the big city.

Next morning was our induction. The Commandant, with the rank of Commander and a lot of scrambled egg on his shoulders, laid out the welcome mat with a few pithy words, then left the room. His place was taken by a drill sergeant, an imposing ex-guardsman with a pace stick under one arm and a vivid red diagonal sash from shoulder to waist. 'While you're under this roof, ladies and gentlemen, we are here to take care of you. You're underage, and three things are taboo: sex, alcohol and tattoos! So no hanky-panky, no visiting the local pubs, and no graffiti on your bodies. Understood?'

We perked up. Here was a personal challenge if ever I heard one – and an initiative test. The girl conscripts were housed three miles away, the pubs were a little closer, and the only place to get a tattoo was 'up west'. By the end of the week we'd accomplished numbers one and two on the song sheet. Number three took a little longer. My tattoo – performed a month later by a so-called 'artist of renown' in a seedy Soho back street parlour – was a six-inch panther climbing up my left shoulder blade. It hurt like hell, cost me a tenner and stayed clinging to my back for the next decade before I came to my senses and had it removed.

Outside our windows lay the concrete expanse of the driving school, and the famous twin skid pans which have helped make the advanced Met drivers the best of the best – and that's not a commercial, just the simple truth. Despite bad publicity of late when too many people have come to grief during high-speed police chases, plus the impression you get from Hollywood cop movies, I'd stake my pension against any other force anywhere in the world.

We would watch in delight as aspiring traffic officers wrestled with the wheel trying to gain control as their vehicles skidded every which way. For those who haven't had the privilege of a front-row seat at these fun and games, I should explain that the pans are greased by oil and water gushing from holes in the side, turning the whole place into an ice rink. These embryo Schumachers are on the 'nuts and bolts' course, which means that after twelve weeks their driving licence has every qualification known to man, and also makes them official vehicle examiners as well as experts in accident reconstruction. I can tell you right now that there is not a single brand-new machine coming off a conveyor belt anywhere in the UK that they won't be able to find a fault in, however tiny.

Traditionally, there's no love lost between the CID and Traffic Division (TD), just as there is huge rivalry between every Scotland Yard department, and in the country beyond. It goes with the game. But speaking personally I always had a healthy respect for the Black Rats, as we know the TD boys. Their proud emblem is a black rat on a white circle – keep a look out for it on the back window of a car, and you'll know there's an off-duty TD man inside. 'For "Child on Board", read Rat!' was the byword when we felt like taking the piss. It was our daily entertainment, sneaking a look through the window during lessons, along with hearing the satisfying thump of car hitting cone.

Years later it would be my turn. Not as a traffic cop, but as a CID detective soaking up the tricks of 'hot pursuit' on specialised surveillance work, tricks that would actually save my life, later, on a far-off caribbean island.

The next months were a stringent diet of physical fitness training, square-bashing on the parade ground and hours of classroom studies involving the law, courts and police procedure. Perhaps it was just me, but you'd never guess how mind-numbing the intricacies of law and order can be, with its mass of paperwork and bureaucracy. But it's a vital and integral part of our whole justice system, so I had to swallow it.

One thing's for sure, they kept us fit. You couldn't fault the state-of-the-art gymnasium above the assembly hall. That gym had everything, even a rock face for climbing. We were up at dawn, scaling ropes, hanging from parallel bars, heaving weights, leap-frogging over a wooden horse, all under the eagle eye of a powerhouse PT instructor in that house of pain. The end result was that we were brought to a remarkable peak of physical fitness, with boxing and unarmed combat as a bonus, and daily 100-yard runs with a pal slung over one's shoulders in a fireman's lift to test our stamina.

I grew more hardened by the minute, and even began to enjoy the daily torture. My particular *bête noir*, though, which I didn't enjoy one bit, was 'race walking'. It's okay for the Olympics, a bone-jarring, undignified method of propelling oneself from point A to point B, keeping both feet (opposite heel and toe) on the ground at the same time, but for some reason the Met employed it to the point of fixation.

No pun intended, it was my Achilles heel. We went round and round the track alongside the Northern Line, an early-morning treat for the rush hour passengers, until we were dizzy.

Race walking. Heel and toe. Heel and toe. I got sore feet, and resented every minute of it. Did the Yard know something we didn't? Is that how we were supposed to chase a mugger, doing our own quickstep while the villain legged it down the nearest alley? But orders are orders, so we just grumbled and got on with it. 'Dig deep, lads, and keep digging!'

And I have to say this. There's always one – and the Cadet School at Hendon actually did produce a flatfoot who represented his country at the race-walking event in the 1992 Olympics in Barcelona. His name was Paul Blagg, and you'll find him there in the record books, at number thirty in the men's fifty-kilometre final. And not a fallen arch in sight.

TEN

BANHAM'S BOYS

After three months came a welcome spot of leave for me to head north for some of Mum's home cooking. On my return I would be assigned to one of three training centres in London for the summer. I nominated my preferred choice: Norwood, then Wanstead, omitting the third one, Sunbury-on-Thames, altogether, as did every other cadet who had heard of its reputation.

Two days before our leave, a notice went up on the board. We crowded round, jostling to discover our fate. I might have guessed it – sod's law. My ticket to ride should have had a black circle round it. Sunbury, where else? A fellow cadet at my elbow groaned out loud. 'That's it,' he said loudly. 'I might have known. I'm putting my papers in.' That's police-speak for resigning, from cadet level to the Commissioner himself. By the afternoon his bed was stripped and the bird had flown.

Why all the fuss about Sunbury? Most people know it as a pleasant riverside village by the Thames with an abundance of nice pubs, a picturesque church and Shepperton film studios close by. You never know if you'll stumble on a famous movie star taking a stroll, or propping up the bar after a gruelling day in front of the cameras. So, why no concerted rush to sign on for Sunbury? In two words – Johnny Banham. Rank: Police Constable, but a qualified Physical Training Instructor (PTI). I ask you to imagine a towering figure, six-foot-plus of muscle, with a broken nose spread like a dumpling across craggy features as a legacy from exchanging unpleasantries in the ring as a noted middleweight.

In fact, PC Banham had scaled the heights of Olympic stardom, and earned the respect of everyone who encountered him, especially in the ring. Long after I knew him, Johnny was one of the first on the scene at the 1988 Clapham rail disaster, which cost thirty-five lives and would leave a lasting mark on him. A few years later, sadly, he died of cancer.

At Sunbury, PTI Banham's reputation had filtered all the way to our police academy and beyond. His task was to lick raw recruits into shape for their next battleground, which would be the streets of London. And his methods? According to legend, brutal. Those who made it back with all their limbs intact could call themselves 'Banham's Boys', and wear the title as a badge of honour.

Eyeing my name on the board at Hendon, I murmured out loud: 'Ah, come on! Is he really that bad?'

A voice replied: 'Put it this way. You don't fuck with him. He fucks with you!'

Point taken.

We arrived at the centre aboard one of the Met's green coaches, a dozen fit young men anxious to please and keen to get on with the business. He was waiting for us. His voice was like a spade shovelling gravel into a deep, dark pit. 'All right, you lot, line up! Let's have a look at you. If you pass my inspection, that's okay, you can relax. Dinner at seven. Have a pint in the pub across the road. If you're not okay, you'll be in the gym in ten minutes.' He walked slowly down the line, eyeing each one of us from top to toe with a gimlet stare.

And to a man, we were not okay. Some hadn't polished their boots properly, others had creases where there shouldn't be any. One cadet had a thumbprint on the vinyl peak of his cap, and that was enough. 'The gym, son. Understood?'

'Yes, sir!'

'Don't you "sir" me. Do you see pips on my shoulder?'

'No – er, Skip –' Skip was the informal word for sergeant.

'Don't you "Skip" me! Do you see three stripes on my arm?'

'Er . . . no . . . er . . .'

'You will address me as Staff. All right?'

'Yes – er, Staff!'

My turn. PTI Banham's X-ray stare was unable to detect a speck of dust on my uniform or my shoes. You could cut yourself on my trouser creases, and my buttons shone like a second sun. But somehow, it seemed, shaving that day I'd missed a single hair on my chin.

'One hair, Staff?'

'Don't you answer me back!'

So the gym it was, for all of us. That first hour PTI Banham showed us what we were in for. Within the ten minutes we just had time to find our rooms, throw down our bags, change into gym kit, and be lined up facing him again. And then it began. Press-ups, squat thrusts, hanging with our backs to a bar and lifting our lower body parallel to the floor – we could handle all that.

But then came his bellow: '*Doggie run!*' and we were off, dashing one way on his command, then at the blast of a whistle stopping in our tracks and dashing off at full pelt in another direction. It may not sound that bad, and we didn't actually get anywhere, geographically speaking. But try it for fifteen minutes and you'll know why some of us were down on our knees at the end, gasping and actually throwing up the day's breakfast all over the polished wooden floor.

For two weeks Johnny Banham ran us ragged. The training centre was an hour from Box Hill, a famous beauty spot near Leatherhead in Surrey that hikers like to climb for a leisurely picnic and where couples can roll about in the grass and get to know one another better. The slope to the top must be close to forty-five degrees, which means they're out of breath before they've even got started.

The heart of leafy Surrey. Stockbroker belt. Rolling hills and lush green trees as far as the eye can see. Today Michael Caine lives a stone's throw away on the Leatherhead road in a converted barn he bought for £1.25 million and on which he spent a further £3 million, turning it into a mansion worthy of Beverly Hills. The area has always been a magnet for celebrities because of its proximity to London, while they can still get a lungful of good clean country air.

But for us, there was no time to admire the view or ask for autographs. We were too busy pounding up and down that slope doing 'log runs' – which meant four of us toting a log the size of a telegraph pole on our aching shoulders. The rest of the day was taken up with cross-country running, six miles around the roads and along the Thames towpath, while our beloved instructor had his own unique method of dealing with stragglers.

We never knew where he'd be hiding. But somewhere along the route PTI Banham would park his car out of sight and sit waiting. If just one kid was caught walking, or stopping to catch his breath, Johnny would mark his card, summon us all together back at the start, publicly name the culprit – and send us all back for another six miles of torture. I can safely say that if you were caught once, you never did it again.

But it worked. A couple of them couldn't take it, and put their papers in. There were no hard feelings on either side – in fact the rest of us felt a twinge of sympathy as they bade farewell to us and to their careers. We all knew it could have been any of us. There but for the Grace of God . . .

After a few days of it, I realised something strange was happening. If not actually liking the guy, I was starting to gain a healthy respect for him. PTI Banham had a job to do and by God, he was going to do it. One example stuck with me. After a particularly arduous twelve-mile run – or 'twice round the block' after some dickhead had been caught stopping for a piss – he called us together, sat us down in a half-circle on the grass, and ordered us to remove our trainers. Then he went round one by one, took each cadet's bare feet in his horny hands with surprising gentleness, and examined them minutely toe by toe. If he spotted a blister or even the smallest cut, it was straight off to the surgery. 'Listen to me carefully, lads,' he said that day, sitting down facing us, his expression serious. 'This may sound like a load of bollocks. But your feet are your greatest asset, and you've got to treat them like your best friend. They may save your life one day. Think about it. You'll be walking around for eight hours a day pounding the beat, possibly for thirty years, and you'll need them to run after people. And sometimes away from people. So you've got to look after them the way a soldier looks after his rifle.'

The instructor eyed our faces, noting a few smirks. His voice took on a sudden hard edge. 'And while I've got your full attention, there's one other thing that you should know. Within a year you'll be leaving here to start your adult training back at Hendon. If you think what I've just told you is so much cobblers, just wait! You'll be taught to do everything by the book – but believe me, that isn't the way it is out in the streets. I wouldn't be sitting here talking to you now if I'd listened to the crap I heard back there.' Back there presumably being Hendon.

He went on: 'Years ago I was a young PC in the East End. A gang of thugs jumped me, and I ended up on the ground having the shit kicked out of me. Like this.' He curled up like a hedgehog, arms over his head, knees drawn up protectively.

'Why didn't you call for help, Staff?' one young voice piped up.

'In those days we didn't have any fucking radios, that's why. Now shut up and listen!' The big man paused to collect his thoughts, his eyes distant. Then: 'I was never going to make it from the pavement. But I managed to draw my stick [truncheon] and lash out at the nearest target – their shins. I cracked at least three of them before the rest broke away and ran.'

Johnny Banham looked around at each of us. 'So the message, lads, is this: tow the line at Hendon, but remember the streets are a different ball game. It's called the real world. And like as not you'll be on your own in it.'

ELEVEN

FIRST BODY!

I found myself in the real world just two weeks later. Not alone, because I went out on the streets on patrol with a veteran police officer beside me whose task was to watch over me like a mother hen. In that summer of 1978 I was cutting my teeth as a police cadet, still eight months short of the magic age of eighteen and a half when I could start 'adult training'.

But in my spanking new uniform I was the dog's bollocks. I looked like a policeman. I felt like a policeman. And I was determined to do my best to behave like a policeman. After two weeks under the ministrations of PTI Banham his 'boys' were assigned to different police stations, mainly in the south-west London area. I wrote to Mum and Dad to inform them proudly that Putney station was my ground – we don't call it 'manor' or 'patch', as you may have heard thrown about on TV by screenwriters who haven't done their research properly. In the Met 'ground' is the word, and ground it remains.

Putney is W Division, and our call sign was Whisky-Papa (WP). All police stations have their own code the same way that airports do. You've all seen LAX or JFK on the departure boards; police stations are no different. London was divided up into divisions (today they're called districts), each roughly coinciding with a borough. All letters of the alphabet are used, apart from 'I' and 'O', which is why on those TV cop shows you're likely to hear 'Oscar' this or 'India' that, which are quite safe to bandy about because they don't exist. But if the radio in the control room crackles: 'Whisky-Papa, Whisky-Papa, from MP –' then everyone sits up. MP is the Yard's call sign, and that means a major alert.

Every police station has its own identification letter, which goes hand in hand with the Divisional letter. One police station in each District is the main Headquarters, and merits the letter D to mark it out. Samples: Leyton is Juliet-Lima (JL). Wandsworth is Whisky-Whisky (WW). Poor old Kingston has the bad luck to be Victor-Delta – VD, right? – because it is the principal police station within V District, and has to live with it. If you're still with me, that's the story in a nutshell. Top of the pile is New Scotland Yard, known as CO, which stands for 'Commissioner's Office'.

Where was I? Ah yes, the summer of 1978, which would turn out to be one of the happiest times of my life. No responsibilities. No paperwork. But plenty of action, even for a fledgling copper. I was a lanky six-footer, ready to fight my corner if I had to, fit as a fiddle and fast on my feet. Somewhere in my bedroom back in Arbroath was the cup from the 100-yard sprint I'd won on the last school sports day, and I was pretty sure I could outrun any fleeing villain unless he happened to have a similar trophy on his sideboard.

When it came to the heavy stuff, meaning a potentially violent situation, it was emphasised that if I found myself face to face with Godzilla the rule was to call for back-up before tackling him. It's not cowardice, just common sense.

Putney police station on Upper Richmond Road was one of the capital's leading factories (our jargon again), a thriving nick bustling with activity. Behind the front office, with its well-worn counter and a desk sergeant with a face that had seen and heard it all, an atmosphere of good humour prevailed, along with a purposeful air of authority.

How was anyone in there to know that the sword of Damocles was hanging over them in the person of the newly appointed Commissioner, David McNee? Just a year into the job, he was anxious to make waves. With him he brought a nickname: 'The Hammer', swiftly and unkindly translated into 'The Rubber Mallet' by the rank and file throughout London, a sobriquet that says it all.

Like most new brooms who feel they need to make a clean sweep, his mission proved to be closing smaller stations in favour of 'central control', rather like local corner shops losing out to the big supermarkets. But he got his gong in 1978, the same year I set foot on the street and Johnny Banham's 'real world'.

Another impact Sir David McNee made on the capital was to transform almost overnight the traditional dark-blue police vehicles into the garish, striped red-and-white 'jam sandwich'. The other revolution was that we coppers had to exchange our blue shirts for white ones, 'Just because they do it in Scotland,' was the communal canteen moan.

Policemen dislike change, and one grizzled desk sergeant summed it up. 'It's the same old story,' he declared, poring over yet another initiative from on high in that week's copy of *Police Orders*, the twice-weekly instruction and information booklet that circulates to each station in the Met. 'Every new Commissioner wants to change the furniture, but all they do is waste the taxpayer's money. You'll see it happen throughout your service. Just watch.'

I watched. All I can say is that the next three commissioners under whom I served all kept the desk sarge to his word.

Meantime, as the new kid on the block, I stepped out along Putney High Street with a newfound authority in my step, a crusading zeal in my loins – and secretly glad of the reassuring presence of PC Eddie Grier strolling beside me, even though he was smaller than me. Like everyone's first love affair, a copper never forgets the first time he actually sets foot on the street in uniform, his baptism under public scrutiny. People look at you differently, for a start, the same as they do with the clergy.

The expressions vary from respectful to shifty. I'd prefer to think it's respect, though these days you can't be so sure with Dixon of Dock Green consigned to romantic fiction, along with the bobby on his bike who was once known to the whole community.

The other fact I now took into account, thanks to PC Eddie tut-tutting at my side and holding me back, is that coppers on the beat stroll, amble, or perambulate. They don't walk at normal speed. And they never, ever run – unless they have to. When they do, watch out! The rest of the world stops in its tracks and gawps. Next time you see a copper sprinting flat out, you'll see what I mean.

Back to Eddie. I felt safe with him beside me, even though he stood just five-foot-eight in his socks and was black as the Ace of Spades. Yes, my companion on my first beat was West Indian, one of the very first black policemen in Britain. I know who got stared at most, and it wasn't me. To compound the situation, the public tended to ask *me* the way to Putney Bridge, or exactly where the Boat Race started. Why? Because I wore a peaked cap while Eddie wore a 'tit' – that's police-speak for the traditional helmet – which seemed to give me the edge.

He took it well, considering the flak he got from his so-called mates in the 'canteen culture' of the time. I was quite shaken by my first taste of racism within the force, as poor Eddie, being the only black copper in the nick, got the brunt of it with daily references to his parentage and ethnic background.

Finally he cracked. 'I've had enough here, Duncan,' he said, as we took our last patrol together along the towpath. 'I've put in for a transfer.' Two weeks later he was gone. The last I heard of him, he was in C Division in Soho, where he was probably more at home.

Soon after, I made my first arrest. Big moment. Big milestone. To be accurate, you couldn't call it an official arrest because I didn't hold the authority of a full constable. But when you're holding a wriggling youth face down in the gutter with his hands locked behind his back, I'd call that an arrest.

All I had were the same powers as Joe Public, powers known to all and sundry as a citizen's arrest. I'd been in the job four weeks, and all in all it had been a quiet month. A couple of shoplifters nabbed by my partner. A cat up a tree – call in the fire brigade for its anguished owner. But this turned out to be quite a day, because I was also introduced to my first dead body.

'Want to come for a ride, kid?' I was hanging around the station waiting for someone to tell me to do something useful. The area car driver was a grey-haired PC called Reg, an old sweat with a reputation for being a tiger behind the wheel.

An area car normally covers two police stations, crewed by two experienced officers and always on the move. A shark cruising dangerous waters, looking for something to bite. The driver's partner is the radio (R/T) operator, and more likely than not you'll find a third, plain-clothes guy in the back. He won't be a detective, but a PC on his normal shift seconded for this duty. Today that third man would be me.

I sat in the back of the souped-up Rover, my eyes scanning every doorway and window, looking and secretly hoping for trouble. Things had been a bit too quiet this past month. Within minutes the radio crackled. 'Whisky Two, Whisky Two from MP. Suspects on premises.' And an address.

We hit the Twos and Blues, the blaring two-tone horn and flashing blue light – and I watched in awe the way other vehicles opened up for us like the parting of the Red Sea. What was that film? *I am the law*! Yeah!

Murder? Armed robbery? A hostage situation? We were at the address within minutes, down a side road by the river. And there were the suspects – a bunch of scruffy kids racing out of a block of flats with various items under their arms. Three doors slammed open. I sprinted after the nearest young tearaway, and caught up with him easily within my allotted time for the 100-metre dash. I grabbed him round his scrawny neck and we both tripped, rolling together like a pair of clowns you see in a circus act, except that there was no sawdust and only a hard pavement underneath us. Hanging on to the collar of his windcheater I breathlessly uttered the immortal words beloved of cops everywhere: 'You're nicked!'

I'd like to say he came quietly, but he didn't. He squirmed and spat like an alley cat before I shoved him in the back of the car. Then I took a long look at my first prisoner. He was a tousle-headed kid with a serious dose of acne, but he must have been some loving mother's son. Or maybe not so loving. The little brat gave vent to his feelings in time-honoured fashion. 'Let me go, you fucker!' Naughty . . . but I'd get used to it. At least I could be proud of one thing: mine was the only arrest. The rest of Fagin's kitchen had split up and scarpered. Seeing I'd got one of them, the officers called it a day and returned to the car. We'd get to the others later.

Reg turned from the front seat, and gave me a broad wink of approval. 'Nice going,' he said. This time, he didn't call me kid.

It wasn't Carlos the Jackal, but it was a start.

A couple of months later I was present when Reg decided his time had come to leave the Force. He had reached the magic age of twenty-seven and a half years service, the bottom line for working your ticket and getting a top index-linked pension as well as a healthy lump sum – provided you're injured. It has become a hot potato in recent times, but in truth it has been going on for as long as anyone can remember. The trick is to get injured severely enough to hoodwink the Chief Medical Officer (CMO) to 'cast' you, meaning to certify you as unfit for duty and, more important, not coming back. It's a ticket to ride off into the sunset, laughing all the way to the bank, and has been abused ever since the rule was first brought in.

Reg played it this way, and it was an award-winning performance. The three of us were in the canteen when a commotion broke out in the yard outside. 'What the fuck's going on?' Reg said, sticking his head through the window. Down below two coppers were frog-marching a noisy drunk towards the Charge-room. He turned and gave Jeff a quick look. 'This is it – my last day on the job!' Then he was gone.

I stared at Jeff. 'What's he mean?'

'He's working his ticket, son. You'll learn something today.'

And I did. Apparently Reg barged into the Charge-room, saw a scuffle going on with the belligerent inebriate, entered into the fray – and ended up flat on his arse, yelling in agony.

Result: one Paddy charged with being drunk and assaulting the police. One long-service PC on his way to hospital complaining of pains in his back. And, later, that same PC invalided out of the Force with a fat cheque in his pocket and a quiet life tending his garden roses ahead.

I realised I had just had my first encounter with the Job's

Compensation Culture, Job being our slang for Police – and the title of our fortnightly newspaper, *The Job*.

It would not be my last.

That was for later. Meantime we left the little tyke I had nabbed at the station, checking him in along with a portable radio set for which he was unlikely to have a receipt. Then the three of us had a quick coffee, and within the hour were back on the streets.

The radio again. 'Got a stiff on the tracks! Putney station.' That meant a body on the District Line. I'd never seen a corpse before.

This was turning out to be my day.

'Ever seen a jumper, son?' The radio operator turned his head.

'You mean suicide – er, Jeff?' Christian names were okay, even for a fledgling cadet.

'Yeah. Or it could be a drunk taking a shortcut. Bloody fool. It's us who have to sort it out.'

I couldn't wait, at least until I saw the body, or what was left of it, lying spreadeagled on the platform. Normally Putney Station is a pleasant open-air building on a branch of the District Line that goes south from Earl's Court to take you over the Thames as far as Wimbledon. There are terraced streets full of upwardly mobile city types, trendy restaurants nearby, and the famous grass tennis courts of the Hurlingham Club down the road, with the river lapping somewhere beyond the end of the platform.

Today was not a normal day for sightseers, tennis players or weak stomachs.

Less than an hour ago the blackened pile on Platform Two had been a man. It lay on its back, the features concentrated into what looked like an expression of surprise, as if he had been taken unawares by a flame-thrower. The scorched remains were still smoking, and the suit he had been wearing was blistered with small grimy holes. A knot of railwaymen stood silently around clutching handkerchiefs to their faces and keeping down wind. Personally, the smell of burning flesh never did worry me too much, but then I'd always had a strong stomach.

'You won't believe this,' the senior LT official said, nodding at the smouldering remains.

'Christ,' said Jeff. 'You didn't tell us this was going to be a barbecue!' Black humour, or what? But that's the emergency services for you, and firemen and ambulancemen are the same. Nurses, too. They see so much death and destruction every day that it's either laugh, cry, or crack up.

Reg looked at me, checking to see if I was going to throw up, but was reassured by what he saw. 'Your first dead body, son? Well, you won't forget this one in a hurry.'

To the railwayman he said: 'What the fuck happened?'

'He was having a piss. Someone who saw him with his dick out thought he was a flasher. But he was only taking a leak, silly bugger . . . straight on to the live rail!'

'Shocking!' muttered Jeff, the humourist in the party. He produced a notebook. 'Cause of death? Umm . . .' He scratched his head with his pencil. 'How about urinary infection?' It occurred to me standing there that I'd have to get used to the jokes as quickly as I was getting used to sudden death. Maybe even quicker.

Reg nudged the body with his foot. It seemed a trifle unnecessary, but I was forgetting the police manual. This is the official *Instruction Book for the Guidance of the Metropolitan Police Force* with which we are all issued on day one, and which I was already reading cover to cover as part of my training. A copper can't sniff or scratch his arse without finding some reference to it somewhere in those thousand pages. The manual is the Bible for our behaviour, and covers everything from Rogues and Vagabonds 'within the meaning of the Vagrancy Act 1824' to 'dying declarations'. Not that we were going to get one today.

One oddity I noticed that day at Putney was Reg sticking his foot into the body. The manual said nothing about kicking a man when he was down, but over the months to come I would find that it was almost a ritual for the head copper called to a sudden death to test the cadaver for himself with his big toe, presumably in case the corpse should sit up and say there'd been some mistake. They all do it. I did it myself. Weird though it sounds, it became force of habit. And throughout my twenty years dealing with bodies I would find myself automatically doing the same. *Prod*! Sorry, sport, no offence! *Prod*! *Prod*!

'We've shut the station, and the ambulance is on its way. The trains won't stop at the platform.' The LT were on the ball, I'll say that for them. 'And a doctor's been called.'

Even if it's not a crime scene as such, a doctor is supposed to attend this kind of fatality to certify the victim is dead, even if it's pretty obvious that he is. The poor bugger's head can be one side of the track and his body the other, but we can't officially reach our own verdict and write it down without a doctor confirming it.

It's there in black and white in the manual. 'Death can rarely be safely assumed,' intones the 'Good Book'. 'If there is the slightest doubt the case should be treated as one of illness or accident.'

In this case I have to say we felt fairly safe.

'Shouldn't we put a blanket over him?' I inquired, mindful of the pasty faces of the onlookers. Reg and Jeff both stared at me. Where do you find a blanket on a station platform anyway? One of the LT workers came up with an old paint-stained sheet. 'We're doing some decorating,' he mumbled, retreating hastily and leaving me to do my Sir Walter Raleigh act to cover the corpse.

It wasn't our job to go through the clothes for identification. That would be taken care of at the mortuary. As we waited for the medical team I mentioned hesitantly that I'd heard of this sort of thing happening to cows straying on to the line out in the countryside, but never to anyone stupid enough to take a leak onto a live rail.

'Listen,' said the senior LT man. 'You won't believe what people do when they're rat-arsed. And even when they're not. Wait till you see the candyfloss . . . '

And by the end of that summer I had indeed seen the candyfloss, and wished I hadn't. This is nothing to do with the kind of spun sugar you find on Brighton pier, but (sorry about this) the technique used to gather what's left from the track if someone's been hit by a train. There can be up to a hundred yards of entrails spread along the line.

Remember your biology lessons? The human body has an incredible thirty feet of intestines tucked away inside, a vital statistic I've never managed to come to terms with, and those innards can take up a lot of space being dragged along by the 8.10 to Waterloo. The only way to get the late Mr Brown together for his trip to the mortuary is by using a pair of sticks that you twiddle like noodles on a fork. Or candyfloss.

Even then the doctor has to certify death. Remember the 'Good Book': 'Death can rarely be safely assumed . . .'

TWELVE

WAYNE KERR, IS THAT YOU?

The summer of 1978 flew by. There were a few downers, such as Scotland being knocked out of the World Cup in Argentina in the first round. As a fresh-faced cadet I spent my time when not pounding the beat in Putney doing one of three things: watching soccer on TV, drinking with my mates in The Flower Pot opposite our section house in Sunbury, or swimming in the Thames across the road.

I still saw Johnny Banham, but only one day a week, and I could wear that. We'd taken all he could give us and come through it triumphant, if a trifle bruised. I was one of 'Banham's Boys', which gave every one of us a big clout among other cadets throughout London, and I knew the fearsome PTI was secretly proud of us.

But now I'd reached eighteen and a half, and that meant I would come of age as a fully fledged police constable. Even with my general attitude to authority I knew it was a solemn moment.

Like most people in the country, I had only a vague idea of the origins of the police force. But now I'd have to learn fast. From my school history books, I knew that the old feudal parish constables had eventually led in 1829 to Sir Robert Peel, the Home Secretary, forming his famous 'peelers'. But I'd sometimes wondered, why Scotland Yard? No one wore kilts. The answer is that the original two Commissioners, Colonel Charles Rowan and Richard Mayne, occupied a private house at 4 Whitehall Place in Westminster. Apparently the rear opened on to a courtyard which had once been a residence of the kings of Scotland, and was later used by Sir Christopher Wren when it was known as 'Scotland Yard'. The back of number four was used as a police station and became the headquarters of the Metropolitan Police. The name stuck, even when the HQ moved to the Thames Embankment and later to its present home in Victoria.

All very interesting, if somewhat academic to an ambitious recruit.

I was sworn in on 25 September with sixty other aspirants at my old training school in Hendon – except now I was with the big boys and would be wearing a tit on my head. There was a fresh intake every week, men and women of all ages, but for my seven days I could claim that I was the youngest PC in the whole of England and Wales.

The candidates came from all corners of the land and from all walks of life. Teachers, university graduates, bank clerks and builders stood shoulder-to-shoulder in line, but most came from the three branches of the Services, men who had seen action across the globe. I was in the minority. Along with three other cadets, I was aware that in the eyes of our prospective tutors we were cocky young upstarts who knew it all and were, as one put it succinctly, 'full of gob'.

The swearing-in was conducted with a disappointing lack of ceremony. If I expected drums, pipes and all the paraphernalia that goes with a benchmark in a young man's career – forget it! The ritual took place in a classroom, with only a whiteboard, marker pens and rows of desks as the trappings. The Commandant wasn't even there to proffer a congratulatory handshake. We had to make do with a sergeant who lined us up in two rows, handed us a small card, and on cue signalled for us to recite the Constable's Oath:

> I solemnly and sincerely declare and affirm that I will well and truly serve our Sovereign Lady the Queen in the Office of Constable without favour or affection, malice or ill-will, and that I will, to the best of my power, cause the peace to be kept and preserved, and prevent all offences against the persons and properties of Her Majesty's subjects, and that while I continue to hold the said office I will, to the best of my skill and knowledge, discharge all the duties thereof faithfully according to law.

Looking back now, I wonder how long it took the others to forget that little homily.

The ragged chorus of voices came to an end, and not all in unison. We signed our names in a large, bound ledger beside the Warrant Number, a number that would remain with us for life. Mine was 172321. That made me the 172,321st person to join the force. Next we filed into another room, where a man with a tripod took our photographs. Finally we were fingerprinted. 'Surely only villains get printed, Sarge?' Not so, though maybe they were trying to tell us something, even at that early age. He didn't bother to reply, but pressed both my hands down on an ink-covered brass plate. The print was then transferred on to paper. It was nothing like the way they roll your fingertips on an ink pad as they do in the movies. But then there's a lot they don't do like it's shown in the movies, as I'd find out soon enough.

'Why fingerprints, Sarge?' I inquired again.

This time he deigned to reply. 'It helps us identify you when you get blown up.' Thank you very much. He could at least have said 'if'.

Then it was off to meet the man who would be our adviser, confidante, mentor, soulmate, judge and jury all rolled into one – our Drill Instructor. Excuse my sarcasm. Sergeant Sid Butcher was a former Guardsman who, so the rumour went, had been too much of a handful for the Met with his methods which, to put it politely, were less than gentle. They chose the simple option to get him off their hands – us.

Tall and broad-shouldered, with hair that stood up in short thick spikes, Sgt Butcher wore a belligerent expression and spoke several decibels above the norm. It scared the shit out of everyone. His stentorian tones blasted you from a foot away as if he was on a permanent parade ground for the terminally deaf. Armed with clipboard and pace stick, he lined us up, then marched down the ranks, eyeing our name badges and checking them off against his list.

'Right, Bryan – student (tick) . . . Duffel – salesman (tick) . . . Denton – piano teacher.' Pause. Then: 'What do we want a fucking piano teacher for?' Denton, a mild-looking chap with a wispy ginger beard, ventured timidly: 'Don't you play then, Sarge?' – and swayed back with the volume of the Sergeant's unintelligible response. Message received loud and clear. He didn't play.

Facing straight ahead, I could hear the heavy footsteps getting nearer. Predictably he tore a strip off the other three cadets, and finally it was my turn. I stared into the baleful gaze as he stood back and looked me up and down. He consulted his board – aha, another smart-ass cadet! Sgt Butcher prodded me in the chest with his pace stick. 'Young man, there's a bit of shit on the end of my stick!'

I knew it was stupid, but I couldn't resist it. 'It's not on my end, Sarge!'

That got me two weeks' 'defaulters', but the muffled laughter was worth it. For the next fortnight I was emptying rubbish bins, cleaning the boards, stacking chairs and doing other menial jobs in the evenings while my three mates propped up the bar and drank toasts to an absent friend.

Meantime we were marched over to the stores to be measured for uniforms. I'd already got two identical outfits from my cadet days, but that didn't seem to cut any ice. 'Bring them over, we'll dispose of them,' said the storeman.

I left the store with a holdall containing the indispensable copper's manual, a wooden truncheon, a pair of ceremonial white gloves (to this day I've never worn them), a torch, an *A–Z* which fell apart within weeks, a whistle, and a key to fit any police box, the only snag being that there aren't any police boxes in the Met district, apart from the single 'Tardis' outside the former cadet school. But they do fit AA boxes, which can be useful. I was also handed Metropolitan Police Form 29 (Protection of Animals Act 1911), which authorised me to instruct a veterinary surgeon to slaughter an injured animal if I came across one or maybe a runaway horse, or a rabid dog, or the Beast of Bodmin. I never did. All the cats up trees, the only four-legged friends I noticed on the beat, seemed to be happily using up their nine lives and emerging unscathed, so I never did make that call.

The Met loves forms, which are their bread, butter and a splash of caviar on top. Moreover every form has to have a number printed on it somewhere. Annual leave requests, expenses chits, witness statements – think of a number, it's there. I made it my personal challenge to find a sheet of paper without a number in the top right-hand corner, and finally found one – on a loo roll. But watch the suggestions box. It'll happen some day.

I was issued with my tit the same day. Otherwise known as the British bobby's helmet, the pride and joy of the Force – even if it is occasionally seen rolling embarrassingly around in the gutter during a scuffle. It's an odd shape, if you think about it, and made of cork so it's both light and strong. Our showcase symbol for the tourists and their cameras, it's as important for the album as Big Ben, Buck House and the Tower. As one of the boys in blue, I would stumble on an unexpected perk: the tit worked marvels abroad. Not just as a calling card, but a trading card too. Especially in the States if the Highway Patrol caught you speeding. Just produce a helmet from the back seat and offer it with the compliments of the Commissioner. How's that for a bribe! I'm not saying I filled my suitcase with a dozen tits, just the odd one or two. But I never did get a ticket – and those boys Stateside play it by the book.

The next fifteen weeks were an intense course of lectures, PT in the gym, swimming and more lectures.

A word about our instructors. They were nice guys, all volunteers. But as time went on I realised that most of them had volunteered for one of three reasons: it gave those with aspirations for promotion time to study;

it gave those who didn't like shift work a cushy nine-to-five job and it gave the shirkers who had woken up to the fact that police work could be a dangerous job an escape route to safety. If you were looking for someone to face down a bunch of yobbos at closing time, or a baying football crowd, or a hostile demo, these were not the guys to put at the top of your A-list.

They took a delight in winding us up. When it came to 'police procedure' and how to address the public, their day was made if they could catch us out with simple humour I thought I'd left behind in primary school. For instance:

Recruit: 'Can I have your name sir?'

Sergeant: 'Why, what's wrong with your own?'

Yes, it was that bad.

Or: 'Okay, what's your name, sir?'

'Wayne –'

'Wayne what, sir?'

'Wayne Kerr.' Pronounced, you've guessed it, 'wanker', followed by one man laughing fit to bust while the rest of us shook our heads in disbelief.

Was it really going to be like that on the beat?

THIRTEEN

FALL OUT!

The one thing we did not learn in all this high-powered brainwashing was how to be streetwise. That would come later, when we were in at the sharp end, learning the hard way. The most memorable bit of advice I can remember was how to deliver what was known as 'the death message' when someone had been killed and it was your job to go round to see the newly bereaved and break the bad news. The instructors drilled it into us: 'Be compassionate. Knock on a neighbour's door first. Explain what you have to do, and invite them to drop by next door in a couple of minutes for a shoulder to cry on. Above all, offer to put the kettle on. There's nothing like a nice cup of tea at a bad moment.'

We took it all in, listened intently and made notes. But anyone can make a mistake, and an example of how *not* to behave came from a character named Angus, actually a friend of mine, who was in my intake. Three weeks after he became a fully fledged copper he was sent with a 'death message' to impart to a lady in a house in East London. He rang the bell, not too long or too loud. Next thing, a flea-bitten mongrel had jumped out and bitten him on the ankle. In his thick Glaswegian accent, Angus (nursing his ankle) addressed the bereaved. 'I've come to tell you your husband's dead – and have you got a licence for that fucking dog?' Angus was later invalided out after being stabbed – not by an enraged widow, as we half-expected, but by some drunk in a pub brawl.

One of the guys in our class was unfortunate enough to have a very soft voice. Nick's brainpower was fine, his vocal power almost non-existent. In their wisdom, the instructors decided to help him project it. They set the scenario as usual, inventing situations where your friendly copper would be face-to-face with Joe Public.

'One of the most frequent situations you'll find yourselves having to handle is a row between two irate motorists. It happens all the time,' a bull-necked instructor intoned. 'Use tact and diplomacy. Remember the Old Testament: "A soft answer turneth away wrath."' With which he called Nick out and marched him over to a wall a good twenty yards away.

Two other instructors played the parts of the angry motorists, finger-wagging and swearing. Poor Nick had to mediate in a soft hoarse bellow as best he could. 'Come now, gentlemen . . . please . . . it's no good taking that attitude . . . calm down . . .' The three-way conversation echoed all the way to the fence and beyond. The rest of us, dutifully watching and learning, nearly wet ourselves.

Now a new word came into my vocabulary, 'mnemonic', the art or system of developing the memory. Put simply, you think up a word with key letters to describe a situation. Like 'POOFS', reminding us what conditions apply for gay sex being permitted: P, for Private (the location); O, only two persons to be involved; O, both parties must be over 21; F, fully consenting; S, for Sane. 'Meaning that you can't take advantage of the village idiot,' an instructor told us. 'Got it?' Got it, Sarge.

Another was 'WOLO DICKY BIRD', referring to indecent exposure. Wilfully, Openly, Lewdly and Obscenely exposing one's penis (Dicky) to a female (Bird). Once I'd got the hang of it – the key word, that is - it proved surprisingly useful, and I remember that extraordinary code to this day. Coppers use mnemonics like a trusted friend, and even if they can't always spell them properly they swear by every syllable. Words like 'PRIMROSE' (dealing with a reported road traffic accident) and 'ELBOWS' (rules for pocket-books: E, no erasures; L, no leaves torn out; B, no blank spaces; O, no over-writing; W, no writing between lines; S, signature) went into our notebooks to be memorised until we knew them inside-out.

Law lectures were a different matter. In short, they were one big yawn, but essential. My eyelids tended to shut before I'd even settled into my desk. I had to keep them open, because we needed to be word perfect on definitions. If one word is wrong on the charge sheet, a case can fold on the spot. Take, for example, the definition of 'robbery'.

> A person is guilty of robbery if he steals, i.e. commits theft, and immediately before or at the time of doing so, and in order to do so, uses force on any person or puts or seeks to put any person in fear of being then and there subjected to such force. (Section 8 of the Theft Act 1968.)

It looks fairly straightforward. But not so fast! Within that little lot lies the word theft, and within that one word I'm supposed to know five definitions. Words like 'dishonestly', 'appropriate' and 'property' abound, and you have to be a legal eagle to get it just right. If it doesn't meet the criteria of the offence, you're screwed! We emerged after each session like one big happy family of barrack-room lawyers, talking nineteen to the dozen about how to put our man behind bars.

Take a bank robbery. A blagger walks up to the teller, and whispers to her: 'I've got a gun in my pocket. If you don't hand over the cash I'm going to shoot the baby in that pram!' Believe it or not, that isn't robbery. Without doubt the guy can be sheeted [charged] for several other offences, but not the one you might think he's committing. If I nick him on the wrong count, a smart defending barrister can spot it in court, and he'll walk.

It gets better. If our friend grabs the baby by his romper suit and drags the kid out of his pram, he's using force within that definition – and committing a robbery. Okay, it's an extreme example, but you get the point. Today's robbers, and their lawyers too, are slippery customers.

The real shaker was the nuclear lecture. No one dozed off then. Once a week Nuclear Ned took the chair, armed with a marker pen, maps, and a pile of videotapes. He was a former army officer, but he'd earned his nickname as he put the fear of God into us by lifting the lid on the unthinkable. We were treated to frightening details about radiation, fall-out and other effects of a nuclear attack, spelled out largely in words of one syllable, and walked out of that room feeling in need of a large drink. In those days the bad guys were the Russkies. Today it's anyone who goes by the overall sobriquet of 'terrorist'.

'On hearing a nuclear explosion, officers at police stations should note the time and test for fall-out with a radiac survey meter,' intoned Ned, a man without a great deal of humour – and who can blame him? He had a pencil moustache that twitched in time with his words as he consulted a home defence manual. A brief and unseemly snigger ran round the classroom at the thought of coppers reaching for their notebooks, licking their pencils and assiduously making a note of the time, presuming the whole place hadn't been incinerated already.

'Fall-out,' continued Ned, unfazed, 'is dust sucked up from the ground by the explosion and made radioactive in the rising fireball. It climbs high in the air and is carried downwind, falling slowly to earth over an area which may be hundreds of miles long.' At moments like this

Nuclear Ned had our full and undivided attention. We coppers would be issued with a 'dosimeter' each 'to measure the cumulative dose of radiation which its holder absorbs', and were assured that 'the intensity of radiation decays with time, a simple analogy being the cooling of a red-hot poker'.

The videos consisted of five-minute commercials, which were also to be broadcast to the public. The voice-over belonged to Patrick Allen, a stiff-upper-lip actor with a steel jaw and a voice to match. He specialised in playing sergeant-majors in military movies, but more recently could be seen leaping in and out of helicopters trying to sell you a Barratt house. The scenario was depressing, to say the least. But then, so was Hiroshima.

Basically our job would be to maintain law and order, protect the public by directing them to the nearest shelter and prevent looting, while those of us who had the training would be issued with firearms, presumably in case we had to shoot someone on the spot.

There was a lot more on these lines, like the signal that the balloon had gone up. They call it 'Red Warning' – a siren rising and falling, the same ominous sound people heard in the wartime Blitz. This means imminent danger of attack, and the order is simple: 'Take cover!' and, in the immortal words of Corporal Jones from *Dad's Army*, 'Don't panic!' 'Black Warning' refers to imminent danger of fall-out, which presumably means the big bang has gone off. This is signalled by three explosions, plus 'gongs and whistles sounding three blasts in succession', with sirens repeating short blasts.

After hearing this reassuring news, the initial consensus among the class of would-be guardians of the streets was 'Fuck it. If the final whistle goes, we know where we want to be – at home with our loved ones and families.' But that, of course, was wishful thinking . . . wasn't it?

I wasn't too impressed with the practical side of defending home and hearth, either. Fall-out shelters for a start. 'Put mattresses over kitchen tables, and hide underneath.' And, 'Make sure the curtains are drawn so the flash won't blind you.' But how do you know when to shut your eyes against the sunburst? It was all quite surreal.

After all the brainstorming and facing up to the imminent end of the world as we know it, we couldn't wait to get into the gym. But another nasty surprise awaited us. It's known in the military as 'milling', or 'choose a friend and kick the shit out of him'! You put on the gloves, pair up with someone of your size and weight, and get stuck in for a full minute. Queensberry Rules go out the window. They sprang it on us without warning. The first hint of trouble was when we mustered in the gym one morning and I noticed Sgt Butcher conferring with the PTI in one corner. Sgt Sid's blue-chinned features came dangerously close to a smile as he nodded and left, and I knew immediately that something was up. I sat by the ring with my mate Ian Hargreaves, another six-footer and similar pound for pound on the scales to me, and we watched in growing apprehension as the carnage began. 'Hard as you can, lads!' the PTI shouted encouragingly. 'No slackers, now!' The gym was a whirlwind of arms, fists, elbows and cracking heads.

The fights had one thing in common; they always seemed one-sided. One poor bugger would stagger off the mat with blood pouring from him to be towelled off and led away, looking distinctly cheesed off, while his opponent marched off in triumph. After half an hour, it was coming to our turn.

'I don't like the look of this,' I muttered, as the latest casualty was helped past us and flung a towel by the PTI to mop up.

'I don't either,' said Ian. 'Tell you what! I won't hit you hard if you don't hit *me* hard. What do you say?'

'Deal!' I said.

Our turn. We were fitted with gloves, and took to the mat. A whistle blew, and we began prancing around like a pair of pansies, tapping gloves lightly and issuing realistic grunts and groans of pain.

But not realistic enough to win any Oscars. We lasted half a minute before the whistle blew again, this time a ferocious blast. 'Ladies, *ladies!*' The PTI's voice filled the gymnasium. 'I take it you don't want to smudge your make-up. Sit down, please! And keep your gloves on.'

By the time that session ended we both looked as if we'd been through a mincer, thanks to the opponents the PTI singled out for us. The bloke who used me as a punching bag was Charlie, the Met's answer to Henry Cooper. But I bore him no illwill, then or now, because it was him or me, even if it was mostly him. Ian emerged in the same condition. As we compared bruises in the bar afterwards, I said: 'Well, we tried!'

Fifteen weeks later it was all over, and for me the course couldn't end quick enough. Final examinations lasted a full morning, but at least the supervisors upstairs didn't leave us dangling for the verdict. We all passed, possibly because if we hadn't it meant staying behind for another month to retake them.

The class instructor read out the list and told us where we'd be spending our first months as fully-fledged qualified police officers – on paper, at least. 'MacLaughlin – N Division.' That meant Islington, a borough in North London with a lot going on. He came to the end. 'Good luck, all of you.'

A hum of excitement followed him as he left the room, with everyone asking each other, 'What did you get? Where are you off to?' Ian got B Division, which I would have liked because it meant Chelsea, Knightsbridge, Holland Park and Kensington, all top of the A-list in estate agents' brochures. Lucky sod.

One of the slower members of the class was writing something on a scrap of paper. 'What you got, John?'

He showed me his *aide memoire*. 'N,' he replied. 'N for Nuckle!'

Islington. Oh, well. 'Good for you,' I muttered, wondering how soon we'd be discussing Pythagoras' Theorem on the beat together.

Our passing-out parade came not long after. January 1979 was a blisteringly cold month, adding to the 'winter of discontent' of industrial chaos, strikes in schools, hospitals and railways, piles of rubbish littering the streets, petrol shortages, workers laid off, even bodies waiting to be buried piling up in church halls and hospital sheds. James Callaghan would soon be packing his bags at Number 10, and Margaret Thatcher was four months away from moving in.

But all this was forgotten for at least one day, as we prepared for the ceremony under the stern gaze of the statue of Sir Robert Peel. My mother and brother braved the snow to drive down from Scotland – by now Ian was carving out a career for himself in hotel management – and I was only sorry that our sister Amanda, now seventeen, couldn't get out of school to be there. As for Dad, he was away again.

The ceremony was not quite the five-star spectacular we'd hoped for. In fact it was somewhat muted, as the parade ground had to be abandoned because of the appalling weather, and we took refuge in the gymnasium. Sir Robert Peel, wearing a white wig of snow on his head, missed out, and so did we. Instead the Commandant walked slowly up and down the thin blue line, standing rigidly to attention in the gym. It was the day we were issued with a black Rover apiece – sadly, not a car, but police-speak for warrant cards which at least afford free travel all over London. He had a word for each man.

'PC MacLaughlin!' He peered at my nametag. I waited expectantly for words of wisdom that would send me off on my new career, full of crusading zeal and zest. He paused, searching for words. Then: 'Umm . . . That's a good shine you've got on your boots.'

'Thank you, sir.' He passed on. If only he knew. Anyone can buy a tin of clear floor polish, and it takes about ten seconds per toecap before you can see your face in it.

The whole thing was a bit flat, nothing like those *Police Academy* movies where they all throw their caps in the air on the lawn and cheer their Super to the echo. Afterwards Mum, Ian and I went for a pint across the road at the local. Ian shook my hand. 'Well done,' he said. 'Congratulations.'

Mum raised her glass of Scotch. 'Shame your dad can't be here. But congratulations from us both – officer!'

FOURTEEN

ON THE BEAT

Every Monday a green coach used to go round London taking eager young PCs off to area headquarters, the police stations where they would start their careers. There would be at least thirty of them, every one eager and impatient to get stuck in.

On that wintry January morning, I was dropped off at King's Cross nick together with four other young coppers, with the crisp number 393N gleaming silver on my shoulders. This is N Division HQ, in the borough of Islington. I'd had a taste of the streets as a cadet, but nevertheless there was a feeling of going out into the big wide world that got the adrenaline pumping just thinking about it.

First things first. We leave our gear in the charge-room downstairs, including our precious tits placed neatly on top, and feeling like the dog's dinner in our crisp new uniforms the five of us are taken upstairs to the office of the Commander of N Division, tall and authoritative, with iron-grey hair and a row of ribbons on his chest. He sits us down and gives us a 20-minute pep talk, telling us what he remembered of his first day and that we were on the threshold of a great career. I find myself thinking 'Sounds like a lot of flannel,' before pushing the unkind thought away. To us young shavers the guy was impressive.

The climax of the big man's talk came; he had saved the best till last. 'One final thing,' he said, his face sombre and the words dropping out with the hollow sound of pebbles down a well. 'You may see unlawful practices within the force, and be tempted to take short cuts. Don't! It's not worth it – and as sure as daylight you'll come a cropper. All right? Good. Now lads – off you go, and good luck.'

So much for Divisional HQ, King's Cross. Outside, a Panda car was waiting in the snow. Two of us, 'Nuckle' John and myself, piled in, to be taken to Islington police station in Upper Street which would become our workplace and second home for the next two years. My first impression was of an old brick building three storeys high and a little run-down, next door to the fire station. Today it's a luxury block of flats.

'Watch out for flying snowballs,' warned the Panda driver, a guy named Kim Smith who, over the months, would become a good mate. He had a great sense of humour, and on one occasion needed it. His particular achievement was to fall foul of a condom company when he agreed to let them put their slogan on his personal Mini car as part of an advertising campaign. He used that car frequently on surveillance operations, and more than once I would be in the passenger seat. His understanding with the condom company was that they'd remove it after a year, and respray the whole car.

Kim thought it would be a small logo. Instead, to his horror, the entire car was covered in suggestive stickers and painted condoms. 'I still drove it – but that put paid to using it for surveillance,' he would admit ruefully, when the canteen laughter died down. At least he got a £1,000 out of it, as well as a good spray job.

He mentioned snowballs? 'Yes, get ready to duck and make a run for the door! You never know when those bastards are going to set up an ambush!'

He gestured up at the fire brigade tower next door, presumably where they practised on the slippery pole, if that doesn't sound ambiguous. They used the tower to nail the coppers next door – and had an unfair height advantage. Over the next two winters I would have my helmet knocked off more than once by a well-aimed snowball.

Now I met a PC called John Watts, an educated Scotsman who was three years ahead of me on the ladder. Over the years we grew very close, both becoming detectives and serving on the Regional Crime Branch. Years later the Commander's words that first day would come back to me when John let slip one job he had been on. He'd been part of a team who arrested a number of people working at the Mint to destroy Bank of England used notes.

'That's one I'd like to have been on,' I said, half-joking, when I heard the details.

'Too right, Duncan,' he replied. 'There was a new car outside my house at the end of it! Paid for in cash.' And he winked.

Several years later John was dead. He had been moved into the Anti-Terrorist Branch as a detective inspector. One morning he went to the squad's office at the Yard, sat drinking coffee with some of his team and then went down to the armoury. He drew a gun from the armourer, signed for it, went back to his office – and put it against his temple and blew his brains out. No one ever found out why. Like everyone who knew him, I was stunned. John may have had his scams, but he was one of the good guys. If he had problems, he kept them to himself. What is it they say about the good dying young?

Now, on day one, came another pep talk, this time from the Chief Superintendent at Islington. He was lower rank than the Commander and with less paint on his chest, but he was still impressive. We were told the shifts: early turn (6 a.m. – 2 p.m.), late turn (2 p.m. – 10 p.m.), night duty (10 p.m. – 6 a.m.) and off-duty. In those days the Met were going through one of their periodic under-staffed phases, a condition which has dogged them ever since they were formed.

'The Metropolitan Police were created on 29 September 1829, and consisted of 1,000 officers.' The Guv'nor knew his stuff, speaking without notes, probably because he must have done it a thousand times before. 'By the following year there were 3,300 patrolling a seven-mile radius with a population of less than two million people. Today, 150 years on, we're around 25,000 in strength, patrolling 620 square miles, with up to 16 million people inside it.

'And think about it, gentlemen. With four shifts, only one-quarter of you can be on duty at any one time. Some of you will be in court, others on courses, others off sick. Can you wonder why the public are always calling for the bobby on the beat – and there isn't one to answer that call? But we're all in it together, and I expect each one of you to pull his weight. Comradeship is the word. We look after our own here.'

Next came the guided tour, with PC Watts doing the conducting. Offices upstairs, four cells on the ground floors – and when I peered round the heavy iron doors for a peek inside, my stomach churned. Manky wasn't the word – the mattresses could have walked out on their own. Stained, plastic and paper-thin, they were crawling with lice. The walls were covered with graffiti. 'Okay, it isn't the Hilton, and you'll know you've arrived when you find your name carved on the wall. Along with your parentage, of course,' said PC John jovially.

My first shift was not quite the *Starsky and Hutch* extravaganza I was hoping for. Because of my age, still eighteen, I was confined to barracks – you're not allowed out on to the streets until you're nineteen, which has always puzzled me since lads of eighteen were regularly being shot on the streets of Northern Ireland in the name of Queen and Country.

So I started life as a full-blown copper behind a counter. Inaction

Man, working in the front office. Dealing with Joe Public producing driving licences, insurance and MOT certificates within five days after they'd been stopped – we used to call them 'five-day wonders' – and keeping the office clean. Oh, and making tea. Lots of tea. 'Very important tea is, sonny,' was the general message from the grizzled veterans who passed through my field of vision those first days. More significantly, I also had my first taste of villainy – the adult kind, not just kids scarpering with radios from a Putney estate. These were people on conditional bail awaiting trial, who had to report to their local cop shop to show they were still around and hadn't done a runner. Coming face to face with them over the counter, I grew to recognise the local rogues. In weeks to come, as I patrolled the streets and got to know each street and doorway as if I lived there, as well as the 'faces', I would take time out to swap jokes and banter with them. It was all part of community policing.

The remainder of my first day behind the desk was spent under the benevolent eye of the duty sergeant, John Glass, tall and slim with sandy-coloured hair and a nose like an eagle's beak. He was the salt of the earth, a real diamond, and he gave me my third pep talk in as many days. 'Forget what those other two have told you, my lad,' he said. 'I'm talking about survival. I'm your reporting sergeant for the next two years, which means it's my job to look after you. So here's the first lesson. The three most important things you need to watch out for are the three Ps.'

I stared at him blankly. 'What – ?'

'Three P's,' he repeated firmly. 'Prisoners, prostitutes and property. More policemen lose their careers through those three little words than for any other reason. With prisoners, it's brutality. With prostitutes it's favours offered, usually a blowjob or a hand shandy. And with property, it's theft. All allegations of course, but you've got to watch your back.' Later, I would add another letter to that lot – 'I' for 'Informants'.

I made the most of the time before I turned nineteen. Like all probationary police officers I had fifteen months of exams to pass, at the rate of one a month, mainly on police procedure, law . . . and more law. These took place in an office block in Holloway, where we'd also attend two days each month for lectures.

The bad news was that you had to study in your own time – and let's face it, I was not the world's most enthusiastic student. You think a college education has distractions – I'm talking beer and girls, of course. Try the junior members of the Force for ways to keep you from your books. Somehow I hung in by the skin of my teeth, though I'd get a regular bollocking and was frequently put on monthly reports. 'Buck your ideas up, young Mac, or you'll be on the next train back to Scotland,' was the usual message.

But unlike all those Old Bill dramas you see on TV, we're actually very relaxed behind the closed doors of the nick. All that tension and shouting – well, we get a bit of it, especially when a big crime breaks on our ground. Otherwise it's very friendly, a lot of pranks and banter, and Christian names or nicknames are the order of the day. Uniformed sergeants are 'Skip' or 'Sarge', or it's first-name terms. A senior officer would be 'Boss'. Nine times out of ten they'd return the compliment by calling me Mac.

After what seemed an age, but was in reality only three months of penpushing, I reached the magic age of nineteen – and my life took a quantum jump, or something close to it, whatever it is. Now I was out in the streets, ready to face any trouble that might come my way with only a radio, a truncheon and a whistle for company.

For our first two weeks, the young rookies were given a 'parent' PC to show us the ropes. It was just like Putney, only somehow I'd grown up in the past months and it all meant more. We'd patrol together on foot, traditional bobbies on the beat, and I'd watch how my minder handled the public and dealt with daily 'incidents' that could be anything from a road accident to a mugging. Sudden deaths are a regular occurrence on any copper's patch, usually taking place behind closed doors and most often alone. Crime, the petty kind, is restricted to shoplifting, breaking into cars, burglaries and assaults.

Now I saw first-hand some lessons that they never touch in the police manual or mention in classes, but are part and parcel of a copper's very existence. I'd had a taste of 'policeman's humour' at Putney, but in Islington it became a daily diet to nourish and sustain us in our hours of need.

My newfound father figure was a PC called Bob. Late-thirties, passed over for selection by the CID, he had got used to the fact that he'd be in uniform all his life. As someone once said about marriage, 'It isn't what you want, it's what you settle for!' Bob had settled for pounding the beat until his shoe leather wore out. He was a good bloke, and he knew the ground like the back of his hand – together with every single pub in that square mile, all ninety-nine of them would you believe, with Islington police station right in the centre. What more could you ask, except at closing time when things could get a bit lively?

People often ask me if I was afraid to walk up to a bunch of drunken yobs and face them down. The fact is, your parent PC is only with you a fortnight, and then you're off like the prodigal son to make your own way in life. Well, policemen are not stupid. It's not so much a matter of fear as simple common sense. If it was all going off, and I was on my own, I'd call for back-up on my radio. There's no point in being cannon fodder for a bunch of drunks outside a pub. It was really very simple: 'November India from 393. Assistance required at King's Head, Upper Street. Got a situation that could boil over. Chucking-out time, and possible disturbance. Can I have some back-up please!'

The police are always polite on the radio, even in times of stress. It is necessary to appear calm at all times, even if your stomach's like jelly. They don't want some hoarse panic-stricken voice bellowing for help down the blower for every copper in London to hear – it would be bad for the image, and wouldn't do morale a lot of good, either. Remember what they taught you, Duncan, I'd think: accuracy, brevity, speed. Get the message across, and forget the fancy words.

With any luck there would be a dog available. Or even two. Dog handlers tend to go around in pairs, especially on night duty, with the coppers up front in the van marked 'DOG UNIT' in heavy capitals so everyone knows they're coming, and with man's best friend behind the grille in the back. We always feel better with an Alsatian or two around – or German Shepherd if, like my dog-breeder mum, you're a stickler for accuracy. They are wonderful animals, as long as they've got their handler on the other end of the leash. But once they're off it and after you, that's a different story. I've actually seen a lone PC and his dog hold back a mob of more than a hundred soccer hooligans at Highbury Corner – Liverpool supporters, actually, who had watched their team lose to Arsenal. It was an impressive sight.

I happen to know what it's like to tangle with a police dog – and I've still got the teeth marks on my thumb to prove it. But more on that later, when I come to my specialised training.

FIFTEEN

INTERLUDE WITH A CARPET-SWEEPER

First day out on the streets with Bob. I checked my 'appointments' – and I don't mean with the bank manager. That's our jargon for truncheon, whistle, torch (if it's night duty) and notebook. I picked up the radio from the cabinet in the front office, booked it out (another form, another number), and went out into Upper Street. These days it amazes me how coppers manage to walk upright with all the gear that's weighing them down.

We only got a hundred yards, walking slowly in step, when both our radios crackled, so we got it in stereo. 'Can you get over to Essex Road, possible sudden death. Ambulance called. Show 393 how to deal with it.' That was me, PC 393N, on his first assignment.

'Right, Bob.' I was raring to go, radiating the eagerness and inexperience of youth. 'Let's get over there.'

'Steady, son. No need to run.'

We found the address, an old terraced house in a tree-lined street. Two women, presumably neighbours, were standing outside, concerned faces turning to relief as we appeared. Otherwise the street was quiet.

'We haven't see him for a while,' the first woman said.

'And there's that funny smell,' the second added.

Bob nodded soberly. 'Watch this,' he said to me. 'A little trick to show you.' He bent and pushed open the letter box, then sniffed. He straightened. 'Yep,' he said. 'We've got a stiff one in there! Anyone got a key?'

The women shook their heads. Without further ado he got his truncheon out, smashed the glass pane, reached inside and turned the knob.

Now my sense of smell is lousy, but even my nostrils could detect something rather awful. It was coming from a door to the left – the living-room. Inside was a sight I will never forget as long as I live, however hard I try.

He was dead all right, and looked like he had been so for a number of days. He had been a young guy in his thirties, and now he faced us across the room, standing up, but slumped on something. His face had a waxen pallor and a curious fixed grin that on any other day might have been a smile of welcome.

Looking closer, I saw in disbelief that he had a carpet-sweeper stuck up his arse.

'Christ,' I said, recoiling. 'Will you look at that!'

Bob peered closer. 'At least he's got a smile on his face, young Mac,' he said. 'Do you think he always cleaned the room this way?' Police humour again. You wonder who writes their scripts.

The giveaway was the selection of gay porn magazines lying around on the sofa, the table and the carpet, littering the room.

Until the Divisional Surgeon arrived, the place had to be treated as a crime scene. Our doctor was a jolly Irishman, a local GP we called out when we had to. Paddy arrived and examined the corpse.

'Ah.' He gave us his diagnosis. 'He's dead all right. He was obviously getting off on them magazines. Poor bugger must have been sitting on it, propped against that coffee table over there, when it slipped and sent him flying backwards into the wall. The handle went right up him. It's embedded in his rib cage.'

The ambulance crew arrived. They shook their heads in unison. 'Can't separate him here,' muttered one. 'We'll have to take him to the mortuary as he is.'

They loaded the body on to a stretcher, put a sheet over it and tried to conceal the bulge made by the carpet-sweeper as they bore it out into the street. 'Come on, lad,' said Bob. 'We've got to see this through. The coroner will want to know the circumstances and the pathologist will need to know who found him. Have you ever been to a post-mortem before?'

I hadn't, and I couldn't wait. It would be the first of many post-mortems I would witness in the years to come. 'Count me in, Bob,' I responded enthusiastically.

It's not like you see on TV. Especially American TV, where they keep the stiffs in individual refrigerated metal compartments. In Britain, we go in for sharing. No such luxury as separate beds – the corpses are stacked a dozen or so in each fridge, as I found when I set foot in the sterile tiled chamber in the basement, accompanying the shrouded figure on a trolley – with the carpet-sweeper incongruously protruding from its rear orifice. You don't see too many carpet-sweepers these days, come to think of it – I wonder why?

The pathologist looked surprisingly young. I'd expected an old man in a white uniform. This one wore a collar, tie, butcher's apron and green wellington boots, as if he'd stepped out of a farmyard. More country gent than city slicker.

He pulled back the sheet and looked down. If I expected hysterics from him, shock, a tot of brandy needed, I was disappointed. Nothing, just the merest twitch of an eyebrow. This man had seen everything – and let's face it, it takes all sorts . . .

'We'll have to leave it in.' I realised he was trying not to laugh out loud, and I could hear muffled sniggers from the autopsy crew, the mortuary technicians whose job it is to prepare the body. This, I was to find out, involves the rudimentary acts of undressing the corpse, removing the top of skull, peeling off the face and laying it on the chest – it's still attached to the neck by the spinal cord. 'This is weird,' I thought. All you see is a crumpled red mask with two staring eyes in it. My rotten sense of smell helped, otherwise I might have thrown up.

Removing the top of skull at that time was performed with a thin saw, and was a work of art in itself. The doc rested the head on a small wooden block before getting to work. All that was missing was the guillotine, and a few old hags knitting alongside it. Into my mind as the top half of the skull was lifted neatly off came an image of my mother slicing into a boiled egg as she used to do at breakfast – except that instead of the yellow yoke, there was a semolina-coloured brain inside!

He then made an incision from the bottom of the throat to the abdomen – just like in a murder case, they always give us the contents of the stomach, which we have to keep sealed up for forensic examination. And all the time he was talking into a tape recorder.

Bob and I hung around for half an hour until the performance was over. When we left the carpet-sweeper was still there.

SIXTEEN

KIDNAP!

The next two weeks flew by, full of road accidents, break-ins, missing persons, the normal daily grind of a policeman's life. I had to breathalyse a couple of people too, one of them a bit-part actor familiar from TV commercials. Also spotting a private vehicle in a bus lane, I had to flag them down when they shouldn't be there. One unlucky man on the end of my beckoning finger surprisingly turned out to be Peter Storey, of one-time Arsenal and England fame, who had his own problems at the time. 'Do I fucking need this?' he said, as I pulled him over in Essex Road, one quote that didn't go into my notebook.

We call it 'process'. Joe Public knows it as traffic misdemeanours: speeding, going down a one-way street the wrong way, bald tyres, missing a red light. 'If you really wanted to make his day, you could have called in the Gestapo,' Bob said approvingly, as if to a favourite son, when I told him. 'Gestapo' is police-speak for the motorbike cops, part of TD, if you hadn't guessed already from their jackboots and black breeches. 'He was lucky to find a nice gentle young copper like you!' My parent cop was being sarky, but he had a point. TD could have taken that car apart and found a hundred things wrong with it.

My attitude was, and has always remained, that we need the public on our side and that there are enough petty rules and regulations around without antagonising them any further. I can truthfully say, hand on heart, that in my eighteen months in uniform I reported no more than a dozen motorists for 'process' offences, and breathalysed three more. I had to play it by the book – up to a point. But, as they say, I allowed myself a certain artistic licence. My interest and my future lay in serious crime, and I had no intention of spending my career walking the streets with a tit on my head and pulling in law-abiding citizens for minor infringements. There's more to life than being a Woody – CID-speak for

Woodentops, as they call the uniform boys. In short, the CID was my goal, and nothing short of it would satisfy me.

All good things come to an end. After two weeks I was off the leash, and ready to set out on my own. 'How about a drink to celebrate?' It was Bob's treat.

'I thought you'd never ask!'

We made for The Florence, a large pub round the back of Upper Street that was close to both the cop shop and the fire station, with one large bar where we'd jostle for drinks. The Flo' became pretty lively at times, even if the only snowball anyone got their hands around there was the kind made of advocaat and lemonade!

'Well, son, have you learned anything? Have you settled in all right?' Bob put a pint in front of me – beer in a straight glass. I had, on both counts. By now I had my own room in the section house, which was only five minutes walk from the nick, I'd chummed up with some good mates, and generally speaking things were rosy.

'That's good,' he said. 'You'll be okay. Keep your nose clean and your head below the parapet.' He put his glass down and reached for his crash helmet. 'I wish I could join you for another, but I can't risk it. I live in bandit country.'

'What?'

'Hertfordshire, that's where I've got to get to. The local Bill are always on the lookout for us lads from the Met. You'd think they could smell us. It's a game with them, to see if they can nick us – and if we're over the top we'll end up in court, and get sacked as a bonus! It's a pain in the arse.'

I was taken aback. 'Don't we look after our own?'

'Yeah, you'd think dog doesn't eat dog,' Bob agreed morosely. 'But you try telling that to the carrot crunchers! It's pure jealousy, because we get paid more than they do, just like our guys who live in Kent, Essex and the other Home Counties. They get the same treatment, so they have to go careful too, or take the train home if they've had a skinful.

'It's worse at Christmas, because the carrot crunchers have a bounty around their manor. They all put money into a pot for six weeks, and first to nick one of us in the New Year for alco. gets the kitty. Bastards.'

Bob downed the dregs of his beer, flipped a hand in farewell and walked out, leaving me alone to think about it.

Twenty-four hours later, it was night duty for the new boy on the block and my first time out on patrol as a lone officer on my own ground. As I walked out into the car park I spotted a curious sight. A uniformed policeman was standing beside his Panda car blowing into a glass phial. I looked closer. A bag on the end was swelling . . . he was giving himself a breath test! The cop glanced at his watch and caught me staring at him. 'Give it another half hour, then I'll be okay,' he said.

Later, when I mentioned it to Bob, I discovered it was routine. 'Well, you don't want to get caught, do you? Think of the embarrassment. Two drunks, same breathalyser!'

It was drummed into all of us that special alertness is called for on night patrol. That's when the ungodly are abroad, going about their nefarious business. This first night I started out with suitably measured tread, radiating superiority, off along Upper Street towards Essex Road. Islington, like its inhabitants, is a mixture of the good, the bad and the ugly. Elegant Victorian houses in a tree-lined terrace give way suddenly to a side street with grimy council estates disfigured with graffiti and torn posters of last month's rock concert.

Islington has some very elegant areas, where at one time or another the likes of Roger Moore, Simon Ward, Jon Snow, Martin Shaw, Angus Deayton and, of course, Tony Blair have had their homes. You could also find families of a different ilk within that square mile: the notorious Adams tribe, for instance, who made the Krays look like wimps, and celebrity villain Frankie Fraser. Another interesting character was Tommy Wisbee, who ran The Trafalgar pub in the area.

My size elevens trudged the pavements at an unhurried pace, leaving the imprint of passing authority on the wet leaves. Like those TV commercials I'd seen of a copper rattling windows and locked gates to check they're intact, I shook the security rail across a store window to make sure it was shut.

Next thing, a deafening jangle filled the silent street. Christ, the bloody thing had gone off! Now my radio was crackling. '393, November India.' Can you get to the supermarket, corner of Essex Road and Rotherfield Street. Burglar alarm's gone off. Can you deal with it?'

Since I was standing right outside the place, that was not hard to do. 'On my way!' I walked down to the end of the street and back. Then, breathing hard, I imparted the information. 'November India, 393. Appears all correct. Can you call out the keyholder?' They'd get whoever was listed on the emergency number out of bed, and I would hang on till he or she arrived. Cause of alarm? Probably a cat, or a wiring fault. We have a mnemonic for the usual explanation: SOBO, or 'set off by occupier'.

'Better have a look at it in the morning, sir,' I advised the manager when his car skidded to a halt beside me. Then PC 393N exited with dignity.

My first week involved me in a kidnapping – my own. A couple of nights after the security alarm fiasco I was patrolling down Essex Road, wrapped up against a biting wind in overcoat, scarf and gloves. We didn't just wear scarves to keep us warm and cosy, or to prevent us from getting a chest cold. They were also used to hide the giveaway white shirts so that we could stand in a doorway unobserved, watching and waiting if we thought there might be trouble brewing. The ears might show, because the tit doesn't cover that part of your anatomy, but they'd be blue with cold anyway.

Out of the night, a Mini with two women inside suddenly screeched to a halt beside me. A window was wound down, a frantic finger wagged at me. 'Officer! Come here, quick.'

The occupants were attractive young girls I judged to be in their early twenties, one blonde, one brunette, older than me but fun-looking with it. I hastened over. 'What's wrong?'

'We need you urgently. Can you come with us?'

'Well – '

'Get in the back!'

I eased off my helmet and squeezed in, thoughts racing through my mind. Was someone injured? Or in labour? Was a cat up a tree? Something hard pressed up against me, and looking down I saw a striped traffic cone, one of those things known in the Force as a 'fuck-off bollard'. And something else, a large fire extinguisher. The girl in the passenger seat was ticking off a list on a clipboard. 'Good. All we need now is a fireman!'

'We'll deliver this one first.'

What the hell? 'What is all this?' I demanded from the back seat as the Mini accelerated and roared off.

'I'm Jo.' The blonde turned and gave me a bright smile from the passenger seat. 'And this is Sophie.'

'Oh . . . ah . . . pleased to meet you. Will you tell me what's going on before I arrest the pair of you?'

'You'll see. We're almost there. Just sit tight!'

I sat tight, six feet of copper squashed in the back of a Mini in a thick overcoat, hardly able to move or breathe. Watching the streets zip past, I realised it wasn't my ground any more. I was on Euston Road – this was E Division's business.

The Mini screeched to a halt outside a large building with a reception area and a warden on duty behind a desk. Someone had scrawled a notice on a piece of cardboard propped against the staircase: 'WELCOME TO THE ASYLUM. FOLLOW THE NOISE.' An arrow pointed upstairs, and music and laughter filtered down from above.

'This way!' On the first floor a party was in full swing. Rock 'n' roll music blared from a record player. Someone pressed a beer into my hand. 'Drink up! Enjoy!' It wasn't an asylum, but a nurses' home, full of gorgeous laughing angels and beer-swilling young men. Nobody batted an eyelid at the sight of a uniformed constable clutching his helmet suddenly appearing in their midst, and then I saw why.

Over in the corner were four other PCs, all in uniform, all with their tits, all drinking beer. I moved in on the nearest and squinted at the epaulette on his shoulder. 'Q – that's Wembley. You've come a long way,' I said. 'What happened?'

'Well,' he waved his can of beer at me. 'It was like this. I was walking down Wembley High Street . . .'

'Don't tell me,' I said. 'I don't want to know.'

London would be five officers short on the beat that night.

It turned out that a dozen nurses were on the prowl as part of a game, looking for objects to 'borrow' and victims to kidnap and haul off to their rave. Half an hour later Jo fought her way through the throng and planted a kiss on my cheek. 'You're a darling, 393. We've got our fireman. And we've won! We get a crate of wine.'

After that I was in no hurry to get back out on the cold streets. Some time in the early hours I returned to my own ground. No one ever sussed it.

Some of the lads thrived on night duty. I wasn't one of them, for no real reason; it just didn't seem natural to hear the sound of my boots echoing on deserted pavements under the stars while all good law-abiding citizens were tucked up asleep. It wasn't right for my body clock, either, and played havoc with my digestive system. And there was something odd about heading back down those same deserted streets at 5.30 in the morning and hearing alarm clocks going off one after the other behind the drawn curtains.

More than anything else, night duty meant drunks. Falling out of pubs, slumped in doorways, inhaling dead leaves from the gutter, throwing up, or simply wandering around spouting incoherent poetry to the night sky, they're usually just a flaming nuisance. It's the older ones you feel sorry for. Homeless vagrants with no chance in life except what they see in the bottom of a bottle of meths, rather than a yuppie who's missed the last train home. On cold winter nights we would pull them off the streets for their own good to give them a bed for a few hours. But occasionally even a drunk could pull a surprise. I'd noticed this white-haired old vagrant a few times, sitting in doorways or on a park bench munching curly sandwiches from a newspaper, but I'd never run him in. We all knew him, and dubbed him 'Steptoe' for reasons that would be obvious to anyone who watched TV.

But one frosty December night I spotted him lurching around outside The Champion long after closing time. He was legless and it was cold enough to freeze your piles off, so I called in the van. It wasn't altogether altruistic, as it would get me off the streets for half an hour, too. But Christmas was coming, and after all it was the season of goodwill.

Back at the station the desk sergeant clocked him in. 'Search him, Mac,' he said, as I propped my prisoner against the wall. The jailer and van driver looked on. I put on my driving gloves and dipped into the pockets of his filthy jacket, to find the usual: an old tobacco tin, a packet of Rizlas, loose change, bits of paper, a soiled handkerchief, a comb with most of its teeth missing – and what appeared to be an empty crisp packet, all scrunched up. I unwrapped it and peered inside. Frowning, I showed the sergeant the contents.

'What do you make of that, Sarge?' It was a gooey, off-white congealed mess.

'Beats me.' He scratched his head. 'Tartare sauce with his crisps? What is it, old man?'

The oldster blinked out through his white fringe. 'That? It's me 'Arry, mate. I've been collecting it for years.'

'Harry?' I said, confused.

'Yes, sonny, 'Arry Monk –'

'Christ!' I let go of the packet as if it was a hot iron, and we all stepped back involuntarily. We knew our Cockney rhyming slang. Harry Monk – spunk.

'You d-e-e-rty old man!' hissed the sergeant, unconsciously emulating the catchphrase that kept millions glued to their sets every week. And to me: 'Get that dirty old fucker out of my nick.'

'But I've just arrested him!'

'Well, un-fucking arrest him, for Christ's sake!' bellowed the desk sarge, his expression turning purple. 'Get him out of here! Now!'

'Come on, Dad.' I stuffed the crisp packet back into his pocket and led him to the door. 'No room at the inn for you tonight. Let's find you a shop doorway.'

Night duty was also good for late-night pranksters, particularly after closing time. One night I was acting as jailer when there was a brief commotion in the front office and two of my mates appeared, Steve and Mike, ushering a portly businessman into the charge-room, complete with pinstriped suit, umbrella and briefcase. He was loudly protesting his innocence. 'What's he in for?' I asked the duty sergeant.

'Drunk,' he answered briefly as I closed the cell door for the prisoner to cool off for a few hours and sober up.

In the canteen later I found myself sitting next to the patrol pair. 'What was all that about?' I asked. 'He didn't look that pissed to me.'

'He wasn't,' said Mike laconically. 'But he caught us on top of a post box.'

'He what?'

'We were having an argument about how wide a post box is. My mate said you could get two guys on top of one, and I said you couldn't. There was only one way to find out. Park the car and get up there. Which we did – and that's when this bloke came round the corner. City type, pinstriped suit, briefcase and umbrella, and he sees us balancing there like something out of Bertram Mills Circus – so we had to nick him, didn't we? For his own good.'

I shrugged. 'Well, you'll be safe in court. No one's going to believe his version of events.'

And they didn't. I wish I'd been there to hear it. 'So, Mr Defendant, you came upon these two officers perched on top of a post box? And you say you hadn't been drinking? Guilty! Ten pound fine. Next!'

Yes, I wish I'd been there.

Early turn. This started at 6 a.m., an hour before breakfast, to give us time to work up an appetite. By 7 a.m. we were famished, and the local greasy spoon café, run by a family of bubbles (bubble-and-squeak . . . (Greek) off Chapel Market did a brisk trade, with a dozen or so orders from the cop shop. This from two sergeants, a handful of us lads, and a couple of plonks – women police constables to the rest of the world. We're plods, they're plonks. But in those days, nobody thought of suing.

The orders taken, a Panda driver would be dispatched to the greasy spoon to collect them, returning a few minutes later to the control room where we'd gathered. Then there was a half-hour break while we sat around munching our rolls, drinking tea and reading the papers until it was time to go back on the street.

'Christ, this tastes salty,' I said one morning, biting into my bacon roll. 'Remind me to have sausage tomorrow.'

'Shut it, Mac,' chided Terry, 411N. 'You're always whinging about something.'

'It's not the first time,' I grumbled. 'Besides, salt's bad for your blood pressure.'

Fast forward three years. By now I was a detective based at King's Cross, and was questioning the youngest bubble from that same café for burglary. The Woodies had nicked him red-handed breaking into a drinks machine in a shop precinct, and we had him bang to rights in the charge-room.

Now it was my turn. I recognised him immediately as one of the local trouble-makers, small fry and cocky with it.

'You're going on the sheet [charge sheet] for burglary,' I told him. 'And while I'm at it I should have you for violating the Food and Safety regulations.'

'What you talking about?' the bubble demanded.

'I'm talking about your bacon rolls. The breakfast deliveries we used to have for breakfast. They were so salty they made me seasick!'

A knowing grin came over the artful dodger's features. 'Salt? That wasn't salt, mate. I used to wank into them!'

'Remind me never to eat there again,' I growled, writing his name on the charge sheet in heavy letters.

Soccer duty was seen as a perk by practically every copper I knew. Maybe I was the only exception to the rule. The truth was that myself and blue serge didn't suit, if you'll pardon the pun. My burning ambition had always been to join the CID, and it burned as strongly now as when the touchpaper was lit back at school. I like football all right, though Formula One motor racing is really my passion, and I would later give my personal stable of informants pseudonyms of racing drivers.

But I copped my fair share of duty in the stands at Highbury and White Hart Lane, as well as other London grounds, with the highlight naturally being Cup final day at Wembley, if you got lucky in the draw. If you looked at your TV set closely enough when West Ham beat Arsenal 1–0 in 1980, you'd have spotted me there behind the goal, third from the left. Closer to home, Highbury Stadium beckoned. Saturday afternoons meant overtime, whether you supported Arsenal or not.

When it comes to football crowds, things don't seem to have changed too much over the years. A soccer lout is still a soccer lout, and probably always will be. As one old-timer in a cloth cap and muffler high up in the stands muttered to me, 'There've been hooligans since time began. I remember them back in the '30s where we're standing now. They dressed different then, but their mentality was still the same.'

As part of the thin blue line, I learned to take it early on, from my first game in fact, when the first globule of spittle landed on my crisp new uniform. We all got used to it, sort of, coming back to the station covered in spit. I can't say any of us liked it, but it went with the game. We used to get cleaning tokens, free, every month.

My first punch-ups were at Highbury, nothing too serious, more of a scuffle than a real ding-dong. The first big rumble was an FA Cup semi-final at the Arsenal ground, West Bromwich against Spurs. The fight took place afterwards, as they usually do, outside a pub in Liverpool Road with a bunch of drunken supporters suddenly going berserk.

I arrived, eager to get stuck in, when someone a lot more sensible grabbed my shoulder and pulled me back. 'Easy, lad. Let them get on with it. Wait for the cavalry. We'll go in and pick up the pieces.' The cavalry being the Special Patrol Group (SPG), hard bastards who went around in special transit vans loaded with anti-riot gear and took no prisoners.

This ruthless band of brothers, formed in 1965 for fast mobile back-up, were only 200 strong, but they wrote their name into history with their heavy-handed methods. They were ultimately disbanded in 1986 after a decade of bad publicity which left a particularly ugly stain with the 1979 death of Blair Peach, a schoolteacher who died in the Southall riots after being coshed across the head. Headlines pointed the finger at the SPG, but the inquest returned a verdict of death by misadventure. Their new name is Territorial Support Group (TSG), otherwise known to us as the 'Thick and Stupid Group' because, with their intake of body-builders, they seem to have more of their share of brawn than brain.

Back to the terraces. Of course I was scared. I wouldn't be human if I pretended otherwise. Not scared shitless, more apprehensive, but at that age you're also hot-headed and physically fit and you honestly think nothing can happen to you.

In those early days I was in a lot of rucks, but somehow came through them virtually unscathed. The worst were the coins, which can take your eye out. Being hit by a sharp coin, especially the 50p bit of legal tender before it became light as plastic, is not an experience I would recommend. It hurts. On particularly lively matches I could hear the things pinging off my helmet like hailstones. At least our heads were protected.

Millwall fans were the worst in those days, closely followed by Spurs and the local lads sporting red and white and supporting Arsenal. Either these oiks on the terraces had money to burn or they were involved in some kind of contest. But at half-time, when everyone was queueing for the loo, we went around discreetly picking the coins up – and usually pocketed enough for a drink in the pub afterwards! Their loss, our gain.

If you were off-duty on a Monday there was another little trick to play to liven things up. Causing a ruck on the North Bank was a public order offence that meant us pulling a yobbo or two into court after charging them at Highbury Vale nick. The court sat on Monday. You had to be there. The magic word 'overtime' flashed up in lights.

The way it went was this. I'd be standing on the back terraces up among the would-be trouble-makers with fellow uniformed officers. At the right moment, when someone had scored and the place erupted, one of us would put a hand between the shoulderblades of the nearest lout and push, hard. The berk would catapult into the crowd with a yell of 'Oi, who you shovin'?' Next thing, the ruck would be on, the cue for us to grab the nearest thug and haul him off to Highbury Vale.

There they faced another opponent, and a formidable one at that – a charge sergeant. His opening line was: 'All right, sunshine, take the laces out of your boots!' The miscreant would automatically put his foot on the only chair, which would immediately collapse under his weight. How could he know it had been primed for just such a moment? 'All right,' said the Skip. 'That's criminal damage.' And into the book it went.

Highbury Corner Magistrates Court is one of the few courts in London that does not enjoy 'extended bail', which means that the person charged goes before the beak on the next available date, always a Monday, following the weekend. For us in the local nick, it was a natural money earner – more overtime, right?

The criminal damage scam went on for months, until it all came to grief one morning. The dulcet tones of Mr Tobias Springer, the elderly and legendary stipendiary magistrate at that court, asked for a message to be conveyed back to Highbury nick after the latest little yob was sent off for a spot of community service. 'That chair really should be replaced.'

SEVENTEEN

DING DONG!

These were the days before PACE. This is the Police and Criminal Evidence Act of 1984, a major piece of legal doctrine bringing all the old laws together under one roof, which basically gives the prisoners more rights, but gives us a few fringe benefits in return, too, like taking 'intimate samples' such as nail cuttings and hairs (pubic and head) to help us out in the witness box. Prior to that act, the police were virtually a law unto themselves. For instance, all that guff about a prisoner making one phone call (usually to his lawyer) was just that – so much guff. I know because I was part of it, and saw it refused more times than I had hot dinners. It was nothing to keep a prisoner banged up for a week while his lawyer scurried frantically around London and the Home Counties, serving writs of Habeas Corpus on police stations as he tried to track down his client.

It was quite uncomplicated to refuse a prisoner's plea. I did it myself, frequently, using words pared to the bone by time-honoured tradition. 'What phone? Fuck off!' It was all within the law. 'We'll be back in a couple of days to speak to you. Think about it.' And we'd leave the fellow sweating in his cell. Today it's a different scenario, with the strictest guidelines imaginable for 'prisoners' rights' laid out in black and white and learned by heart by every fresh-faced constable walking out of the gates at Hendon.

In those days you could be in for some nasty surprises. It was nothing to throw a suspect in the pokey and leave him there for up to ten hours without checking on him. More than one jailer has opened the cell door to find a dead man instead of a live one lying on his bunk. Then the doctor had to be brought in, and this is where things could get a trifle touchy.

I was given some useful guidelines on my first time out as acting jailer at Islington nick. The desk sergeant beckoned me over. 'Listen young Mac. If you open the cell door and find a stiff in there, you know what to do.'

'Call the doctor?' I remembered the manual.

'No!' The sarge's brows shot up, then descended again into a frown of rebuke. 'That's the last thing you want. It's dereliction of duty not to have supervised him.'

'Strewth! What do I do, Sarge?'

'You call one of us, and together we prop him up against the radiator until he warms up. *Then* you call the doctor.'

I was learning.

Night duty again. But this time I had something to look forward to. The Force likes to show it's a caring organisation by keeping victims of crime updated on the investigation or the way a court case is going. It's part of fostering the community spirit. I had been involved in a domestic violence incident where a man had whacked his partner across the face, fracturing her nose. Let's call her Caroline. She'd chucked him out of her flat in Oakley Road, and he'd gone back to his mum in Surrey. Then she told us. I took a day trip out to Woking armed with a warrant for his arrest and returned with him on the train. He was a rueful and sad man, a model prisoner, no handcuffs needed. He was charged, bailed and pleaded guilty.

A couple of weeks later I went round to Caroline's flat to bring her up to date. Let's just say that one thing led to another and within a week I had moved in. I must say it was handy having a second home on my ground, and made a welcome respite from the section house. I kept it totally secret, of course. Shagging on duty is next thing to a hanging offence if you're caught, even though you could write a TV soap about the number of times it happens. There's something about a uniform . . .

On the night in question, as we say in the witness box, I was out of the station by 10.30 p.m. and in bed with Caroline for a spot of r and r by 11 p.m. before continuing my rounds. My big mistake that night was to leave my radio switched off – well, you don't want a shout from headquarters butting in when you're approaching the moment of truth, do you?

An hour later, back on the streets, the radio came to life. An irate voice demanded: 'Where the fuck have you been?'

'Sorry, Sarge. My radio's up the spout. I'm on my way back to change it.'

My route back took me past a factory in Southgate Road, with a big expanse of grass in front of it. The premises were protected by six-foot spiked railings, enough to make a man speak in a high voice if he sat on them. To my astonishment two men *were* sitting on them, or near enough as makes no difference. One had just flung a holdall on to the pavement and was poised to jump down after it when I spotted them. Talk about a fair cop! It doesn't happen often, but when it does it brings a warm glow to your soul.

'Hey, you two! Stay right where you are!' Dialogue straight out of *Z-Cars*, but that's what we say and somehow it's more civilised than 'Freeze!'

The shadowy figures did freeze, then moved like greased lightning, leaping down and scarpering in opposite directions. I had two choices, and chose the smaller and less fleet-footed. Well, I'd just got out of a warm bed, hadn't I? For once I could have done without the glow in my soul and settled for a quiet walk back to base. It was not to be.

My long legs were still fast enough to overhaul him in under a minute. By the time I caught up with his fleeing figure I'd got through to control room on my radio, miraculously restored, to pant: 'Three-Nine-Three. Chasing suspect, Southgate Road towards New North Road.' Then I jumped him. He put up a struggle, threshing and kicking across the pavement and into the road, but he was trying to escape rather than lay me out and the only scrapes I got were from the tarmac.

Despite my recent indoor exertions I finally managed to subdue him. By this time we could both hear the 'da-da da-da' blare of the two-tone horn, picked up from all directions like an echo chamber as other police cars answered the call. Then the street was washed with eerie blue light, vehicles surrounded us, men raced in from everywhere and my captive went limp.

'Okay, you're nicked!' I gasped out, as willing hands helped me to my feet and others, less gently, snapped handcuffs on the suspect.

Back at base camp, I booked him in and left it to CID to pick up the traces when they came in next morning. At midday I was woken by a knock on the door. It was the section house warden. 'There's a phone call for you.'

The voice on the other end belonged to the local detective inspector. 'You awake, Mac?'

'I am now, Guv!'

'Any idea who you nicked last night?'

'Some two-bob burglar as far as I know.'

'He's more than that, son. He's Les the Bell.'

'Who?' I'd never heard of him.

'The Flying Squad's most wanted man, that's all. Get dressed and get your arse over here. Someone important wants to meet you.'

The 'someone important' turned out to be DI John Bassett, a real-life version of Jack Regan in *The Sweeney*, and the man who much later, promoted to detective superintendent, was in charge of the sensational Rachel Nickell murder inquiry.

I got my arse over there in a hurry. In the CID office, a grey-haired, authoritative figure in a dark suit shook my hand. 'Well done, Mac. We've been after this character for months. Now you've nailed him.'

'Why, what's he done?'

'Just about everything to do with major thefts right across the capital. Every team of villains wants him. He's a genius at getting into alarm systems. That's why he's called Les the Bell.'

They kept him there for days – pre-PACE, remember. I don't know how many writs were flying around for his release as lawyers tried to find him, but they never fluttered our way. Eventually Les the Bell was charged with a string of offences as long as a plateful of spaghetti and sent down at the Old Bailey for enough years to take him off the Sweeney's Most Wanted list for keeps.

For me it meant my career had taken a sudden lift. The big man raised a questioning eyebrow. 'Ever thought of the Department, young man?' The Department meant the CID, everything I'd ever wanted.

'Has Rose Kennedy got a black dress?' I replied.

EIGHTEEN

SCALY AIDE

January 1981. My two-year probation before I became a full police constable was almost over. The final examination took place in Beak Street, off Regent Street. It was called K and R, standing for 'Knowledge and Reasoning' – which is roughly our version of a taxi driver 'doing the Knowledge'. They called it the 'Probationers' Final Examination'. Funny thing, nobody ever said to me 'You're on probation,' presumably because that always has connotations with someone from the other side of the wire.

The questions got my brain cells stewing. Example:

> At 2 a.m. you are patrolling an industrial area when you hear a muffled explosion from a nearby factory. As you go towards the scene you see three men run from the entrance, get into a large saloon car and drive away.
>
> On entering through the open factory door you find the watchman lying in the office, unconscious with head injuries. He is not in danger of dying. The safe has been blown open and there are some tools, a battery, a length of wire and some small copper tubes on the floor near the safe.
>
> State fully your action.

And another:

> At 11 p.m. you are on duty outside a main-line railway station where you see two women soliciting prostitution. Their action is not blatant.
>
> One of the women, aged about forty, is known to you, and ten months earlier you were present in Court when she pleaded

guilty to a charge of prostitution and was fined £20. The other woman, aged about twenty, is not known to you. You later ascertain the two women are mother and daughter.

Detail your action fully from the outset.

And a third:

You are on duty at 4 p.m. when you are called to a railway embankment where you see the decapitated body of a man lying across the live rail. A witness says: 'I saw him walk up the bank and stand by the line. As soon as the train came along he just threw himself under the wheels. He must have been depressed.'

There is no railway employee in the area and the train did not stop. The duty officer is not immediately available.

Detail your action from the outset.

The last one had a familiar ring about it. Been there, done that, give or take the head. The rest were all examples of actual incidents. Other questions varied from what you did when you spotted a Peeping Tom to handling a situation where a woman was about to give birth at a bus stop. All human life was there.

The examination took up half a day, but at least we only had to gnaw our nails for a week before the results. I got through with a gratifying 75 per cent pass mark. When the letter dropped into my pigeon hole, I nearly shouted out loud. 'You've done it, Duncan! You're a cop – and no more shitty exams!'

Seventy-five per cent was a pretty good pass all in all, considering that I was never known for my academic prowess. Now I had some security. They could only throw me out if I did something really stupid. The beer flowed like water in our local that night.

On the personal side, it was time for a change of scenery. Above all, I wanted to get out of the section house. My top-floor room had become too small, with its single bed, washbasin, wardrobe and a few drawers. It was smaller than your average hotel room, and hardly worth one star. It was also quite noisy. You were allowed to bring girlfriends back twenty-four hours a day with no questions asked by the wardens, and the corridors would echo with cries of ecstasy or despair, largely depending on how much beer had been consumed by the parties involved.

In all, there were a hundred rooms. Ninety for the plods, ten for the plonks, WPCs who were segregated from the rest. We paid £2 a month nominal rent, with the run of two canteens, two TV rooms and the use of facilities like showers and washing machines.

Coppers aren't rock stars or sporting heroes. But I have to tell you this: there is a virtual army of groupies who go gaga at the sight of a police uniform, and not just in London but throughout the entire country. Young girls hung around us in pubs and bars like leeches, and somehow found a way to smuggle themselves into the canteens at the section house where the bunch of us testosterone-fuelled lads normally gathered. Like I say, Olive House was not known for its cathedral silence.

Eventually I was able to move into a nearby flat in Highbury with two other Woodies, Fred and Steve. We hung our helmets in a three-bedroom pad, which cost a bit but gave us more freedom. Without too many regrets, I packed my clothes, cassettes and books, stripped the wall of that famous Athena poster of the tennis girl showing her bare backside (later identified as an eighteen-year-old Birmingham University student named Fiona Butler) and got out of there.

There was a second opening, so to speak, waiting for me with Caroline. She would have welcomed me with open arms, and frequently did. But two Woodies were better than a bird in the hand, and made for fewer complications. There was also one little problem with this very nice girl. She smoked dope. Nothing too heavy, but Caroline enjoyed a spliff. Which spelled b-i-g trouble if I was caught on the premises, even though I never touched the stuff myself.

The first hint I got happened one day when I was in the kitchen admiring her floral arrangements. Our relationship had become a very loose affair and I hadn't seen her for a few weeks. But now I couldn't help noticing a profusion of potted plants dotted around the place – on top of the fridge, on the sideboard, on the table. Then more in the lounge on top of the TV, and in the corner by the cushions on the floor where we used to watch soccer and the *Morecambe and Wise Show*. All of them were positioned well away from the windowsill and any passing stranger with a roving eye. The display was quite fetching – elegant green plants about two feet tall with serrated edged leaves. But it didn't take Sherlock Holmes to identify them for what they were. Marijuana plants.

I broached the subject delicately. 'What the fuck's all this?'

'What's it look like?' She was in the next room, watching soccer on the TV from the cushions. 'Come here! Do you want a drag?'

Up to then I'd never tried it because I don't smoke. But anything for a quiet life, so for the first and last time I succumbed to the dreaded weed. I joined her on the cushions and took a drag. Big mistake. The resultant coughing fit, streaming eyes and burning throat made me a candidate for the nearest first-aid post.

'Typical non-smoker,' Caroline derided, with a marked lack of sympathy. 'Poor boy. Let's try it another way.'

I thought she might be baking it in a cake. Instead she produced an innocent-looking bottle of white wine with a blank label, and waved it at me. 'Home-made plonk! Plus a little extra something.'

I poured myself a glass, took a sip, then another. The effect of the little extra something was extraordinary. I found myself staring at a picture on the opposite wall. It was an abstract painting, all zigzag shapes and bright colours, and as I finished the glass it became even more abstract. The picture started to move up and down, then sideways. I slid down the cushions, watching my feet recede across the carpet. I felt extremely relaxed.

'Hey, darling. This didn't come from the Savoy's private cellar!'

'No. It's home-grown and home-made!'

And that's how I found out about spliff wine.

You might care to know that the cannabis plant produces ten grams of the drug per foot per year as it grows. So if you've got a four-foot plant, you can harvest forty grams per year – close to an ounce and a half. Not a lot, but multiply it and it becomes something significant.

So what was the recipe? She handed me a sheet of paper torn from an exercise book. I focused hazily. Even the lines were moving. Dimly, written in her neat hand, I read:

> Fill wine flagons with the stems and leaves of the plant. Add sugar or honey to boiling water. When cool add yeast, and top the bottles up with extra water. Shake and cork the bottles before storing in a dark place to ferment. After four to six weeks the wine should be ready for filtration and bottling. Leave for another four weeks, then chill to keep the wine fresh.

'Christ! Where did you get this from?'

She touched the side of her nose with a pert finger. 'Secret!'

By now I was too far gone to care. I lay back on the cushions, closed my eyes and slept like a baby. Next morning there was no hangover, but I never touched a drop again. And I figured it was time to call it a day with Caroline.

Now, more confessions. It wasn't just the grass she was growing that sent danger signals. I had met another girl, a pretty young nurse from Bart's Hospital named Cathy, and dividing my time between two ladies and keeping it secret from both of them had become something of a strain, even for a twenty-year-old with a highly charged libido. Besides which, my twenty-first birthday was fast approaching, and the long-awaited, though ultimately disastrous, Israeli holiday with Phil was on the horizon. Well, we know all about that, and the less said the better.

I left it till I came back to make the break, and ran into some heavy flak when I called round to her flat with my speech all prepared to let her down gently. Instead of the welcome mat, followed by tears and pleading, I found a virago reading the riot act. Somehow she had found out about my double-dealing. King Rat never had the chance to make his speech – she did it for me.

It emerged that while I had been striving to do my bit for Britain in the Holy Land, I had been stitched up by someone who was not only a fellow copper but a bloke I'd trusted implicitly. I have to admit my jaw hit the carpet. Worse still, and out of revenge, she told me triumphantly that she had let this guy have his way with her, as they say in polite parlance. Fair enough, with twenty-twenty hindsight, looking back now I can't blame her.

As true friends do, my pal Phil wanted to rearrange the Judas's features. I held him off. 'Wait,' I said. 'You know what they say; revenge is a dish best served cold.' I waited a year, by which time the chill factor had turned to frostbite. In that time the snitch found himself a bride, a plonk we labelled 'luscious lips', pure temptation, of whom a number of my station colleagues had availed themselves. I didn't expect an invitation to his stag night, but that didn't mean I couldn't gatecrash the bride's hen night at a local boozer.

Drinks flowed. Likewise the chat, all the way to the bedroom. That same night I ended up in the nest – hers. What was that about sweet revenge? The bride was unfazed. 'Don't worry, Duncan. When the cat's away, the mice and all that,' she purred between the rumpled sheets when I mentioned something about a wedding.

Summer 1981. Phil and I were on the Crime Squad. My application was approved, and suddenly the blue serge could be locked away. The uniform became academic within a week anyway after someone banjoed (broke into) my locker and pinched the lot, including my tit. This annoyed me, as I wanted to keep it as a memento. I found out later that my prize exhibit ended up in Florida, no doubt saving someone a speeding ticket. I didn't bother making a complaint – who wants to be branded a grass?

Day one in plain clothes. I arrived at the Crime Squad office in a suit because I didn't know what else to wear, with rising excitement and anticipation fighting for space inside my stomach. Later my gear would be anything from torn jeans to boiler suits as I started learning the A–Z of undercover work. My new boss was DS Dennis Morse – no relation to John Thaw, or to the character, except that he was ex-Flying Squad and an equally brilliant detective in real life as his namesake was in TV fiction. Dennis was big and burly, with lank black hair hanging over a broad, open face. Here was one guy who knew the job inside out. He had a slightly unnerving habit of speaking out of the side of his mouth as if he'd seen too many gangster movies. I warmed to him immediately.

The Crime Squad Office was a spacious third-floor room at the back of Islington Police Station, filled with desks where twelve embryo detectives – acting DCs – gathered expectantly each morning to await instructions. On the career ladder the Crime Squad was the stepping stone to the CID, consisting mainly of officers who, like me, had ambitions to become 'real' detectives. For some reason we were called 'Scalies' – apparently short for 'Scaly Aides'. It's a word everyone used, but no one seemed to know exactly why. I didn't think we looked that reptilian – but then the CID are known as 'The Filth', and actually wear the epithet like a badge of honour.

Dennis Morse sat at a desk at one end of the room where he could keep an eye on everybody, with his aide, a DC named Andy, at his elbow. He spotted the stranger, called me over and shook my hand. 'Welcome aboard, Mac.' Then he sat me down and spelled out the ground rules.

'Listen carefully. We're a team. We work hard, we play hard and we watch each other's backs. Our dress code is shit order; you'll dress for the job, anything goes, you won't need a short back and sides, and it's Christian names all round.

'Now, your hours. We work Monday to Friday, 9 a.m. to 10 p.m. Weekends we're entitled to "black time" on both days on our duty states – whether we come in or not, though you may well have to.'

'Black time' meant overtime. It sounded like I could be having a lie-in on Sunday mornings while still earning a whack, and no questions asked. The mortgage for the house I'd started to think about suddenly came a few steps closer to reality.

Dennis was still talking. 'You're not yet a full-blown detective, but you still get to see the bodies on the hearth rugs. You'll get a mountain of paperwork, and that goes with the game. Basically you're back-up to the main men in raincoats. When we're called in, it means a load of slogging round on door-to-door inquiries, collecting evidence, cross-referencing witness statements, that kind of thing. But it's still detection work.'

He leaned forward, fixing me with his hard, shrewd gaze. 'Remember this. If you want to make detective you've got to listen and learn. You'll be doing what I tell you – that's when you're not being lumbered helping out on a murder or some other major inquiry. You'll be paired up with someone, and I expect a regular turnover of bodies, live ones. I want results.

'We are the pro-active arm of the CID. You're out there to stop crime, not wait till it's happened. You spot some guy at a bus stop, and he lets three number 73s go by without getting on – I want him dragged in for Sus.'

Ah, the infamous S-word! 'Sus' came under the Vagrancy Act of 1824 which gave us the power to stop and arrest people on suspicion. Of what? Suspicion of anything! It was repealed shortly after I joined, replaced by the 1982 Criminal Attempts Act (CAA) which in fact makes it even easier for us to pick people off the streets. Sus required us to witness two overt acts from a suspect before we could sweep him up third time around. A guy might be walking round a car, touching the handle (once), peering through the window (twice), moving to another car and doing the same thing. Three strikes. Bingo! We had him.

The CAA was a strong piece of legislation, covering a variety of situations which up to then had been borderline. It can get complicated. For instance, if a man attempted rape on someone he thought was a woman, only to find it was another man in drag, he could still be charged with the *intention* of raping the person, whereas before he couldn't. It happens. As for sus, Dennis had his own way of spelling it out.

'If I tell you to bring in a spade wearing pink socks and a trilby, I want a spade in the charge-room wearing pink socks and a trilby. Understood? Otherwise *you'll* be back on the streets wearing a top hat.' Top hat was another word for tit, or wooden top. Funny how one innocent helmet could create so many images.

Sure, Dennis. Whatever Dennis wants, Dennis gets.

The big hurdle ahead of me would be the CID interview board, an ordeal held once a year which either opens the door to your future or slams it shut in your face. You're jousting with scores of other Scalies from all over London after the prized few places to make full detective, and you've got to be right up on your toes to get through. A trio of gimlet-eyed top brass ranged behind a desk will sit you down in front of them and put you through the mangler.

Meantime, Dennis again: 'I want drums (houses) turned over, because sure as I'm sitting here there are places out there with shooters in drawers, stolen property waiting to be fenced, and kiters waiting for the January sales.' 'Kiters' are cheque fraudsters, so called because the cheques bounce as high as a kite. 'That means warrants. You're going to start kicking doors in, and I want to be authorising more warrants than you'll have hot dinners. Don't worry – you come to me with the goods, I'll back you all the way. Okay?'

Okay, Skip. Okay all the way.

I knew about search warrants, having spent so many hours in uniform sniffing the Islington air for cannabis. They're a bore to get, those official scraps of paper, when you'd rather go steaming straight in, mob-handed if possible, to nail the beast in his lair. But before breaking into anyone's privacy you have to go through the motions.

Search warrants are actually two documents. One is called the 'Information', which you type out before you go off and put the boot in the door, and is retained by the magistrate who has signed it. The other is the warrant itself, which gets the police through that door, legally and by whatever means. You can pull up a warrant twenty-four hours a day because every police station has a list of magistrates authorised to sign it, even if it means getting their worships out of bed to do so. Many's the time I've gone round to a magistrate's home in the early hours with the documents, following a quick phone call to wake him up, then found myself swearing on a dictionary, because there's no Bible handy, that the 'information contained herein is basically the truth'.

You'd think every Muppet would have the Good Book by his bedside. Muppet is what we coppers call a lay magistrate – rather apt, when you think of them sitting up there in three's behind the Bench like dummies on a fairground rifle range. After all, any half-decent hotel in America has got the Gideon next to every bed. But no. I've even sworn on the Beano Annual before going off to look for a sledgehammer.

But in the early hours, when Rip Van Winkle is standing there in his pyjamas rubbing the sleep out of his eyes, no one's going to bother too much about the small print. So the Muppet signs the warrant, and usually there's a whisky in it before he sends you on your way. Incidentally, you never go alone to execute a warrant – 'teamed and tooled up' is the order of the day, though often it's just you and your partner, with a couple more muckers as back-up.

Normally we'd apply for them in batches, hauling our arses off to the local Magistrates Court on a Tuesday morning with half a dozen or so warrant applications. These would be slapped down on the Bench while the copper involved stepped up to the witness box and went through the 'information contained herein' litany. The Muppet normally leafed through them like a spin dryer before getting on with the more serious business of the day.

One evening when I was propping up the bar at The Flo' a fellow copper and a known humorist gave me a nudge. 'Tell you what,' he said. 'I'm off to the court in the morning. What do you bet that I can't get a search warrant for Number 10?'

'Downing Street?' I was taken aback, which made me a bit slow on the uptake.

'Where else? I've got a whole wad tomorrow. I'll slip it in somewhere in the middle.'

'You'll never get away with it. What if you're spotted?'

'I'll risk it. For a tenner.'

'You're on,' I said.

I went with him next morning, not for moral support but to see if he went through with it. From the back of the court I watched the usual formalities take place. My mate handed the clerk of the court the wad of warrants, ten of them in all, stepped into the box and swore the information contained therein was the truth. The magistrate bent his white head over the pile and riffled through them, signing each one with a fountain pen with hardly a second glance. Finally he pushed the wad back to the clerk, who gave them to my joker friend.

Outside, I shook my head. 'Phew!' I said. 'That's got to be a first. By the way, what's the excuse for raiding Number 10?'

'Possession of drugs on the premises,' he replied laconically. 'Where's that tenner you owe me?'

The warrant went up that day on the noticeboard, and stayed there a week. Personally, I think we should have framed it.

It was good to have a partner. No more lone patrols, pounding the pavements in the wee small hours. We had wheels now.

'You're into the big league,' DS Morse informed me. 'You won't hear about half the stuff, so you need to get out there and cultivate informants and 'turn' prisoners. There's a slush fund for paying snouts, sitting there waiting to be used. Convince me it's genuine and I'll get the cash for you.' His final word to me was, 'You produce the goods, and you'll get beyond Scaly.'

I was curious. 'Who's my buck [partner] going to be, Sarge?'

Dennis looked up with a glint in his eye. 'Hitler Youth,' he said. 'Your faggot friend Phil.'

Obviously word had got back from Israel.

NINETEEN

INFORMATION RECEIVED

I spent the next fifteen months looking for trouble. And let's not cloud the facts, causing a lot of it too. If it moves, it gets nicked! That was the standard I endeavoured to live up to, and so did the rest of the Dirty Dozen in the Crime Squad.

My first snout came to me the easy way. He approached *me*! This may sound unusual, but in fact they usually know they're in the shit and want to do a deal. People don't actually like doing time, not even if they're the Birdman of Alcatraz. Your average snout? There's no such thing. Forget the popular image of a little weasel sidling up to you in a doorway and whispering, 'I've got something you ought to know. But it'll cost!' We used to say they're usually desperate for a leg-up in life, as distinct from a leg-over. They don't want to go inside, and if they are inside they want out.

A snout can be the person selling you flowers down the road, or a local newsboy. They are officially classed as an informer if they're doing just that – passing on information to you. The official part means they're put on a list and given an alias to disguise their true identity, thus saving them from becoming part of a concrete pillar holding up a flyover on the M4. We needed names because when we paid them it had to go through official channels. So Mickey Mouse, Donald Duck and a whole cast of other showbiz characters were getting rich without knowing it.

Often informers can be pub landlords, and sometimes they may not even realise they're informing. I'd be called aside in the public bar, and the owner would mutter: 'I see so-and-so's back in the area.' Or: 'I've got these four guys come in every night and I'm sure they're dealing in puff down the end of the bar.' Puff, of course, being cannabis. A landlord could lose his licence if that sort of thing is caught happening on his premises, so if we made the bust we made sure it was down the road or some other place far away.

Back to my first snout. I'd never set eyes on Billy until I nicked him for 'going equipped'. We were driving along Caledonian Road, three of us, Phil and myself, plus another PC named John at the wheel. We spotted a figure acting suspiciously in the street, walking up and down a line of parked cars, and John recognised him as a face with a track record. 'That's Billy! Let's have a chat.' In fact when we finally pounced and bundled him into the back, we did hand him a 'few doors', meaning that we accused him of actually touching some of the vehicles – even though his sticky fingers had been lodged firmly in his pockets. But we found a bunch of keys on him that could have opened anything from a Roller to a Reliant Robin, so we knew we had our pigeon.

It was not uncommon in those days for some cops to plant a few lumps of cannabis resin in the pocket of a known suspect. Times have changed, but not a lot. In fact, to avoid the indignity of being stitched up by the boys in blue, clued-up gangs resorted to a simple solution: they actually sewed their pockets up before going out on the streets, thus doing their own stitching up before we got to them.

The chat turned out to pay dividends beyond our expectations. We picked him up on sus, found the keys in a poacher's pocket and hauled our catch down to the station for further questioning.

Back at the factory they ran his details through the computer. I was in the fingerprint studio – a small room with a camera for mug shots and a brass block for prints similar to the one they had in Hendon – doing the business when Phil poked his head round the door and addressed the prisoner. 'Hey, sunshine, you didn't tell us you're on a bender!'

This meant our Billy was in more trouble than we'd realised. He had a suspended prison sentence hanging over him for theft. So when the door closed and the two of us were alone together, he suddenly blurted out, 'I'm in the shit, aren't I?'

'You could say that,' I agreed, with a tinge of sympathy. He wasn't the usual stereotype of a car thief, but a plump little chap with a round moon face which right then was a picture of concern.

'I can't go back inside. She'll throw me out this time.' I took it he meant the girlfriend.

'Well, Billy, you know what to do. You scratch my back . . .' I left the sentence hanging in the air.

He knew what to do, and now the picture changed to hopeless indecision as he wrestled with the dilemma of shitting on his own doorstep or having to be constantly watching his arse in the showers at the Scrubs, and above all not dropping the soap.

'All right,' he said finally. 'There's a job going down in two weeks, and I know where the shooter is hidden.'

I looked up. 'What sort of gun?'

'Pair of nostrils.' That meant a sawn-off shotgun, one of the deadliest weapons around. To give you an idea how deadly, when I was on my firearms course the instructor posed a hypothetical question. 'Three men are coming at you. One's got a Smith & Wesson revolver, the sort you're carrying. Another's holding a Heckler & Koch MP5.' The latter is the kind the SAS used in the Iranian Embassy siege, a machine gun that fires fifteen rounds a second. 'And the third has a sawn-off 12-bore. Which one do you take out first?'

To a man, we all chorused, 'The one with the MP5.'

'Wrong! The body can absorb several bullets and still live. If you get it from a shotgun, you're wasted!'

None of us ever forgot it.

Meantime, back at the ranch, Billy had come up with the goods. 'Now, where is it?'

'An underground garage in Packington Estate.'

I knew the place. One of the shithole estates, a zoo where even patrols in police cars wouldn't venture too close because the inhabitants liked to drop flower pots on you from a great height. You may have seen the place featured in the Pink Floyd video 'Another Brick in the Wall'. One of my mates once foolishly left his unmarked car outside while making inquiries in one of the flats – and came back to find he had acquired a sun roof, with an indoor fridge buried in it. The thing would have killed anyone inside the car. It was that kind of estate.

Mention of a gun tends to galvanise coppers into instant action. More brownie points for me, as I prevailed upon Dennis to okay a ticket (warrant) – immediately if not sooner. Two hours later four of us hit the garage without even bothering to find out whose it was. A set of bolt cutters snapped the padlock, a couple of sledge-hammers did the rest, and sure enough there was what we were looking for: a happy bag (an armed robber's holdall for carrying his gear) stashed in an old cooker in the far corner. Score one to Billy! And Duncan had his first snout. I got him off the hook with a caution.

Back at the factory we booked the bag and its contents in triumph into the stock sheet. Boiler suit, balaclava, gloves – and a sawn-off 12-bore shotgun, complete with cartridges. The first rule was to get the weaponry out of circulation. Later you could worry about the owner, whoever he might be. Meantime, we'd earned ourselves a beer.

At The Flo' I spotted Dennis putting on a show with a broomstick. This was his party piece and it took place on the pool table. He was so good at the game that he would challenge anyone for a fiver a game – 'And I'll play with a broomstick!' It always worked. I never saw Dennis lose a wager.

He caught my eye across a crowded room, and beckoned me with a peremptory finger.

'What is it, boss?'

'Outside! And leave your beer.' Why did I suddenly feel a cold breath of apprehension?

In the street, away from wagging ears, I found my back suddenly up against a wall. Morse thrust his moon face into mine. 'Where have you just been?'

'We just spun the garage.'

He knew all about it, of course. After all, he'd authorised the warrant.

'And what did you find?' His voice was quiet and controlled, but I sensed an ominous undertone.

'A happy bag, Sarge, with a shooter. A sawn-off!'

'And where is it?'

'Next door, in the safe.'

'And the prisoner?'

'Oh . . . ah . . .' The red warning light flashed at last. 'We're working on that.'

'So you're telling me you've got a sawn-off, and no body?'

'Er, yes.' My voice tailed away.

'*What the fuck have I been teaching you for the past two months?* You're never going to prove the owner of that garage is the blagger, so you've just wasted a perfectly good happy bag.'

'Sorry, Den . . .'

'Listen, Mac.' He wasn't going to let me off that lightly. 'If you want to stay in this outfit, you'd better learn to engage your brain in future. That's what we do around here. You're not a helmet any more. Now get your arse inside and buy me a beer!'

That was Dennis, short and sweet and no hard feelings. I said he was ace.

TWENTY

SNOUTS INC.

Snouts became my bread and butter. In this game I was to discover that every prisoner was a potential informant. The trick was to turn them. It's a strange, some may say bizarre, relationship between cops and robbers. They feed you the goods. In turn they become dependent on you to keep them out of prison, as much for their own security as for their continued freedom. They also depend on you for other things. Many a time in the middle of the night I was woken by a phone call that sent me hastening off to a cash point to draw out £200 which I would use to buy a couple of grams of heroin from a source I knew, open all hours. Maybe it was a Turk in neighbouring Haringey near the area they call 'Little Cyprus', or a black guy in a tea-cosy hat operating from a room above a shop in Brixton. All this just to get an informer the fix he desperately needed before he started biting the carpet.

In those heady Crime Squad days the informant system was ad hoc and relaxed. Real names were never put on paper. If you went to your guv'nor and told him you had an informer called Joe Bloggs whose palm needed to be greased, he took you on trust and charged it to 'incidental expenses'. Nothing too big, just the odd tenner here or a pony (£25) there. If it was a major snitch, like a significant seizure, the reward could go into five figures, and this had to be okayed from the top, superintendent level.

Those were the good old days. Today everything has changed – and not for the better, from the snout's point of view. Today if you turn someone you have to log it into a system, which makes all concerned feel distinctly uneasy.

In my fifteen months with the Crime Squad I collected a small team of informants whose information was classed A1. Only half a dozen, but that was six more than the average copper. These guys – they were all men at that stage, before I opened the club to women – worked their bollocks off for me. Out of those six, five were crooks. The sixth was a publican who ran a place near Upper Street, a gaff which had its regulars but also a lot of passing trade. This area was the gateway to the West End, and numerous underworld figures from the East End and the Crooks' Corner of Essex made it a watering hole for meeting their mates before heading up west.

Though years later, and by now a Yard detective, one of the most colourful characters I bumped into from that neck of the woods was Frankie Fraser, 'hardest of the hard'. I have to tell you that he was one of the few to resist my advances – the monetary kind, that is. In an Italian trattoria off Goodge Street we had a meal together with a couple of mutual acquaintances from TV, and over the spaghetti and wine I tried to turn him.

'I know you're into things, Frankie. But you could also be useful to me – and I could repay the compliment,' I said carefully. 'If things get too hot, and you want to take out your opposition, I could make things easier for you.'

I deliberately kept it vague.

'Oh – and if we lay our hands on a good load being divvied up at a slaughter, it'll be a nice little earner for you. Compliments of the Home Secretary.' Translation: 'If we can raid a gang in the act of sharing out a drugs consignment in a venue where illegal goods are distributed, etc . . .'

The nice little earner would come courtesy of a special fund recently set up to entice informers to spill the beans on drug movements, the only proviso being that to get a lump of it the seizures had to be 'significant', i.e. strictly big time.

Frankie got the message at once. He gave me that crooked smile of his. 'I'll think about it,' he said.

I handed him my business card, and said 'I hope to hear from you,' knowing full well I never would. And I never did. Frankie was nobody's grass, and despite my disappointment he earned my respect for that.

Back to my own team. Of the five on the wrong side of the fence, three were fraudsters, one was heavily into drugs and one was an active burglar specialising in jewellery shops in the Clerkenwell area. Like I say, they had funny names to protect their identities. Just to be different, I chose a World Cup winner's name for each of my merry men: Geoff Hurst, Alan Ball, Bobby Moore, Martin Peters, Roger Hunt and Gordon Banks. Sorry about that, Martin, because you were my boyhood hero. I even wrote to you asking for your autograph, which I've still got. The names only went down on paper when I needed payola for them – a reward for services rendered which had to go through official channels.

My report on a drug seizure would end up on the desk of the detective chief superintendent, the head honcho for the whole division who was based at King's Cross divisional headquarters. It was the end of a complex paper trail starting with Dennis, moving up the ladder to the detective inspector, then to the detective chief inspector, all of whom added their comments, and finally to the top man who made the decision on how much to shell out.

I know the Guv'nor got a quiet chuckle out of signing a century (£100) or even a monkey (£500) away to England's goalkeeper for alerting us to an armed robbery, while some of the other aliases used by the Squad would not have looked out of place in a Hollywood movie.

My best informant in those days was the one I called Geoff Hurst. Geoff (real name Alfie) could have stepped straight out of a Damon Runyan story from Chicago in the roaring '20s. Alfie had his finger in every pie, knew every scam, yet he was only in his mid-twenties. Jack the Lad I called him, with his lank hair and pinched face, but he was the most streetwise kid I ever came across. He even looked like the snout of everyone's imagination, a scrawny weasel on two legs. Alfie moved so fast you had to keep him on a leash – but in the end, not fast enough to save his life.

We had nicked him tendering a stolen credit card in an off-licence. It was a roundabout way of getting currency. Alfie would simply buy a couple of crates with a nicked card, load them into his van, then take the booze round to a local publican and flog it at a cut rate. That way he had cash in his pocket, and the publican was saved a lot of paperwork. It's a common ploy, and at the factory we often found ourselves unexpectedly benefiting from it. The bad lad would be caught leaving the off-licence with a crate of the hard stuff under each arm. Body and goods would be hauled off to the station, where we'd charge him and retain the crates until the end of the trial, which is when they become the property of the credit card company. The company's team of investigators, usually based out of town, more often than not can't be bothered to make the trek to collect it. A phone call tells us, quietly: 'Do a moody [false] signature to show it's been signed for and collected, then divvy it round the office. Enjoy!' Cheers to that!

Alfie had been caught almost literally with his hand in the till, and with a collection of other people's credit cards on him, usually pinched from coats or handbags in a busy hostelry at lunchtime. You see the warning signs in every pub: 'We do not accept liability for stolen valuables'. But either people can't read or they don't take any notice. It's the 'can't happen to me' mentality – but I know it can, and does. And here was Alfie to prove it.

The off-licence owner, sharper-eyed than most, had spotted something wrong with the proffered card and phoned 999. We were there inside three minutes. Back at base camp I sat the shivering weasel down, decided he was putting on a good act and gave him the full verbals. 'Is it inside or out – and I'm talking about Parkhurst?'

Carrot and stick, bullying and cajoling by turns, finally did the trick. Alfie caved in – and became Geoff Hurst. For the next few months, every time he gave us a successful operation it called for us to meet with a detective inspector in some discreet pub to sign his name when the cash was handed over. 'Good luck on Saturday, Geoff!' was my guv'nor's usual heavy-handed parting shot after he passed over the brown envelope, watching the weasel make a fast exit.

One of Alfie's best tips came out of the blue. 'Can we have a meet?' said his low voice on the blower. It was always one-to-one and never over a phone. An hour later, clutching a beer in the bar at King's Cross railway station, he was imparting the goods, and it was pure gold dust.

'There's a guy I've done time with who's nearing the end of a six-year stretch. Armed robbery. He's allowed out during the week to get himself used to society and to find a job. But I know that on a certain day he's meeting up with his uncle in a car, and his uncle will be tooled up and they're going to do a wages snatch.'

'Just the two of them?'

'Yeah. The guy wants a bit of bread waiting for him when he comes out.'

'When and where exactly?'

Alfie spelled out the date, time and place. It was to be a factory job, round the corner from Theberton Street, jumping a Securicor van as it approached the gates loaded with the week's wages. These were big beans my man was spilling, the best he ever did. I passed the information to the Flying Squad.

Later I heard the details from a mate who took part in the ambush, part of an armed Sweeney team who were there waiting when the pair turned up. Alfie had been spot on. The car was a bright yellow Triumph Dolomite, a nippy little job but rather the wrong colour for knocking over a security van and making off with the wages. Bright yellow, I ask you! The Squad nabbed them both.

As further proof of how thick some precious pairs like this were, a mate divulged some details later about a similar type of job. 'You won't believe this, Mac. But after we descended on them with our shooters out and spread them on the ground, we looked inside the glove compartment. You know what we found there? A load of cartridges – but none in the shotgun. Securicor was due any moment, but the stupid buggers hadn't even loaded up. So we helped them out. By the time that 12-bore got back in the nick, there was a shell down each barrel!'

I knew what that meant – an extra year or two when the blaggers were sent down. But it didn't bother me. Big boys' games, big boys' rules. I'd have done the same myself.

I wish the sequel to the notable success of Alfie's tip-off could have been better, with more plums dropping off the tree. Sadly, it wasn't. Alfie, alias Geoff Hurst, earned himself a couple of centuries for his efforts, but didn't live long enough to spend them. I missed his death by minutes.

What happened was this. Two weeks after he picked up his £200, we met at another neutral venue, The Queen's Head in Essex Road, to discuss a further sensitive matter. Alfie had heard a whisper about a stash of cannabis being grown in a loft somewhere off the Cally – that's the Caledonian Road – down the street from Pentonville prison. 'It's under heat lamps, and there's a lot of it. Around four hundred plants.' Four *hundred*! Christ! He gave me an address, but he hadn't seen the gear himself. 'It's only a whisper, Duncan, but I think it's kosher.'

'Thanks a lot, Alf. I'll check it out.'

Sadly Geoff Hurst never lived to collect his winnings. He left me in the pub to make his way to the Angel tube station, and was standing with other pedestrians waiting to cross the road when round the corner came a large skip lorry with a loose chain swinging at its side. The flailing chain caught Alfie across the face, nearly taking his head off. The Black Rat said he was probably dead before he hit the ground. The verdict was an accident.

His final tip-off checked out. Four hundred plants takes a lot of heat. I dialled the electricity board. 'I'm running a check on this number in Caledonian Road. Any unusually high bills from the top-floor flat?'

The supervisor rang me back within the hour. 'You're right. There's something going on there. I don't know what it is, but they're using enough juice to be plugged into the National Grid!' That was good enough for me.

The world sleeps, but others are awake. We usually go in before dawn, waving sledgehammers and crowbars, making a lot of noise. This one was a big Georgian house off the Cally. Three unmarked cars slid up to the kerb in the darkness. Silent approach. Until . . . Crash! Bang! Wallop!

The first sledgehammer hit the front door. With a drugs bust you are entitled to use as much force as you want to gain entry. Repairs and questions come later. Our job is to get in before the stuff can get out. Normally the scroats try to flush it away, though the idea of four hundred cannabis plants being stuffed down the toilet is pushing it a bit. Six of us in rough clothes (jeans and leather jackets) stormed in. You don't dress for dinner in a dawn raid. We took a dragon light with us, a hugely intensive beam that you don't look into unless you want to go blind, which turns a black interior into day. First sighting: a flight of stairs going up into darkness. Threadbare carpet, peeling wallpaper. Somewhere up there was our target. The first essential was to secure the place, starting from the bottom up. So we bomb-burst in through every door, sweeping the rooms with our torches, turning on lights.

In the first room I found a couple sound asleep on a mattress, wakening out of a pot-shrouded stupor to a stranger in their midst. 'Sorry for the intrusion, folks. This is your early morning call!'

There was no resistance. In fact, we had left the hardware behind. This time we had a pickaxe handle apiece to do the work of a truncheon and crack heads if anyone wanted to start playing the hero. A single whack would usually be enough, but on this occasion it was mainly exchanging verbals as they were in no condition to put up a fight.

Pickaxe handles have their uses. I had briefed the troops at Cally police station down the road. In the CID office you couldn't help noticing a pickaxe handle hanging on the wall. On one end was a blob of blood and beside it, with an arrow pointing to the bloodstain, some wit had written: 'George Davis Was Here.'

Let me explain. George was a London cabbie convicted for an armed robbery at the Electricity Board offices in Ilford, Essex. The blaggers escaped after a high-speed chase in which shots were fired and a policeman wounded. George was picked out by several officers in a series of identity parades, and sentenced to twenty years. He always protested his innocence, and became something of a folk hero in the East End through a 'Free George Davis' campaign mounted by his friends. Children even played hop-scotch on the pavements, echoing the slogans that were calling for his release.

The robbery didn't make that much of a ripple, but the campaign did. Two of George's relatives climbed to the top of St Paul's Cathedral, while a friend crashed a van into the gates of Buckingham Palace to make their point. But it was only when saboteurs ruined the 1975 Test match against the Aussies at Headingley by pouring a gallon of oil onto the pitch that people, particularly cricket lovers, sat up and took notice. It happened on the fourth day, and the Test was abandoned as a draw. A few months later George walked free from Albany jail on the Isle of Wight with a Royal Pardon in his pocket. He didn't do his image a lot of good when he was caught red-handed in another hold-up a year later – which is where that pickaxe handle comes in. Detectives were lying in wait at the Bank of Cyprus in Holloway, and ambushed the gang in the street. An American tourist actually caught George and his cronies on camera, and the pictures were all over the front pages the next day. George went down for another fifteen, this time with no repeal. Some people never learn.

So much for George and pickaxe handles. Off the Cally, things were getting lively. Boots pounding on stairs. Doors crashing open. The lads of the Crime Squad were in their element, creating a disturbance. By now we had achieved a certain notoriety with our methods, earning ourselves the tag of 'Wild Boys' from within the ranks, which is no bad nickname when you want a drink in a packed bar. A couple of years later Duran Duran would come out with their hit song 'Wild Boys', and we always liked to pretend we were the inspiration for it. Okay, we weren't. But a few gullible souls believed it.

Voices rose throughout the house. 'What the fuck?' 'Get out of here!' 'Piss off!' Followed by the gruff order: 'You're nicked! Get dressed!'

At the top of the stairs a metal ceiling ladder led to the loft. I clambered up, and pushed open the flap. An eerie blue glow filtered out of the square gap. Cautiously, I put my head through the hole, flashing the dragon light around. Inside it was like stepping into a greenhouse. The air was warm and cloying, the aroma sweet and overpowering as a call-girl's perfume. The loft had been lined with hardboard. Every square inch had a yellow gro-bag, full of earth, normally used for growing tomatoes. Each gro-bag sprouted six plants, copies of the ones in Caroline's flat, fighting for space. A thick hosepipe snaked around the interior of the loft, punctured with holes, creating an irrigation system that may have been primitive but was certainly effective. The ringleader of the outfit was another Jack the Lad – Islington was full of them. Late-twenties, stark naked in bed with a bird, but still able to come up with a smart-ass remark even at that hour.

'What's wrong with growing tomatoes?' he tried.

'Full marks for enterprise,' I replied, throwing a pair of trousers at him. 'You're nicked, sunshine!' There were cartons of the stuff stacked in the kitchen, too. As for the gardeners, we bagged eight of them.

It took us all morning to clear that loft, and by the end of it we were on a high, every man jack of us. Call it the sweet smell of excess. The scent of marijuana was in our hair and nostrils, and clinging to our clothes. That was one day we didn't put our faces into The Flo' or The Mail before a shower and a complete change of uniform, even if the uniform was a pair of torn jeans and a T-shirt. But it was a great bust, worth thousands in street value, and I'm only sorry Alfie wasn't there to get his cut.

I found his replacement the very next week. Phil and myself, along with our third mate Bob at the wheel, were cruising the streets – in the strictly old-fashioned meaning of the word – looking for potential wrongdoers. We found one in the shape of a lanky youth in his early twenties meandering down Liverpool Road – a kid surprisingly tall for a burglar, which is what he was.

'I recognise that bloke!' exclaimed Bob suddenly alert. He had a memory like an elephant. 'We've got a docket on him.' A docket meant someone had lifted a set of fingerprints at a scene-of-crime, and they'd been matched with an identity and a face.

We slid alongside, and Bob wound down the window. 'Hullo, Frank!' The youth looked round, startled. 'Get in the car. You're nicked!' Those magic words. It makes a long debate unnecessary.

Frank could have done a runner. He didn't. He knew that odds of three to one, possibly accompanied by half a ton of metal, were not so good. He got in at once, and demanded, 'What you lifting me for?'

I thought for a moment. Anything to enliven the day. 'How about flashing?'

'What? I wasn't fucking flashing!'

'Oh yes you were,' I said. 'We saw you with your todger in your hand, waving it around.'

'And the women at the bus stop were horrified,' Bob chipped in from the driver's seat.

'Todger? Me? What women? Leave it out! If you're going to charge me, anything but flashing.'

Like any sane mortal, Frank didn't want 'indecent exposure' on his record. Who does? Those kinds of things look bad on your CV, especially to those of the criminal fraternity. Word gets around, particularly after it has been published in the local paper.

I relented. 'Look, Frank. Bob's not the fastest of drivers, but we're going to be at the nick in five minutes. You've got those five minutes to rectify the situation. The ball's in your court.'

The implication sank in. Finally he sighed, and nodded slowly. 'Okay . . .' Another pause. 'There was a job done at M&S last week. I can tell you where the clothes are.' It was good enough. We had ourselves another grass.

'Welcome to the club . . . Alan Ball!'

TWENTY-ONE

THE RUBBER-HEELERS MOVE IN

The year rolled on. Drums were being spun (houses raided), people lifted off the streets, the property store was bulging, prisoners came and went, and the courts were kept so busy the staff even invited us to their Christmas party. The flow of 'bodies' was so impressive that we became the talk of the division. As a team, we were nothing less than brilliant. The arrest turnover of the Dirty Dozen was hitting the stratosphere.

'Thursday is blagging day. That's the day we're likely to be busy.' Dennis was right, as usual. He always put his money where his mouth was, my boss. Every Thursday he would strap on a Smith & Wesson and slide into the back of one of our cars to be part of the patrol. Although he had a mountain of paperwork to plough through during the week, Thursday was always Action Day. Once a squad man, always a squad man.

But with our arrests came the complaints. Not of theft, as you might expect, as there was plenty of opportunity. No, this was equally as serious: allegations of assault, planting fake evidence, perjury, that kind of thing. The low life and their lawyers came out of the woodwork from everywhere to put us on the spot. Even a muppet or a judge had a few sour things to say after a case had folded with the hint that one or other of us had told porkies.

There's a certain twisted logic in all this. The harder a copper works to bring in the dirt littering the streets, the more complaints he's sure to get. In short, more bodies mean more squeals of 'foul!'

The complaints mounted up, showering in like confetti. Every day it seemed that one or other of the Crime Squad was being dragged off to Room 101, or the equivalent of it, for a grilling. Personally I had more than my share of it, facing a chief inspector plus a sergeant from uniform branch across a table in a small, overheated room at area headquarters in King's Cross police station.

The scenario invariably went like this.

'Sit down, MacLaughlin.' (No friendly smile, handshake conspiciously absent.)

You were allowed a lawyer, or one friend, the friend being a colleague from the Force whose job would be to see fair play and give you advice. I never bothered with a lawyer when Room 101 beckoned, but if the kitchen became too hot I was permitted to stop the hearing and call for a legal eagle. I settled for a veteran pal from the CID, DS John Corner, a good bloke to have on your side with a load of experience under his belt. This guy was Socrates. His attitude was equally profound: 'Keep your fucking mouth shut, Mac! Let them prove it!'

You were handed a sheet of paper marked 163, the standard complaint form. Two pairs of steely eyes stared across the desk at you while you studied it. 'We are now serving Form 163 on you,' intoned the chief inspector. 'I will read the contents.'

Those were the days before tape recorders, and the sergeant's role was to take a 'contemporaneous record' of the proceedings. Like the bloke who couldn't swim but fell down the toilet, they had to go through the motions. Their job was to prove that the allegations can stick, which might well result in dismissal from the Force, or even an appearance in court.

An example of the contents of Form 163:

> On the afternoon of 23 July, together with another officer, you had reason to stop one John Smith in Essex Road. It is alleged that you searched the complainant, and during the course of the search a quantity of heroin was found in his coat pocket.
>
> It is alleged that you secreted the said substance in that pocket. Following his arrest, the complainant alleges that he was taken to Islington Police Station, where he was assaulted in a cell. Records at the police station show that you were one of the arresting officers.

The chief inspector would look up, then go on: 'Following these allegations, I must caution you. You are not obliged to say anything unless you wish to do so, but anything you do say will be taken down in writing and may be used in evidence against you.'

All this might sound a case for bicycle clips and a change of underwear, but despite a plethora of 'allegations' I was usually confident that I could walk away with a clean sheet.

Looking him straight in the eye, my immediate answer was always the same. 'I totally refute the allegations, and do not intend to answer any questions.' After that it became a formality, bordering on a charade, with them asking the questions and me looking out of the window, playing dumb.

'Is this going to be your answer to every question?' the chief inspector would finally demand. I would nod. 'In that case I see no further point in continuing this interview, which will now be terminated.'

Weeks, sometimes months later, the final scene of this one-act drama would be enacted. Form 163A would appear on my desk, referring to the case with the postscript: 'No further action.' I lived to fight another day.

Over the months this long-playing record was repeated again and again until it merited a place in the bestseller list – but the crime figures fell and the streets became cleaner and safer. For heroin and assault on the complaint sheet against us, you could substitute keys, bolt cutters, cannabis, flick knives, coshes, and sundry other miscellaneous items of potential illegality.

They could have added bribery and corruption if I'd succumbed to my first-ever approach from someone who wanted to cross my palm with silver – a well-known boxing promoter, no less. We had pulled a relative of his for assault, and hours later he turned up unannounced at the factory, took me to one side and said quietly: 'Look, son. We're both men of the world. How about you having a nice holiday on me – and let him go?'

I looked at one of the most famous faces to adorn the back pages of the tabloids. 'I'm not one of your boys,' I said, equally quietly. 'No thanks.'

'Maybe another time,' he said, and turned on his heel and walked out. I went back inside and charged the relative. Gilding the lily is one thing, taking an out-and-out bribe is another.

One of us did nearly come a cropper with a car thief, a known ringer I'll call Ted who was stopped in the street and 'found' to have around thirty car keys in his possession. A ringer is someone who completely changes a car's identity by welding on new parts, removing the chassis and engine numbers, respraying and sundry other dodges.

Our friend pleaded not guilty. But instead of alleging that the keys had been planted on him, he stood up cool as a cucumber in the dock at Clerkenwell magistrates court and called for them to be handed to him by the usher. Then, to the mutual astonishment of the police who had nicked him and the court who recognised a familiar face, he went through them one by one.

'That's my Ford. That's my old Rover . . . that's my dad's spare Austin . . . and my sister's Sierra. Oh, here's Uncle Joe's Transit van . . .' And so on. We had to sit there and take it.

The verdict, of course, was not guilty by dint of being not proven, eliciting a wintry glare from the magistrate in our direction. At the end, as Ted walked free with a quiet smile on his face, he winked at us. We didn't wink back, but metaphorically speaking we had to take our hats off to him.

All I could mutter as his retreating back vanished through the swing door was: 'You'll be back, smart-ass!'

It was inevitable that we would come to the attention of CIB, the Met's Internal Affairs Department, known within the Force as the 'rubber-heelers' because you can't hear them creeping up on you to feel your collar. Their official name is the Criminal Investigation Bureau. This department is there to investigate alleged criminal activities of police officers, and basically try to give us all the shits if we knew their sleuths were loose in the building. We knew we were in trouble when Dennis called us together to make an announcement from his desk. I had never seen him so worried. 'We've got a problem, lads. I want you all in the hothouse in one hour. Round up anyone who's not here and make sure he's with you.' The hothouse was the sauna attached to the public swimming baths off Clerkenwell Road, a place we used to go to sweat out the toxins of a hard day at the office, along with the beer we had consumed during the week. Normally we'd go in pairs or small groups. Having the entire Dirty Dozen in there for a communal wash was a first.

Sixty minutes later we were sitting around on the wooden slats, wrapped in towels and sweating profusely. The room designated for our Extraordinary General Meeting was no bigger than a normal sauna, which meant that we were squashed together like peas in a pod, hardly able to move a muscle. 'This is all very friendly,' I muttered to Phil, pressed next to me. 'Just watch where you put your elbow.'

But Dennis knew what he was doing. This way there could be no possibility of anyone being wired up, with a Nagra body recorder taped to the small of their back, the listening device I would later use myself for undercover operations. Indeed, the infamous Kenneth Noye, currently serving time for the M25 'road rage' killing, regularly employed this ploy when calling a high-level 'meeting' with his cohorts in a hotel near Brand's Hatch. He'd sit them down in the hotel sauna stark naked to make sure the talk was kept secret.

So our sauna wouldn't be tapped – unlike our Crime Squad office, which was open season to the eager-beavers of CIB, who had a history of bugging their own men. If you doubt my word, not long after our sauna session someone in Enfield CID decided to make a sweep of their office and found a radio transmitter secreted in the strip light in the ceiling. How long it had been there no one ever revealed, but the shit hit the fan that day and caused the most enormous fall-out and ill-feeling in the ranks.

Through the steam, Dennis addressed us. 'Listen up! I've had a tip-off. We've got a visit from the big house tomorrow.' The big house was the Yard. 'I want you to clear out all your desks. Anything that shouldn't be there – weapons, drugs, bottles of booze, letters from your mistresses, naughty pictures. Do it tonight.

'And bring your keys in tomorrow in case they want to open your drawers or lockers. I don't want any excuse for them to break into anything. Also, make sure all your diaries are up to date.' Diaries are the desk books detailing our day-to-day movements, our arrests and our expenses. 'I want you on parade at 10 a.m. sharp, and everyone to be as squeaky clean as Snow White. Got it? Above all, don't forget to be polite.'

They came at ten on the dot, eight strong, without knocking, led by a detective superintendent and his bag carrier, a detective inspector. The big man, formidable and fair-haired, spoke for all of them. He was wearing a raincoat which he kept on throughout the proceedings, as if to indicate he wouldn't be staying that long before discovering what they'd come for. Nice bit of psychological pressure.

The detective super set down his briefcase, put his hands on his hips, looked around and said loudly, 'Well, well, well. So this is Islington's Crime Squad! I was expecting something out of *Hill Street Blues*.' We exchanged glances at each other from our desks. What was he on about? Was that a compliment or not? *Hill Street Blues* had high ratings, but we weren't sure if they were the kind of ratings that impressed CIB.

'These gentlemen are going to search the room, and search your desks.' His sharp eyes swept the office, taking in everything, looking for guilty faces. It was obvious they'd heard something, a whisper that all was not as hunky-dory as it should be on our squad. I sensed they knew what they were looking for.

Behind him, the posse got busy. They went from desk to desk, taking us apart like a Customs and Excise rummage crew. I put my feet up on the blotter, leaning back with my hands behind my head, and gazed out of the window. The rest of the Dirty Dozen feigned equal disinterest, though a few butterflies were fluttering under our belts. We'd done our own sweep the night before, but had we overlooked anything?

We had.

'Move your feet, will you?' One of the plain-clothes boys was standing over me. 'What's this?' He picked up a book from my desk, *The Old Man and the Sea* by Hemingway. 'A little light reading?'

'Put it down. There aren't enough pictures in it for you!' Dennis's admonition to be polite had temporarily slipped my mind, but you can only take so much stick.

The CIB bloodhound found nothing – which didn't mean there was nothing to find. There's always a weak link in a chain, and I suddenly remembered ours. '*Shit! They're going to find the Stop Book.*' Every police station in the country has a Stop Book, the size of an A4 desk diary, in which details of members of the public who are stopped for any reason whatsoever are recorded. It tells you how, when and why they were checked, and which of us did the stopping. Also whether they were searched. If they're arrested, they go into the book in red ink.

Every policeman, whether in uniform or plain clothes, is encouraged to make 'stops'. The top brass love us for it. The fact that you're out there at the sharp end, ferreting about, making waves, demonstrates devotion to duty. We always grumbled that it was pure politics, so that the hierarchy could show the mandarins in Whitehall a bit of paper with enough figures on it to prove the thin blue line is doing its job. With better things to do, a lot of uniformed coppers became experts in visiting graveyards and telephone boxes to find names to put in their notebook. Me, I never bothered. Why go into a graveyard or a telephone booth when you can make them up in your head? It was a pointless exercise unless you had the power to back it up and demand ID. As for an arrest, if you were in uniform the odds were probably less than one in twenty, if that. Once in plain clothes, it was a different ball game. You became more selective. You weren't just doing it to get a name in your book, but because there was a genuine suspicion that something was wrong.

But the Stop Book was still an Achilles Heel. There was a lot of resentment in those pages, and if CIB followed the names up, some of them were sure to want to drag us through the mire. Normally the Stop Book was kept on a desk by the door. I looked casually over. It was gone.

While his bloodhounds went through our desks, the big man kept the small talk going with Dennis, who admirably managed to retain his cool apart from one brief lapse when he raised his voice so the whole room could hear it: 'I think if you want to ask me that question, you should caution me first!'

'I just want to know where that book is!' the big man told him ominously.

'The Stop Book? It went missing last week.'

'Why haven't you got a new one?'

'No one's stopped anybody yet.'

The big man's mouth tightened, but he kept silent.

At the end of an hour the leader called his team together. They shook their heads. Nothing. 'Okay, DS Morse. We'll be on our way.' He paused. 'But I have no doubt we'll be back.'

'Won't you join us for a beer?' Dennis asked, all hospitality and innocence. He didn't get up to shake hands.

'Some other time.' And they were gone.

We watched them from the window as they marched out of the building and climbed into their cars. At last Dennis relaxed. 'CIB? They'll never be detectives as long as they've got a hole in their arse. And as for *him*,' and we knew who he meant, 'he couldn't run a bath, let alone a search team.'

At which point our guv'nor reached beneath his ample posterior and produced a red-covered A4 ledger. It was the Stop Book, of course. He'd been sitting on it all the time.

He tossed it at me. 'Here, Duncan. Your job tonight. Burn it!'

It was warm already. 'My pleasure, Skip!'

TWENTY-TWO

ROOFTOP RENDEZVOUS

Despite the subterfuge, someone had to be the fall guy. CIB weren't happy, and made their displeasure known. A docket landed on someone's desk in a faraway office, and within a month Dennis and Andy, his number two, had gone. They simply vanished overnight. On a Friday he'd said his usual 'Cheerio, lads, have a nice weekend. I want you in bright and early on Monday.' He never came back.

It transpired that both of them had been quietly moved back into the main CID office – shifted sideways. In the month of the investigation someone in the squad had managed to heap more coals onto the Crime Squad's battered head. 'He's a bit moody at the moment, he's got a lot on his plate,' one of my mates had confided in me.

'Why? What's wrong?' The guy was certainly looking unlike his usual cheery self.

'Yesterday he mowed down someone on a zebra crossing.'

'Christ, that's not good.'

The story came out. A police dog handler had reached him first after the accident, and found him swaying around on the pavement. 'You've had a skinful,' he said, stating the obvious and producing a breathalyser.

'But instead of sticking it in his mouth,' my colleague went on, 'he simply drops it on the pavement and grinds the phial under his boot. At which point a Black Rat sergeant turns up in his jam sandwich, sees the chaos on the pavement and takes control of the situation. Naturally he makes a move to breathalyse our bloke.' Then, it seems, the scenario went as follows.

Dog handler: 'It's okay. I've bagged him, Skip.'

Black Rat: 'Then why isn't he in the back of the car?'

Dog handler: 'He blew negative.'

Black Rat: 'I can smell him from here.'

Dog handler: 'Well, it didn't turn green.'

Black Rat: 'Are you taking the piss? I'll bag him myself.'

The dog handler was already making notes. Without looking up, he said: 'Can't do that, pal. You know that under the Road Traffic Act we've got no right to bag him twice. That's it.' He didn't need to add that he was in the clear, because they weren't allowed to take a urine or blood test either now, since he couldn't be nicked. Not even on suspicion.

It cost our boy a crate of Scotch. Who wouldn't look moody after that?

25 November 1981, 1 p.m. A crisp autumn day, full of sunshine and falling leaves. This day would be the biggest day in my life so far, though I didn't know it at the time as the three of us cruised through the streets in our unmarked car, Gerry Willmott behind the wheel, myself on the radio and Phil in the back.

We were on our way to the Metropolitan Police Laboratory, a stone's throw from Lambeth Palace on the south bank of the Thames. This is the place where everything connected with forensic and scientific investigation is submitted. There is even a double garage with no windows and infra-red lighting where they rebuild vehicles blown up by bombs, piece by tiny piece. Word is that the lab is one of the few buildings that would survive a nuclear attack because of the soft foundations on which it is built, which somehow has a stabilising effect. You'd never believe what lies beneath the streets of London – and I'm not just talking about sewers, cables, water pipes and underground train tunnels. I had my first hint of the oddities you might find when I arrested one of the few people I ever nicked for drink-driving. He was a nice enough guy, who told me he was a diver when I asked for his occupation.

'You're a long way from the sea,' I said, trying to ease the pain.

'You think so? I'm up to my neck in water every day, and I don't mean the Thames. There's all these roads under London, in case the balloon ever goes up, and right under Holborn is the canal I'm working on now. It separates a dual carriageway. You'd be amazed at what's down there.'

Somehow Nuclear Ned had missed that one.

Suddenly the main set on our dashboard came to life and a female voice, clear, clipped and precise said: 'November One, November One, from MP' [Information Room at CO calling King's Cross area car]. Premises of Midland Bank, Exmouth Market, WC1. Suspect on roof armed with a rifle.'

Another voice: 'All received November One, MP [King's Cross area car acknowledging].'

A third voice: 'Show November Two assisting, MP. [Neighbouring area car Islington acknowledging].'

And a fourth: 'Show Alpha Seven assisting, MP.' The City boys were in on the act. The City of London police have two area cars, Alpha Seven and Alpha Eight, who tend to stray into the Met's territory out of sheer boredom – after all, the City turns into a ghost town at night. To reach Exmouth Market they'd be coming up Farringdon Street, which becomes Farringdon Road where it left their patch. There are no 'roads' listed in your *A–Z* in the famous Square Mile, only 'avenues', 'lanes', 'rows', 'yards', 'streets' etc.

More voices over the airwaves. 'Echo One, MP . . . November Delta One . . .' And another: 'India Nine-Nine, MP. We're two minutes away.' That was the police helicopter whirring in for moral support.

I looked at Gerry. 'Do you fancy taking that shout?'

He shrugged. 'It's on our way. Why not?' He slammed his foot down.

As my back pressed against the seat with what seemed like G-force, I managed to gasp out: 'Steady, mate. Slow down! We don't want to be first on scene! Let someone else be a hero.'

He ignored me, of course. If anything, his foot stamped on the floor harder, feet working overtime on the pedals and gloved hands going through the gears like Nigel Mansell.

We were there inside a minute, the first on the scene, to find a throng gathered outside the bank and all of them staring skywards. I followed the pointing fingers – and there was a man with a rifle, aiming it straight at us.

I was in a brown leather jacket, jeans and trainers. I had long hair and a scruffy beard. Thank God, at that moment I did not look like a policeman. The one thing I didn't have was the thing I needed most – a gun.

'Get back, everyone! Back, all of you!' And to the stragglers: '*Fuck off out of it*! You want to get shot?' There are always onlookers reluctant to leave the scene of a crime, behaving as if they're extras in a TV episode of *The Bill*.

By now the sound of India Nine-Nine's threshing blades filled the sky as she circled above us. The wail of two-tone sirens seemed to be everywhere, coming in from every street, growing louder by the second. Gerry, still in the car, caught a radio message from the chopper. 'He's still there, right above us!'

We raced into the bank. One of the clerks pointed to a door. 'That'll get you to the roof!' We crashed through it like young bulls. Inside, rough stone stairs led upwards from a dark landing filled with empty boxes. The three of us pelted up – one, two, three flights, gasping for breath at the top. And still not a weapon between us, not even a truncheon. A thick door blocked the way to the roof. We took it in turns to plant our size elevens on it, and finally it came off its hinges with a splintering crash, magnified in the confined area.

As the door crashed in and a cloud of dust enveloped us, we caught sight of a black youth kneeling down in the firing position twenty yards away, waiting for us to come through. The rifle was on his shoulder, and his finger was on the trigger.

I know that in such circumstances this seems stupid, but sometimes the best form of defence really is attack. Which is why the three of us charged forward as one instead of diving for the nearest cover. '*There's the bastard!*' All for one and one for all. But suddenly there were only two of us off the starting block. The gunman had fired and Gerry caught it full in the chest. As he fell, Phil and I went on running, and I had a glimpse of our quarry desperately trying to reload.

He was big, but not big enough. We hit the yob as he raised the gun again, and dived on him like a pair of backs in a rugger scrum. A wild mêlée took us across the roof, punching, kicking and cursing. Finally I managed to whack the gun out of his hand and send it skittering across the asphalt. Then we started kicking the shit out of him. Two fit coppers against one arsehole makes fair-to-middling odds.

'Shall we sling him over?' I meant it, indicating the wall and shouting against the thunderous roar from above. Gerry was dead, wasn't he? An eye for an eye, what's wrong with that? 'Go on, you take his feet!'

Phil shook his head, and pointed upwards.

India Nine-Nine was still there, hovering like a dragonfly, and she might well be pointing a video camera at us even now. Point taken. I took in gulps of air, trying to calm down.

I gave our man a final thumping, and he lapsed semi-conscious on to the roof. Phil started dragging him towards the exit where the door had been while I ran back to see if I could do anything for Gerry. Amazingly, he suddenly sat up, gingerly feeling his chest. Then he got to his feet, a trifle unsteadily – but at least he was up. I grabbed him in disbelief, turning him around, searching for blood and gaping flesh. Nothing. Gerry said hoarsely: 'What the fuck happened?' He felt his chest again, winced. 'Something hit me . . .'

'He shot you!' I exclaimed. 'But there's no sign of anything!'

I ran back and picked up the rifle, looking at it more closely. 'It's an air gun.' It was, too – a .22 air rifle, but still a lethal weapon.

Our prisoner was in no shape to put up a fight any more. I kept hold of the rifle, grabbed his other arm and yanked him towards the stairs. Phil cocked a quizzical eye at me. 'Just as well we didn't tip him over,' he said.

'You're right,' I said. 'Thanks, mate!'

The outcome to all this excitement was not one award, but two. First off was a recognition from the Bow Street Magistrates Court Police Reward Fund, a cheque for £75 apiece. Now that may not sound a lot, but it was the thought that counted.

I framed it, and to this day it hangs in my bathroom, where I can see it from the loo and indulge in a spot of nostalgia whenever I feel the urge. When anyone asks me if it shouldn't be somewhere more select, I refer them to Glenda Jackson, who used her two Oscars as garden gnomes. I believed that was the end of it, appreciated the gesture, and thought no more about it.

But then out of a clear blue sky came the second award, and this was the real dog's bollocks. The Commissioner's High Commendation is the top award he can bestow, and it came a whole year later for the three musketeers after a lengthy process of discussion at top level in the Yard. The citation read: 'The courage and dedication of the three officers was in the highest traditions of the Service, and they have been awarded the Commissioner's High Commendations.'

My parents flew down to be at the ceremony, which took place at Scotland Yard, with Commissioner Sir Kenneth Newman shaking my hand and murmuring the usual pleasantries for such an occasion. Most importantly for me, Dad was there to see it.

Subsequently I learned that we had all been considered for the Queen's Gallantry Medal, but the relevant board decided we hadn't been gallant enough to deserve it. After hearing the citations for some of the other officers at the Commendation ceremony, I had to agree with them. I felt very humble being in such company with my fellow officers, men and women alike who were being rewarded for selfless feats of true courage.

I said as much to my father. 'It was only an air rifle.'

'You weren't to know that,' Dad replied.

After the ceremony the family went to a pub opposite King's Cross nick, where some of the boys had laid on a spread for me. It was great to have them all there.

'Well done, son.' Dad shook me by the hand, clinking tankards. 'I'm proud of you. We all are.'

Those were the only words I really wanted to hear as I entered the next phase of my career.

TWENTY-THREE

THREE WISE MONKEYS

September 1982. The Falklands War had been won, everybody was on a high, and I was on a list of 100 or so Scalies hoping for higher things. The immediate higher thing on the agenda was being promoted to full detective, with one last hurdle to surmount – the selection board. I was twenty-two years old and I knew that 25 September would be one of the most important days of my life. Out of the 100 candidates, maybe twenty would get through.

I was determined to be one of them.

To show what a competitive bastard I am, I have to tell you that I was prepared to shaft the opposition. Maybe not my three colleagues from King's Cross who were also up for it, but certainly the other hopefuls who gathered in City Road police station that morning for the big ordeal. The interviews were held in a conference room, and would take place over two weeks.

I sat with eight interviewees in a side room, waiting my turn. I'd arrived as instructed at 9 a.m, by taxi, even though I knew my interview wasn't until 11.30 a.m. Some of the other poor sods would have to wait all day, twitching. 'What are they going to ask us? Have we done our homework?' The silent questions filled the room. Out of the blue, someone would pipe up: 'Does anyone know what you should do when . . .' If there was a silence, I would rattle off an answer, all of it duff info, smile encouragingly and lapse back into my own inner space. This was one day when Mr Nice Guy wasn't at home.

Looking around I could detect only one serious rival, a thickset man some ten years older than me, with thinning fair hair. Working on the principle of 'know thine enemy', I got talking to him.

'What did you do before you joined up?' It was nervous small talk, but anything to get through the morning.

'Ex-Army, ex-Box Five,' he said laconically. Box Five and Box Six are how the police refer to MI5 and MI6. The derogatory term for MI5, incidentally, is MFI, as I would later learn when I had to work with them.

'What are you doing here, then?' Why give up the life of James Bond to pound the pavements? 'Bit of a comedown, isn't it?'

'Let me tell you, being a spook is the most boring job on the planet,' he responded darkly. 'I've had more fun with the Old Bill than I ever had chasing Russkies.'

I liked the guy straight away. We sat together, comparing notes, until a face appeared round the door. 'Mr MacLaughlin? Will you come this way, please?'

Behind a wooden door, three faces looked up at me expectantly. Two sleuths and a helmet. The Three Wise Monkeys, they were called behind their backs. The main monkey, chairman of the board, was Commander Bill Taylor, a man who had risen rapidly through the ranks. Commander Taylor was widely respected, and went on to become Commissioner of the City of London Police. I expected a grizzled father figure, but instead I found myself looking into the keen eyes of a man little more than fifteen years older than myself.

To his right sat Detective Chief Superintendent Geoff Chambers, known to one and all as 'Fag Ash and Confusion'. I'd seen the reason for this perjorative nickname first hand at more than one murder scene. I can visualise him now, standing by the body with legs spread belligerently apart, gut protruding over his belt, cigarette drooping from his mouth and ash tumbling down his waistcoat – with confusion writ large across his features. This was a gross and deliberate deception, I should add, because the sad bloodhound eyes disguised a brain as sharp as a razor.

Word was that DCS Chambers, the most senior detective in the combined boroughs of Haringey and Enfield, had handled more murder investigations than any other copper in the Met, including a nasty arson revenge attack on the music centre of Tin Pan Alley in Central London, as well as the notorious serial killer Dennis Nilsen who carved his own swathe through North London's gay community.

I couldn't help noticing his tie: dark blue with a gold eagle, claws extended, the symbol of the Flying Squad. I wondered how many other ties he had hanging up in his closet at home. It is not generally known that police squads sport a variety of ties, not unlike regimental neckwear, while certain major investigations merit a special tie for those involved in them. All ties have to be approved by a committee at the Yard. For example, the Central Drugs Squad boasted a Chinese Dragon as its emblem, based on the famous phrase 'chasing the dragon', where addicts sniff the swirling smoke from burning heroin to inhale into their systems and get themselves into fantasy land. The Fraud Squad has a quill, the Regional Crime Squad has the little red flower of the scarlet pimpernel ('We seek him here, we seek him there . . . that damn'd elusive Pimpernel'), while the Anti-Terrorist Branch, otherwise known as the Bomb Squad, sports a Bible, a candle and a bell as the insignia on their neckwear, ostensibly a religious artefact used for the 'exorcism of terror'. Personally I always thought they should have a round black ball with a lighted fuse on it.

This form of neckwear occasionally got the owners into trouble. The Brixton Robbery Squad are a case in point. Their tie depicted a hand of cards, a fan of four black Ace of Spades. The tie had been worn for months, appearing as day-to-day attire in court, at crime scenes, even down the Brixton market, before someone in high office spotted it. The manure hit the fan, possibly because this was the time of the Brixton riots and not exactly the most sensitive moment to parade it around.

'What does that tie signify?' one of the top brass in the Yard demanded, deducing the worst. 'Is this some kind of a wind-up for the local community?'

'Not at all, sir,' came the quick-thinking response. 'It stands for "A fair deal for everyone."'

The top brass didn't wear that one. The tie was banned on the spot, and is now classed as a collector's item.

Back to the Board. The third wise monkey was cloaked in the full uniform of a chief superintendent. He left such an impression on me that I can't even describe him, let alone remember his name. But he must have been highly regarded by somebody, or he wouldn't have been sitting there. The Commander motioned me to a chair in the middle of the room, which suddenly felt as wide as a desert with no oasis in sight.

'Good morning, sir. Good morning, gentlemen.' I had been groomed by my DCI at King's Cross, a splendid and charismatic individual named Bill McLaurin, who would go on to become deputy head of the Central Drugs Squad, and on his retirement head of security at Nat West. 'Keep your breathing deep and regular. Don't fidget. If it itches, don't scratch it,' he'd advised me, along with a few other tips that I had revised until I knew them backwards. I was aware of one detective who had to face eleven Boards before being accepted. I intended to get through in one.

The opening remarks were encouraging. The Commander himself congratulated me on my award. 'Reading your file, Mr MacLaughlin, I'm sure you'd rather have been in the Falklands War than in London.' So my father's influence was still alive. 'You also have an impressive recommendation from your division.'

This was good news, because it confirmed that I had the backing of my guv'nors. Four people had been put up from our division, and I had been told on the quiet that I was number one in the pecking order, meaning that I was favourite on our ground to come romping home.

There was a bit more chat to relax me, questions about my family and background. Then the hard stuff, questions firing on all three cylinders. Law, rules of evidence, police procedure, courts, warrants, informants, more law. Then, out of the blue, from Commander Taylor: 'When was your last arrest, Mr MacLaughlin?'

I glanced ostentatiously at my watch. 'About eleven hours ago, sir!' This time I knew I had them. All three looked up from studying their paperwork. Three pairs of eyebrows rose in unison.

'Er . . . would you like to tell us for what offence?'

'Sus, sir.' I'd said it without thinking, but made it look like a slip of the tongue. 'Sorry, I mean an offence under the Criminal Attempts Act.' The two detectives looked at me with a glint of approval, the Woody guv'nor stared stonily. He knew what I was doing – being a smart-ass, trying to create an impression.

But he was outnumbered two to one, and the odds came down on my side. Besides, since when has it been illegal to manipulate a panel?

'Would you care to elaborate?'

Now it can be told. The previous night myself and two other officers had gone out deliberately looking for someone to nick, purely in order to help me bat off this question, which was high in the probability stakes for the asking. We had trawled the back streets of Clerkenwell in an unmarked car until we spotted a face we knew, a known car thief with a lot of previous on his record, mainly small stuff like radios and forcing the boot – which can still be highly inconvenient for a motorist, what with replacements, insurance claims and the shards of broken glass embedded in the car mat for weeks. The youth was hovering around a line of parked cars, and that was enough for us. If he wasn't guilty now, he would be sooner or later. And no doubt he'd got away with a few things in the past. Call it summary justice, but he was well overdue for a nicking. 'In you get, sunshine!'

Back at the station, I 'showed the body', meaning that my name went down on the charge sheet as the arresting officer. Then I called it a night and headed back to the section house for a spot of kip, leaving my two loyal colleagues to get on with the paperwork. I had a big day in the morning.

'Eleven hours? Ah!' The Commander made a note, and so did the others.

Pardon me for feeling smug at that moment, but I knew I'd put up a good performance and sideswiped everything they'd lobbed at me. But then came a handful of grenades. The last questions went for the jugular, designed to test your conscience and what is known among the chattering classes as the moral imperative.

'Mr MacLaughlin,' the question came from Blue Serge, in deceptively quiet tones. 'You are out with your detective inspector who has told you he is meeting a source. You witness the contact hand over a significant amount of cash, which the detective inspector pockets. You overhear the contact thank him for dropping the charges. What do you do?'

Fuck! Aloud I said: 'Well, sir, I'm sure such things don't go on in the Metropolitan police.' Brown-nose MacLaughlin, or what? I pressed on: 'But in those hypothetical circumstances, on returning to the police station I would make notes on what I had seen and heard, and then report the matter immediately to a senior officer.'

It was the answer they expected. But of course such things do go on, as everyone who lives in the real world knows, and not just in the Met either. But if I'd really seen it happen, what then? The short answer is that I'd have turned a blind eye and kept clear water between us in the future.

That's it, I thought, noting the nods of approval all round. Ordeal over. Then DCS Chambers popped up with one final salvo. 'You've obviously given evidence at the Central Criminal Court. What is engraved in stone above the door?'

I had been to the Old Bailey loads of times, though never once had I actually looked up as I went in. But without pausing I replied: 'Defend the children of the poor, and punish the wrongdoer.' Fag Ash and Confusion gave me a wry grin of approval. Mr McLaurin had briefed me on that one, too. 'It always comes up if Fag Ash is on the Board.' Thanks Bill, that's another one I owe you.

In fact, my first appearance at a Crown Court had been at the Old Bailey, where I blew it big-time when it came to the important matter of protocol. As a nervous young greenhorn copper, I was giving evidence in a drugs case. I had helped arrest two dealers following a car chase through North London after they finally ran out of road. In the back of their van we discovered a large slab of cannabis. Testifying in the witness box I had repeatedly called the judge 'Your Honour', as is normal in a Crown Court.

Mr Justice Grant never batted an eyelid under his imposing wig. But a court usher, a not unattractive female in the standard black robes, kept winking at me and mouthing something. Was it my lucky day? I couldn't read her lips.

It wasn't. As the lunch interval was called and the Court rose for the judge to leave, she grabbed my arm. 'Couldn't you see what I was trying to show you?' She held up a sheet of foolscap. On it was scrawled, in large capital letters, 'MY LORD.' 'That's what you're supposed to call him.'

'Why? It's not like that anywhere else.'

'It is here. The Old Bailey is the only place in the country where the judge is representing the Lord Mayor of London. So he's M'lud to you.' And after lunch he was. M'lud even acknowledged it with the ghost of a smile when I got it right.

Commander Taylor again. 'Thank you, Mr MacLaughlin. I think that's all. Now, before you go, is there anything you'd like to ask us?'

There were a dozen things I wanted to know – like, had I passed? Instead I remembered the words of wisdom from my mentor. 'Don't ask questions, and above all don't make any smart speeches about what you have to offer the Department. Don't try and be clever. Just keep stumm!'

So, like Long John Silver's parrot, I repeated what he'd told me to say. 'No thank you, sir. It's been a fair Board. Good day, sir. Good day, gentlemen.' And I left.

Just one week later I was a member of The Filth.

PART TWO

TWENTY-FOUR

THE FILTH

October 1982. They found a desk for me in the CID office at King's Cross, and I walked in at 9 a.m. sharp to find a lot of old faces around, and by old I mean friendly. There were handshakes and back-slapping all round. It was a temporary posting while they found a more permanent home for me elsewhere in London, but I would stay there for the next twelve months. In that year we had thirteen murders, which I thought was a bit much, even for that busy part of the metropolis. We solved them all bar one – and we knew the culprits, a well-known family, via our informants and the mob's trademark weapon, a .38 revolver adapted to take a .410 shotgun cartridge. It did a lot of damage to this particular victim's private parts before he expired, the latest victim in an ongoing drug war.

My biggest fear was to be sent to Stoke Newington, popularly known by both police and criminals alike as Cokey Stokey, a reference to alleged police involvement in drugs and corruption. I wasn't frightened for my own safety, more for my sanity. Thirteen murders? That was child's play compared to what went on in that next-door borough, separated from us by Green Lanes which is one of the main arteries into Central London from the north. In my year at King's Cross there were so many murders across the border that they had to bring in portakabins as overflow incident rooms.

Contrary to the public's image of Brixton, which always seems to get into the headlines with street crime, I can tell you here and now that you don't want to be walking around parts of Stoke Newington on a foggy November night. If you want to picture it, think of London's answer to the Bronx, and then think of the biggest shithole you can imagine. Every conceivable kind of villainy goes on in that area, which you might care to note is in p48 on the London *A–Z*: drugs, vice, rape, robbery, every degree of violence from a slap on the face to a knife in the gut. They even had a murder in the police station, for Christ's sake. In case you're wondering, this was a domestic dispute which carried on outside the family home and got slightly out of hand. The couple came in for counselling, continued arguing and were left alone for ten minutes to have a quiet kiss-and-make-up chat, during which time the husband suddenly leaped on the wife and stabbed her to death with a kitchen knife he had somehow seen fit to bring with him.

The other blot on the station's copybook – 'and wallpaper', as one cynical sergeant put it – was a much-publicised suicide a few years earlier. A black guy named Colin Roach, obviously very disturbed, parked his car outside the nick, walked into the front office, put a sawn-off shotgun into his mouth and pulled the trigger.

The whole area is an ethnic soup, which is all right until it boils over. You can feel the constant tension in the streets and bars, where Greeks, Turks, Kurds, West Indians and Africans are all flung together, along with the 'Stamford Hill Cowboys', the name given to the orthodox Jewish fraternity because of their wide-brimmed black hats. Shalom, pardner! When you get a group walking down the hill with the sun behind them it's like a scene from *Gunfight at the OK Corral*.

One of my mates, with twelve years behind him, went so far as to resign from the Force after being told that he was being transferred there. 'This I don't need,' he told me. 'There are better things in life than dealing with shit twenty-four hours a day.'

All in all, I didn't want Stoke Newington.

King's Cross had its moments too. At that point, though still wet behind the ears at twenty-two, my attitude to the job was already hardening. You couldn't call it Murder Incorporated, quite, but now I saw more than my fair share of the citizenry who had met their demise sooner than nature intended. In fact, detectives do not rush out in a scrum to an actual murder scene, fighting to get a look at the body. We go out singly or in pairs, and when we do we're advised to keep our hands in our pockets as much as possible, to keep us from contaminating the scene. Spotting clues is the job of the SOCOs, Scenes of Crime Officers, the guys you see in white overalls dusting for fingerprints, scraping blood samples, using tweezers to pick up hairs from the carpet. They'll also 'lift' prints with sticky tape, the images then being transferred on to glass.

My job as a detective was to gather evidence, do a lot of research and cross-referencing, detect anomalies in stories, look for the hidden secrets. There are always two inquiries going on in tandem. The visible side, which the SOCOs deal with, gathering the pieces of the jigsaw, and the other side, us putting them together. But the basics are the same: find a suspect, then close all the doors on him to make a case watertight.

Most murders, as is commonly known, are domestic. Most victims know their killers. Every now and then you'd get a 'sticker', which usually makes the headlines because detectives are stuck on it, either knowing the killer without getting proof, or having no idea at all.

My first murder, I got lucky. At nights there is always one detective on duty – and as the representative of the detective chief superintendent for the Division, he'll be the man in charge. In my first month, I found myself put on the roster for night duty. Around 1 a.m., a phone call to the CID room interrupted my paperwork. It was control room on the line from downstairs. 'Uniformed officers at St John Street asking for CID presence. They've got what looks like a murder.'

'What do you mean, *looks like*?'

'Well, his head's missing.'

Ask a silly question. 'Okay, I'll be right there.'

The head was missing, at least from the body. The street was elegant and tree-lined, but the sight would do nothing to help the neighbourhood. When I pulled aside a rough blanket, I saw that the head and body were lying side by side in the gutter. 'He looks like a Rasta,' someone observed acutely, noting the dreadlocks strung out from under a woolly tea-cosy hat like the furry legs of a squashed tarantula.

'Have you called a doctor?' I asked one of the Woodies laying out tape to keep a handful of gawpers at a safe distance. I had to play it by the Good Book, which demands the presence of a doctor. 'What happened? Some kind of drug war?'

The PC filled me in. 'Not quite, Mac.' He knew me from the station. 'By all accounts there was a bit of an argument. This guy's not a spade, he's a Paki. The stupid wanker was throwing stones up at that window to attract his girlfriend.' He gestured across the street, two floors up. 'He hit the wrong window, witnesses heard a bit of verbal from the occupant of the flat, a Scots guy, leaning out of the window telling the Paki to fuck off.

'The Paki's apologised. The window slams down. Next thing our friend here picks up another stone, aims it at the next window, misses, and hits the same one as before. Down comes the Scots geezer spitting bricks – and he's got a Samurai sword with him. Whack! There's a head rolling in the gutter.'

'Fuck me! A Samurai sword! Where is he?'

'Well gone, mate. Probably heading for the border, back to Gretna Green.'

We pulled in the runaway three days later, shacked up with his family in Glasgow. He hadn't even bothered to cover his tracks. Some time after that he took up new lodgings – in Parkhurst. The only blades he gets there are plastic.

One day a helmet put its head round the door and issued a challenge. 'Any of you lot got the bottle for a game of footie, Woodies against the Filth?' We rose to it as one man. The CID had a soccer team going, run by a DC called Tom Whittaker. Tom was a Geordie whose speciality was funny money, i.e. counterfeit currency.

It was Tom who alerted me to the problem with a duff tenner or a twenty, or even a fifty. 'If you're caught with it, you're stuck with it,' he said. 'A bank won't give you the time of day if you try to exchange it over the counter for the genuine article.' The only solution is to pass it on, preferably somewhere dark and dingy like a night club where it should pass unnoticed. Okay, you've been done. But you're cutting your losses, having a drink when you don't need one to get a few quid back after you've been stung.

Tom, our team manager, had shouted back: 'You're on.' When the door closed, he started looking for volunteers. I put my hand up. How was I to know that this one simple action would end with a trip to the altar? But there's the fickle finger of fate for you. We played the Woodies the following weekend, and that was how the fuse was lit for my combustible marriage.

The Met have four sports clubs, one roughly situated in each corner of London: Chigwell to the north-east, the Warren off to the south near Bromley, Bushey in the north-west and Imber Court in the south-west by Kingston, which also has an impressive array of stables for its other capacity as the Mounted Branch's training school. If you want to get on a horse, you go to Imber Court and saddle up, though it will take you a passable few months to win your spurs. The clubs are all well appointed, beautiful grounds with changing-rooms, restaurants and tennis courts. Imber Court even has a swimming-pool. And they are very popular for weddings, where you have to book up months in advance.

Unfortunately for me, our game took place at a local ground, and on Astro-turf. I was a speedy winger, but not speedy enough for the Woody who floored me – all sixteen stone of him, and yards from the ball, ref! As I lay on the ground, I realised the bastard was none other than one of the jokers who had balanced on a pillar box for a bet. Not for the first time, I wondered how there was room for two of them on that box, because he was a such a big bugger. But with two broken wrists I had other things to worry about. I had hit the Astroturf in a forward dive, put out my hands to protect my face – and snap, they both buckled under me. Ouch!

At Bart's Hospital they found a fracture in each. I could only put one in plaster, as I was living alone in a cottage I had bought in Woodford Green and needed to have one hand functioning. I elected to put the right one in plaster.

Two days later I somehow got myself invited to a medics' party, and there across a crowded room was this ash-blonde nurse with the most beautiful grey-green eyes I'd ever seen. I forgot all about my impediment. Think of Fiona Fullerton with Charlotte Rampling's eyes, and that was Beverly. She was stunning, a baker's daughter from Ilfracombe, North Devon. We got talking, and towards the end of the evening she said 'Can I sign your plaster?'

'Of course.'

She wrote on it, 'I said get pissed, not plastered.' Luckily she added her phone number – and soon after Bev was in residence in my small homestead in Woodford Green. We walked down the aisle in Ilfracombe parish church, and eventually I was to be the proud father of three lively children, son Ashley and daughters Sara and Anna.

Before the big day there was a whip-round in the office. One worldly sergeant, a dour Yorkshireman, dispensed some advice about marriage with the tenner he shoved into the hat, having gone through the most horrendous divorce and come out the other side with battle scars that would last a lifetime. 'Take my word for it, Duncan,' he said, pulling me to one side. 'Marriage and detective work do not go hand in hand. It all ends in tears.' It was the voice of experience. 'You'd be better to go out and find a woman in the street that you don't fancy, sign over your house to her now, write her out a large cheque and be done with it. That way you're ahead of the game.'

I stayed ahead of the game for fifteen years before his words bore fruit.

Bev and I were happy enough, but gradually the rigours of the job took their toll: long hours spent on investigations, some overseas, late nights checking with informants, knocking on doors, following up leads. It all meant hours away from home and hearth. It hit me one day when I heard my little Anna, aged two, singing 'Twinkle, twinkle, little star!'

'Wow,' I said to my wife. 'She knows all the words!'

Bev pursed her lips. 'She's been singing it for the past four months,' she said. I was in the doghouse again.

But kids can be useful in other ways than giving you a cosy feeling by singing 'Twinkle, twinkle!' On more than one occasion I used all of mine as junior sleuths. It's amazing what you can get away with by using a football, a dog leash or your family as a prop. One time, down in the salt marshes of Kent, we were expecting a boat to come in from Holland loaded with amphetamine and ecstasy tablets. It was the usual story. The gang had bought up an old disused set of outbuildings close to the water, where they would moor the vessel and offload the contraband. We had the place photographed from the air, but aerial pictures and Ordnance Survey maps never give the full picture. You can't beat being on the ground having a good sniff round yourself.

So I was dispatched to recce the area and check on alarm systems, guards and dogs – the normal precautions before a bust. The best approach, I decided, was the brazen one, so I roped in my three kids for company. Ashley was ten by then, Sara nine, and little Anna was five. They all trooped along with me, with my little daughter's hand in one of mine and a dog leash in the other.

'Here Prince, where are you? Come here, boy!' Bold as brass, we walked up a track leading right into the property, and past the outhouses beside a creek where I could see a fishing boat moored. I noted the red, white and blue striped flag behind the wheelhouse, and caught a glimpse of the name.

'*Oi, stop*! Where do you think you're going?' A gruff man in a Barbour came dashing out from one of the huts. 'This is private property!'

'I'm sorry,' I apologised, waving the leash. 'Have you seen a black Labrador?'

I was praying little Anna wouldn't open her mouth. 'But we haven't got a dog, daddy!' Luckily the little sweetheart kept mum. She was getting used to Daddy's silly games.

The man shook his head. 'No, I haven't. I told you, this is private. Didn't you see the notice?'

I apologised again. 'Do you mind if we just go on to the next fence?'

He gave a reluctant nod, and watched us walk innocently off through the ramshackle huts, oil drums and piles of broken timber. I made a mental photograph of the whole set-up, and once we had reached a gap in the far fence I took out my camera to take a real one, a happy snap of the family – with the boat in the background. There were figures moving about in the wheelhouse and we might just get lucky with an ID.

Then we were gone before we pushed our luck too far. The kids thought it was a great game of 'I Spy' when I questioned them on what they'd seen.

But as in so many marriages where the husband is wedded to his job, it couldn't last. Something had to give. As our rows grew in frequency and bitterness, the verbal conflict with Bev grew more intense. The end came after one particularly noisy shouting match, and she finally broke. 'Please leave!'

I was stunned. 'Leave? But this is my home.'

She turned on me. 'Don't give me home! Your home is where the blue light is.' And she was right. In that moment I joined the thick blue line of coppers who can't juggle a marriage and a career. Our divorce went through in the summer of 1999. End of marriage. End of story.

Meantime, back at the ranch, life went on apace with at least two armed blaggings a week, muggings virtually by the hour, burglaries and dippings, not forgetting the shootings we never heard about. Doctors are not compelled to report violent incidents to us if the victim doesn't want us to know, just as a victim doesn't have to cooperate. Cajoling, yes. Compulsion, no. So we probably missed a few flesh wounds, and maybe the occasional corpse.

The arrests I made had one thing in common. The public never volunteered to help. It was the same when I'd been a Woody. As long as it looks as if law and order are winning, passers-by do just that – pass by and look the other way. Fair enough, that's okay. There have always been mixed views on whether Joe Public should have a go or not. Mine is unequivocal: we're paid for it, you're not. If a copper's getting the worst of it, we like to think some help may be at hand, but nothing is writ in stone. Reason and timidity hold most people back. Nobody wants a smack in the mouth or a broken nose, or worse, and I can remember blokes who told me they would have joined the scrum but didn't want to get their suits dirty. Usually we can handle it best ourselves anyway. So if you've ever walked past on the other side of the road, don't lose any sleep over it.

More than once I knocked on a door to find a bandaged figure facing me. Sometimes he'd been shot, other times it was a knife. Most times it was a gang dispute, and he'd be a scroat anyway. The dialogue invariably went like this.

Me: 'I'm from the local nick, mate. Word is that you've had a run-in with someone and come off worse.'

Bandaged figure: 'No idea what you're talking about, Guv. But I'll be sure to let you know where to pick up the pieces later.'

That meant more claret on the carpet and maybe bullets flying, but as long as they weren't flying our way I didn't give a damn. Let the slags take each other out – it was doing society a favour!

TWENTY-FIVE

FLASH IN THE PAN

January 1984. On average they move detectives around every three years. In the Met they have Central, Inner and Outer divisions, and they try to jockey you about from one to the other. The principal reason is to avoid corruption, though you'll never find anyone putting that in writing. I went from King's Cross, N division, to Enfield, Y division. From Inner to Outer – and you couldn't get more outer than Enfield.

One of my new bosses was a detective chief inspector who lived for opening time at his local, drank port and lemon, and suffered from gout. On my first day I was dropped off in the afternoon to get settled in. I knocked on a door – no reply. Squinting through the frosted glass, I could just make out a figure slumped over a desk. I pushed open the door to find the man with his head on his arms on the blotting paper, fast asleep and snoring contentedly. I retreated to the main CID office, and mentioned my presence to one of the detectives.

'I've just met one of the guv'nors,' I said. 'At least, I haven't. He's asleep.'

'Passed out more like,' said the other unfeelingly. 'He's sleeping off his lunch. You'll get used to it.'

Four months later I was moved again, this time to one of Enfield's satellite stations, Ponder's End, where I found myself breathing a new kind of freedom. There were just five of us in the CID office – one DS, four DCs, all of us answerable to Mr Port and Lemon at Enfield. But he never called. Out of sight, out of mind.

'You're in for a few surprises here, son,' the DS, Bob Webster, said with a welcoming grin. 'There's no other nick in the Met quite like us.'

When I looked at the crime book I saw what he meant. Leafing through the pages, it became apparent that virtually every other entry related to a sexual offence of one kind or another. If it moved, someone shagged it. Mums were shagging sons, sons were shagging sisters, granddads were shagging daughters, brothers were shagging brothers. It was all logged and proven.

Talk about getting your Ponder's End away! There must be more nutters walking around that place through in-breeding than anywhere else in the capital. One thing that was missing was grandmothers shagging grandsons, because that's the only relationship in a family that is not illegal, for the reason that the law, in its dubious wisdom, has decided that a grandson can't make his granny pregnant.

If there was shirt-lifting going on behind the curtains, there was tail-lifting too – horses being the prime victims. There are a number of stables in Ponder's End, being close to Green Belt country, and the area went through a phase of mane cropping soon after I arrived – pure coincidence, I assure you. During this investigation, we were tipped off by Social Services about a girl they were counselling whose father was abusing her. I had a quiet chat with him in his living-room. Under my questioning he admitted not only to having intercourse with his daughter, but going out at night and shagging horses, too.

This was a first. I stared at him in disbelief. 'You can't be that well-endowed. How do you reach them – standing on a box?'

'No, I catch them lying down,' he said, almost proudly. 'It's really quite easy when you know how. And they don't seem to mind – I never get kicked.'

This made him prime suspect as a mane cropper, taking souvenirs from each of his conquests, but he wouldn't put his hands up to that. We charged him with incest and bestiality, he was convicted on both counts and we shut the stable doors on him for a three-year stretch. The horses of Ponder's End breathed again. More importantly, he was away from his daughter.

One nugget of information I gleaned from this bizarre episode might be of interest to any Mrs Worthington out there thinking of putting her daughter on the stage. The offence of bestiality does not apply to female entertainers who use snakes in their act, however suggestive the performance. An animal has to penetrate a human with its vital organ, or in turn be entered through one of its own orifices to be subject to that particular piece of legislation. So if you see a snake slithering headfirst into the nether regions of the Amazing Jungle Queen, there's nothing you can do about it. Except, perhaps, avert your gaze and head for the exit – or call the RSPCA.

At the end of that summer I was sent away on a specialised course at the CID Detective Training School, back to my old stamping ground in

Hendon. This was ten weeks of intensive stuff, attracting would-be Sherlocks from all over the country. There was a price to pay. If you failed, you were back in uniform. I knew I was into something special on Day One when DI Bob Melrose, in charge of our twenty-five strong class, stood up to address us.

'Ladies and gentlemen, I would like to welcome you to the most exclusive club in the world. The Criminal Investigation Department.' That was all the introduction needed. It was what he didn't say that mattered. If we didn't apply ourselves day and night, we'd be back on the beat. This time it was purely academic, all brain, no brawn. No gym, no running round the block. Just study, study and more study, and all of it to do with the law and 'stated cases' – Regina versus Joe Bloggs, a vast library that had our heads reeling.

'You're dealing with a different level of crime now, the kind of things you don't cover as a basic copper.' Bob was a policeman body and soul, he loved the job and would rise through the ranks to become head of the Flying Squad. During the weeks that followed, the CID course made all the earlier law I'd learned at Hendon seem like kindergarten stuff. By the time I came out I was thinking and talking like a barrister – it's no surprise that a number of my colleagues actually went on to take law degrees and qualify for the Bar.

But I surprised myself with the high marks I achieved – up in the high seventies, after a whole last day sweating over questions that made my brain spin. Here are some of the easier examples:

1. BROWN, a drug pusher, is kept under observation by Crime Squad officers. He is seen to make deals at the doorway of an illegal gambling club. The officers see him accept a five pound note in exchange for a small silver coloured packet. The receiver of the packet, GREEN, is stopped further down the street and is found in possession of the packet which on analysis contains cannabis.

   What offences, if any, have been committed contrary to the Misuse of Drugs Act 1971? Quote penalties as appropriate.

2. After keeping observation for several days, the officers decide to raid the club and search it for drugs at 11 p.m. at night.

   What powers exist under the Misuse of Drugs Act 1971 to carry out such a search? Discuss what power is most appropriate.

3. WILSON enters a bank, points a shotgun at a cashier and demands money be given him. Because she is behind a bulletproof screen the cashier is not afraid and refuses to part with any money. WILSON then tells the cashier that unless she hands over money he will shoot an old lady who is standing near the door out of earshot. The cashier still refuses to hand over money so WILSON repeats his demand and threatens, in a louder voice, to shoot the old lady so that she hears him and faints. The cashier becomes worried for the old lady's safety and hands WILSON £100 in notes.

Discuss fully the criminal liability of WILSON in connection with robbery, blackmail and criminal attempts only, using any relevant authority to support your argument.

Challenging, or what? On my return to the station, nothing had changed. Ponder's End was still going its merry way. Except for one thing: in my absence it had suddenly become trendy for club bouncers to stand in their doorways with a python draped round their necks, the weirdest costume jewellery I'd ever seen, but suddenly all over the area pet stores were being broken into and the reptile corners plundered.

It wasn't an investigation I relished because I don't like snakes. But inside a month we had raided houses and recovered half a dozen of the slithery creatures. Next move was to pop them in a bag and deposit them in a friendly pet shop to keep as evidence – luckily a store was right across the road from the police station.

'How do we know they won't be nicked from here?' I asked the owner.

'My guard dog has free range of the place,' came the answer. Then a pause. 'Well, he's not exactly a dog. He's a ten-foot anaconda. No one in their right mind is going to break in here!' Sadly, there must have been something wrong with the place. Not one of those snakes ever made it to court – they all died in captivity. I know, because the owner showed the corpses to me, worried in case we accused him of selling them on.

Otherwise life went on as usual. Burglaries, assaults, a couple of murders, sex games behind the lace curtains and their less-than-infrequent aftermath in court, the usual. One day I had been down at the lock on the River Lee after a suspected drowning, seen the divers drag a body out, and since it wasn't foul play had wandered back to the cop shop. I checked the crime book. One reported flashing – a routine occurrence, but somebody had to follow it up. I phoned the lady who had reported it. 'I understand you've had a bit of a shock, madam?'

'I wouldn't have bothered you, but it's the second time this week.' She was a local factory worker, and seemed remarkably unperturbed. 'There should be a law against it.'

'There is,' I said. 'But unless you know the person or catch him in the act it's very hard to make these things stick.' I was thinking of the usual flasher in the bushes or jumping out from behind a parked car to open his raincoat.

'Know him! He's the bloke who runs the bus company – and he bloody does it from his front porch at all the girls going past on the way to the factory! I see him regular, and he's at it all the time. But twice a week is too bloody much!'

I knew the factory, which made televisions, and I knew the area. Our todger-wielding friend ran his own one-man business, picking up people in a coach to take them to parties or outings. I could picture the cheerful bus, fresh white paint gleaming, parked in the street at the side of his house.

My first stop was the factory, where I questioned a few of the girls. 'Know him?' It was a positive chorus. 'You mean the wanker on the end house? Course we know him.'

That was good enough. The problem with a flasher is that if you don't catch them on the job you have to go through the whole boring procedure of getting a warrant. Two days later on a dark winter morning Denise, a trusted WPC attached to the CID, was despatched to walk past his house.

'Give us the signal when you see him,' I instructed her. 'Take out a handkerchief and blow your nose. Then we'll move in.' Myself and a Scaly parked our unmarked car within sight of the house, and waited. Through the mirror I watched Denise approach in jeans and a jacket, just another factory girl going to work. Sure enough, the fish rose to the bait. The front door opened and a figure appeared in the glass porch. Now most flashers at least keep their clothes on. This one stood there stark bollock naked, unashamedly waving man's best friend at the world outside. Denise had no time to sniff, let alone blow her nose, before I was out of the car and running towards the house. Our man didn't even try to shut the door, but stood there stark naked, still clutching his most vital possession.

'Can I 'elp you?' he inquired as I stormed up. Give him full marks for bottle, at least. He seemed totally unfazed.

'You certainly can – back at the nick,' I responded, trying not to look down. 'Get dressed. And stop waving that thing at me. There's a nice warm cell waiting for you, my friend!'

He was probably nobody's friend, elderly, skinny and without a lot to boast about in the hardware department. Back at base I questioned someone who had suddenly become a pathetic figure, a tearful old man who only got his kicks out of life by being a pest.

'Listen, Granddad. I'm going to charge you with three sample flashings. There's obviously a lot more. Do you want to tell me now, or do you want me round at your house every morning nicking you for the next few weeks?'

He merely shook his head, tears rolling down his cheeks.

'Do you know what a TIC is?'

He shook his head again.

'It stands for "Taken Into Consideration". It's a way to get things off your chest, and the important thing is that if you admit them you can't get arrested for them again. The Court will be made aware of it. You'll have a clean sheet.'

He looked up. 'What are you trying to get me to say?'

'I've been to the factory. I know this has been going on for some time. Let me spell it out. Do I have to take statements from every single girl there, which means coming back to interview you about every single one? And then charge you? Or would you like to tell me roughly how many times you've flashed at these girls in the last year or so?'

I was expecting a couple of dozen, maximum. Instead he looked at me with watery eyes. 'I'd say about three 'undred, or thereabouts.'

Three *hundred*! Christ! The man must be insatiable. The beak at Tottenham Magistrates Court in the morning shared my incredulity. He eyed me with a sharp gaze in the witness box as I summarised the prosecution case. I could read his thoughts: *Is this some kind of a stitch-up?* 'Three hundred? Are you sure, officer?'

All I did was gesture at the dock. 'The man is before you, sir, and here are the TIC forms, all duly signed.' This was an admission of guilt.

The magistrate peered over his glasses at the dock. Our friend simply nodded his head. 'It's true, my lord.' He was remanded for 'nut and gut' reports from the doctor.

We fed the TICs through the monthly statistics in batches of fifty to side-track anyone from asking awkward questions. Each TIC counts as a 'clear-up crime', and goes into the system. Call it massaging the figures, but for the next six months the Ponder's End clear-up rate broke all known records.

During one of our regular monthly meetings, the DI finished the business, then said: 'Sorry the guv'nor can't be here today. However, it gives me the opportunity to let you know that he'll be checking mileometers next week.' That meant the he would be checking our private car readings against the Duty State – the daily diary where we logged up our daily events, minor expenses and mileage from our own car if you used it. Most of us possessed an old banger we used as a work vehicle, in addition to our own cars, with the number plate blocked from the DVLA so that no outsider could find out where we lived. It was common practice to alter the figures, just as it is whether you're a captain of industry or a local councillor fiddling his expenses, and I had no qualms about getting myself an extra £200 a month, working on 27p a mile allowance.

When the meeting was over I checked the book, then my car. Shit! I was 2,000 miles under what I'd declared. I thought fast. That meant either totting up 2,000 miles in six days, spending a night going round and round the M25, or a friendly garage. I chose the easy option. My mate John had a small workshop off the Hertford Road, and when I took my battered Mini Clubman in he gave me a friendly nod and said: 'What is it this time, Duncan?'

'I need a favour, in a hurry. I want my mileometer put forward a couple of grand.'

'Put *forward*!' His eyebrows went up. 'You're an odd one. Most people want it put back.'

'Can you do it, or can't you?'

'Give me ten minutes.'

He fiddled with the dashboard, then suddenly laughed out loud. 'Hey, look at this!' He extended the mileometer casing, and I saw written in Tippex: 'Oh no, not again!' John gave an involuntary chuckle. 'Someone's been here before us . . .'

Safely back at the station, with two thousand more miles on the clock, I found a veteran DC pacing up and down the CID office, chain-smoking vigorously. He was one of the old school, an office sweat with well over twenty years behind him. One of his claims to dubious fame was when he faced a disciplinary board for striking a superior officer, in this case superintendent level.

He had faced a three-man bench and pleaded mitigating circumstances. 'What are they?'

The DC looked them full in the face. 'He touched my arse.'

'What?'

'I was talking to him, when he suddenly stroked my backside, sir. So I did what any man would do. I lumped him one.'

The man bringing the charge spluttered furious denials. My mate got off, but was immediately moved to Ponder's End. There I asked him: 'Why did you belt him?'

'Listen, Mac. He'd had it in for me for weeks, and he was just winding me up all the time. He was asking for it.'

'But did he really . . ?'

'Course not. But there's no smoke without fire. Let's see him talk his way out of *that* when the word gets round that he's a shit-stabber!'

Now he looked at me through the haze of cigarette smoke. 'You're looking like you swallowed the cream, Mac.'

'Should do. My mileometer's just gone up by 2,000 miles. I'm in the clear.'

'Kid's stuff,' he snorted unexpectedly. 'I've done better than that. I'll buy you a pint in The Swan and tell you about it.' The Swan was next door to the nick, and run by an ex-Black Rat. For the DC to buy anyone a pint, something must have happened. He was known for having short arms and deep pockets. In the bar he leaned forward. 'Listen to this. While you were up there fiddling with your car, I took a call from Avon and Somerset Old Bill. They had a delicate matter to discuss, and didn't want to go through usual channels in case one of the Woodies leaked it. They wanted to know whether Cecil Parkinson lived on our ground.'

'Really?' We both knew the former Tory chairman lived in the Cuffley area, six miles away.

'I told them, "Yes, he does. Why?" A voice said: "It's a bit sensitive. We just nicked his daughter Mary for tomming [prostitution] and possession of smack [heroin]. She's given that address for a bail inquiry so she can be released."

'I told them: "If you've got the right woman, and she is Parkinson's daughter, that's a legit address." And of course it was. I was thinking to myself "Fuck me!"'

I said: 'Bloody hell, that's red-hot info. But why the celebration?'

'Too right it's hot. I put down the phone, picked it right up again and dialled *The Sun*. I've just made myself £400. Drink up!'

TWENTY-SIX

PC BLAKELOCK

A lot has been written about the Broadwater Farm Estate riots and the terrible night of 6 October 1985 that ended with a brave PC hacked to death with knives and machetes in a maniacal mob attack. But there's a lot that hasn't. His name was Keith Blakelock, and his killing in that mindless, frenzied slaughter belonged to the darkest side of the street. It left a lasting imprint on everyone who was there, myself included, especially the thin blue line trying to keep some semblance of control on the baying mob running wild through that menacing block of council flats. Some of the soft-soapers tried to make out that it was never a no-go area. But I can tell you – it was. Particularly if you were one of the hated pigs.

I was lying in my bath when the call came. For once I was home early from Ponder's End and treating myself to a good long soak and an early night after a particularly strenuous week. It was 10.30 p.m. I took the call with a towel wrapped round my middle and water leaving wet patches on the hall rug.

The voice on the other end was low and urgent. 'Phone Winchmore Hill police station. Right now. It's a major incident. There's a riot gone off.'

Riots, thankfully, are unusual in Britain, and this isn't a word you use lightly, even though the CID usually leave it to the uniform boys to sort it out. The definition of a riot in law is 'any assembly of twelve or more persons deliberately using violence to perpetrate breaches of the peace', which on that level can extend to a bunch of soccer hooligans creating wanton mayhem inside a pub.

The major disturbances of the '80s were both racially induced – Brixton in 1981 and Broadwater Farm – while the Notting Hill Carnival sometimes came close to the edge.

This sounded bad. I phoned the shop. It got worse. 'There's been two policemen killed. We're pulling everyone in. Get over here!' It fact it would turn out that just one, poor Keith, was dead, but that three constables had been shot.

I was living at that time in Woodford Green, which is quite some distance from Winchmore Hill nick. But I was in my Ford Escort and haring off down the North Circular Road in minutes. By the time I got there it seemed as if someone had put a match to a fuse and the whole of North London was going up.

The circumstances have been recorded in scrupulous and agonising detail over the weeks, months and years that followed, and none of the records are more meticulous than those of the Yard itself. Cause and effect, blame and counter-blame, lessons to be learned – they're all part of the massive dossier on what the official *Encyclopedia of Scotland Yard* describes as 'the most traumatic of all the London riots of the 1980s'.

Only recently, as late as January 2000, news came that the case was being reopened with a 'virtual reality' reconstruction of the events that stunned the entire nation with its savagery. DNA technology was being brought into play to retest clothing and weapons that had been retrieved from the crime scene and kept in storage for fifteen years.

From my viewpoint, I entered the seething furnace of Tottenham around 11 p.m. when the riot was at its height. The violence had begun at 7.15 p.m, when a police van with a dozen men aboard drove into the grim concrete estate to respond to a 'disturbance' in a shop. It was a hoax call. Instead they ran into a prepared ambush, as a hail of petrol bombs, bricks and bottles rained down, and masked black youths emerged from the dark lanes, swarming over the van. As one shaken officer who had been trapped inside said later: 'They were after our blood. They were not out to loot, but to kill.'

Reinforcements were there within five minutes, and the battle was on. A supermarket in Willan Road was set ablaze by a flaming canister of petrol. The tension had been sparked off the previous day when four police officers went to search the flat of Mrs Cynthia Jarrett, whose son Floyd was in custody for giving a false name when being questioned about a car offence. She was knocked over as they went in with a rush and suffered a fatal heart attack. That did it. For days the tension had been mounting. A week previously, the local Tesco complained that a number of their trolleys had gone missing. They were later found on the rooftops of the farm, used to transport concrete blocks to the roof that would become missiles to hurl down on the police vans. They were also used to move petrol bombs around.

Reporters and a TV sound man were hit. At 10.15 p.m. PC Blakelock, defending firemen from hurtling missiles as they fought to put out the blaze, was chopped down by the mob of baying youths. He was rushed to Whittington hospital two miles away, where he died on the operating table.

I would be the one sent to the Whittington to take a statement from Dr William Innes, the doctor on duty who suddenly found himself in the front line as the A & E was flooded with injured officers. He told me: 'I couldn't believe it. He died in front of me. I had to say to the nurses, "That's it. We've lost a policeman."' Keith had been taken there by a paramedic driving his own ambulance, which was well-intentioned but sadly turned out to have weighed the scales against his survival. In his statement Dr Innes said he believed that if PC Blakelock had been picked up by a proper London Ambulance crew he could have lived, despite a knife still being buried in his neck when he was rushed through the doors of the A & E wing off Highgate Hill. I saw the photographs, and they were truly sickening.

Back at the Farm, twenty buildings were ablaze. Around 1 a.m. the first rain came slanting down to drive the remaining rioters away. By 4.30 a.m. the estate was quiet. So much for the statistics of a world that for a few hours had fallen victim to anarchy. The climate of hatred I walked into was almost palpable. In those first hours, I was grabbing any young black tearaway I could find on the streets of Tottenham, hauling them away and getting them into an interview room before their parents had a whiff of it.

More than 150 officers would be injured that night, and for many their lives changed for ever amid the hatred, petrol bombs and fear that exploded over Broadwater Farm. The word went out to every copper: 'zero tolerance'. No parents, no social workers, no lawyers . . . not before we got every ounce of information out of the rampaging youths. The number of arrests I made went into two figures, and people asked me afterwards how I had the bottle to feel someone's collar knowing that other hostile eyes would be on me. The answer to that was, we just did it.

The bile spouted from the mouths of youngsters, some of them under twelve years old. They'd hacked a copper to death, and now the rumours spread that they'd had his fingers off and intended to post them to the Yard. It made grotesque sense in those early chaotic hours – he'd be putting his hands up trying to defend himself, wouldn't he? 'More than that, you pigs, we're going to stick his head on a pole and parade it around the Farm.' I got it myself, full in the face, from squirming, foul-mouthed kids who should have been tucked up in bed long ago.

In that explosive air of unreality it was all too easy to believe. The fingers remained intact. But in the pathologist's report the injuries to Keith's head and neck were commensurate with assailants trying to decapitate him: 'Injuries to the head and neck were consistent with blows from a machete, or axe-like weapons.' Equally ominous was the word, later verified, that a WPC was the mob's next target: she would be snatched and gang-raped. As a result, those few women officers allowed on the estate were given at least two male companions to accompany them.

The final toll was as follows. Thirteen people shot, including three police officers, 193 injured. Damage amounted to £293,000, and 346 crimes were reported, including 34 of arson and 53 of criminal damage.

For myself, I would spend six months in that hostile arena and my second child, Sara, was born in the second month of it. This added to the general pressure at home, and I made a point of never talking about it, not one word to Bev of the daily tension I was under. Eventually the headlines faded, and media interest waned as a sullen truce settled over the area. But for those like myself, who spent months investigating the 'incident', every day was a tense affair.

Watch your shoulderblades, Duncan. Make sure there's an escape route when you venture into the graffiti-smeared stairwells to reach the upstairs balconies. Above all, don't take the lift. You never know what might be facing you when the doors slide back and you're stuck inside. I got to know the Farm like the back of my hand, as I was practically living there.

On the morning after the initial eruption, I had a taste of what was in store. I stayed too long into the dusk as the October night closed in. That first day when I returned to the Farm I was a zombie, a man in a trance. Everything seemed to be happening in slow motion, yet it felt eerily normal. The estate was a mess. Smoking cars still lay upside down. Smouldering debris and refuse emitted their own stench like an invisible cloud of accusation. Yet outside, less than 100 yards away, life went on as usual. People were shopping. The supermarkets and corner shops were open, even if there was only one topic on everyone's lips.

They caught me on a third-floor balcony of Tangmere House, known to the locals as 'the Deck', and ironically the site of the supermarket where the first fire was started. All the blocks on Broadwater were named after World War II airfields, Denham, Rochford, Stapleford and the like.

One can only surmise what the young pilots – some no older than the rioters – who took off and never came back would have made of their names being associated with such madness.

The gang of black youths had gathered by the stairs. I was at the far end closing the door on an interview which had in fact proved useless, and now I realised it was time to call it a day.

Only I'd left it later than I realised, or intended. 'Get out of there in daylight!' the chief had warned back at the pre-dawn briefing. 'Don't try to be heroes. If you're outnumbered, just leg it.' Dusk was coming down fast.

'*Babylon! Get the fucker!*' I was casually dressed and generally of unkempt appearance, but they could smell copper a mile away. They charged in a bunch, five or six strong, but the balcony was too narrow for them to come at me in more than single file. All you can do in a situation like that is obey the old adage about discretion being the better part of valour – and run. Almost without thinking I vaulted over the rail on to the pebble-dash roof of a garage block, raced across it, hung by my fingertips for a heart-stopping moment half-expecting my pursuers to appear over the edge above, then dropped on to the pavement at the back. Thank God for some iota of fitness.

At this point I felt safe. I knew the uniforms were a shout away, in white control vans parked at vantage spots throughout the estate. The pack knew it too. The sounds of the chase died away, and I straightened my jacket and walked as nonchalantly as I could to the van. Although I was no longer a Woody, I still kept my truncheon with me, plus a sheath knife which shouldn't have been there but was concealed in a jacket pocket. I didn't want my kids to be fatherless. At the back of all our minds, like a spectre, was the image of Keith and what they'd done to him.

Today his uniform jacket is on show in the Yard's Black Museum, with squares of yellow tape marking the blade wounds, graphic evidence of the savagery inflicted on him. Thirteen weapons recovered from the scene are placed alongside it. Keith's helmet was never found, and it is believed someone took it away as a trophy.

During my six months on Broadwater Farm, the strategy remained the same: get yourself invited through the door by decent black families who had wanted no part of the violence and were as shocked as anyone at the scale of it. Ask questions and get answers. Reading the fear behind the initial wariness and hostility, the softly-softly approach worked seven times out of ten. Not bad, considering everything.

Many of them – particularly the mothers who knew the boys running wild on the Farm – were in a state of delayed shock, and the wall of silence I had anticipated proved to be paper-thin. People actually like to talk after a tragedy, especially to a sympathetic stranger. It's cathartic, a kind of release. My job was to keep my eyes and ears open, collating scraps of information which, when put together, might just add up to something. At Southgate station the Incident Room had photographs plastered round all four walls, including an incredible montage of events that was like a film unfolding, called an Anacapa. This is an analysis-graphic system created by Anacapa Sciences Inc., based in Santa Barbara, California, designed to 'clarify relationships among individuals, organisations, locations and other types of entities'. In other words, an at-a-glance chart of who did what to whom, and why. Extraordinary. I'd never seen anything like it.

At the sharp end, every time I stepped out on that estate my eyes were peeled for a face, a giveaway jacket, or maybe a baseball cap with a particular logo captured at the murder scene by one of the police photographers.

Over the next days I developed a certain sympathy for foxes, stags and hares. I must have been chased at least once a week by gangs of black youths, mostly with scarves over their faces, pelting insults and sometimes stones after my flying heels. I got to know the alleys between the fortress-like blocks of Rochford House, Martlesham House and Northolt House the way a rabbit knows its warren, as these became bolt holes to safety.

The pack of young wolves melted away when I made it to the corner where the van was parked. But don't get me wrong. There were others in the same boat, and the uniforms probably got it worse than the CID. But we were there to do a job, and after a time the job got done.

There was a price to pay, on all sides. One copper I knew cracked under the strain, and actually tried to commit suicide by walking into the estate one night and inviting them to attack him. 'Come on out, you bastards, and take me!' The last I heard he was in an institution, detained under the 'nut and gut' Mental Health Act.

One decision – or lack of it – caused huge controversy in the ranks: whether rubber bullets and CS gas should have been used. I had it from an eyewitness how the Commissioner himself – Sir Kenneth Newman, dubbed somewhat unkindly 'E.T.' after the little movie alien – issued an order via Wood Green station to do just that very thing. The person who was given the dubious privilege of being the first man to order rubber bullets to be fired on mainland Britain was a uniformed superintendent.

Personally I would have been all for it, knowing what was going on outside the windows. But the prospect horrified this man – I won't name him. So much so that with an armed escort he made his way to a local resident's house in the early hours, knocked on the door and asked if he could use their phone. He wanted the call to stay confidential, away from other officers at the station.

For thirty minutes he pleaded with the Top Man to let him off the hook. 'Sir, I don't want to have that on my conscience,' he was overheard to say. The order was rescinded within the hour. I'm not saying rubber bullets and CS gas would have saved poor Keith Blakelock, but it would have saved a lot of his colleagues from injury.

How do I know all this? Because I took an official statement a few days later from one of the Superintendent's bodyguards, a firearms expert who told me grimly: 'I've been sitting here boiling for days, and wanted to get it off my chest.'

A large number of people who agreed with him called it 'mismanagement'. I had another word for it, and four months later I had the chance to voice it direct. By chance I spotted a car for sale in a newsagent's, gave them a call and went round to the house. A young man answered the door, and after a chat and a look at the car, a modest family saloon, we agreed a price. Back in the living-room I had just handed over a cheque when the door opened, and in walked his father – the Superintendent!

I'd seen him around the station from time to time, but never actually met him. 'Ah,' he said heartily. 'So you're buying my car. She's a good little runner.' I gawped at him, then looked down at the logbook to confirm it. Yes, this was the man. I'd already paid the money and signed for the car, so it was too late to go back on the deal.

I introduced myself and looked at him hard. 'I know who you are, Guv. If I'd known it was your car, I'd never have bought it. I consider you totally lacking guts for what you *didn't* do that night.' He watched open-mouthed as I turned on my heel and walked out of the house. Our paths would cross a few times afterwards, but he never mentioned it again.

Feelings ran high within the Force in the months following that surreal night, and the main cause was the unhappy postscript. It was a boil that was never lanced. We thought we had the case sewn up when Winston Silcott was arrested. It was not to be. Silcott, then twenty-six, was a local greengrocer who lived in Martlesham House. Along with two others, Mark Braithwaite and Engin Raghip, he was charged with murder and jailed for life. I'd heard the names in every flat I visited on the Farm.

All three had their convictions quashed by the Court of Appeal in 1991 after tests found that police notes had been tampered with. Two senior detectives were themselves charged with perverting the course of justice. Silcott, widely reported to be a ringleader in the rioting, successfully sued the police over their handling of the case and accepted a £50,000 payout – from a cell, where he was serving life for another murder.

It was all very unsatisfactory, and left a nasty taste all round. But that was for the future, and the casebook still remains open today, unfinished business.

You always get high-wire tension in the air at a big crime scene. It goes with the game. You've seen it countless times on TV and at the cinema, and believe me, that's the way it is. People yell at one another, they pull rank, they let off steam with bawdy humour and bad jokes, and you don't need to be a psychiatrist to know why. Harrowing scenes, violence and danger are enough to tax anyone's state of mind. My abiding memory is a night that I was in the local Southgate Conservative Club, which the police had commandeered as a watering hole where they could unwind. I heard raised voices from the bar. A detective sergeant was head-to-head with a top-ranking detective chief superintendent, a sight you seldom if ever saw in public.

The DS's voice carried across the room, hoarse and outraged. 'I tell you, Guv'nor, if you don't drag that bastard in, there'll be another murder on your hands – and the Old Bill will have done it. And this one will never be solved.' We all knew which bastard he meant and at that moment, in the sudden silence, the outspoken detective had the support of every man and woman in that room.

TWENTY-SEVEN

CON TRICKS

My three years on Y Division were nearing an end. I was summoned to area HQ at Chigwell to be asked by a uniformed chief inspector where I saw my career going. Dave Peatty was in the personnel department, and remembered me from my days in Islington. 'What do you want to do now?' he asked, with genuine interest in my future.

'Central Drugs Squad, boss,' I answered promptly. That meant Scotland Yard, the central nerve system of crime detection and base camp of the elite squads – Drugs Squad (SO1[4]), Flying Squad (SO8), Anti-Terrorist Branch (SO13), Serious Crime Squad (SO1[7]), in other words, the big boys. 'SO' stand for Specialist Operations. We call SO squads the Circle Line, and I wanted my ticket to ride.

He made some notes. 'How about Criminal Intelligence? SIS are looking for a couple of experienced men.' The Special Intelligence Service is part of SO11 based at Jubilee House in Putney, and part of their *modus operandi* is gathering intelligence from technical sources, which means they're able to tune into every message pager in the country. No doubt these days that includes text messages on cell phones. The idea of sitting at a desk all day reading other people's messages didn't appeal to me, nor transcribing tapes from bugged rooms, which is another facet of their operation. 'Thanks, but I'd rather hang on for the Drugs Squad,' I responded after a suitable pause for thought.

'I'll mark that down,' he said. 'We'll let you know in a couple of months.' My posting came through just as he said it would, except that instead of drug-busting at the Yard I found myself destined for the routine grind of Leyton police station in East London. Luckily it was a great little place, one of the happiest cop shops I ever served in, with plenty of good humour, jokes and camaraderie to send the days spinning past.

Like most police stations, though, it had its share of bad apples. While I was there a series of stabbings terrorised the borough, and the local paper, the *Waltham Forest Guardian*, launched its own 'weapons amnesty' in a purge to drive knives off the street. We were only too pleased to help, and placed a metal bin inside the doorway of each of the half-dozen stations in the manor. A nice little idea, and there was a surprisingly good response.

But I have to say that some of my uniformed colleagues had light fingers, and they couldn't resist a ready supply of weapons for the express purpose of stitching people up. The next time you saw that knife would be on the charge desk, and some young tearaway protesting his innocence.

One or two plain-clothes boys weren't squeaky clean either. I was leaving the Leyton nick one day with a colleague to go over the road for a spot of lunch, and he automatically flipped the lid and glanced into the bin. 'Hullo, what have we here?'

He pulled out something wrapped in a dirty towel. 'Christ!' A stubby Smith and Wesson revolver lay in his palm, with six .38 bullets beside it. The gun gleamed like a new toy, and I could smell the oil on it. Someone had taken good care of it, someone anxious to get rid of it.

'You found it, you can do the paperwork,' I said. All firearms are submitted to the lab in Lambeth for comparison by the forensic scientists there.

'Fuck that,' he said. 'I'm joining the Flying Squad next month, and this will come in useful on some early-morning turnover.' Meaning that he'd plant it in some deserving villain's gaff when the time was right.

I just shrugged. Big boys' games, big boys' rules.

In case you're wondering, I didn't have a chip on my shoulder at being passed over for SO1(4) as you might expect. My time would come.

Instead I submerged myself in the day-to-day business of J Division, and as one of the station's senior detectives I found myself with a number of unexpected responsibilities on my plate. In those days the Crown Prosecution Service (CPS) was in its infancy, and I was appointed as Liaison Officer between Leyton Police station and the CPS.

All prosecution papers would be served through me, and I could either submit them to the CPS or NFA them, meaning No Further Action, if I thought there was insufficient evidence. I thought at first I'd been lumbered, but as the days wore on and I found myself handling anything from GBH to drink driving and shoplifting, I started to enjoy the work.

Also, I ate well. Part of the chores required hobnobbing with senior prosecutors, where we could discuss forthcoming cases over a drumstick and a glass of wine at fortnightly meetings at CPS headquarters in Wood Green. A lot of it was getting to know each other, so we could put a face with a voice you'd hear on the end of a phone.

It wasn't all paperwork. To keep in the front line, I volunteered to work some weekends. Our factory covered Leyton Orient FC, but since they were Fourth Division, there wasn't a lot of aggro or activity. One day a uniform said: 'We've got two Herberts in downstairs for climbing over the wall to get in the ground without paying. It's a CID matter.'

I went downstairs and eyed the two kids. 'I have no intention of taking this matter any further.'

The PC was a bit put out. 'Why not? I caught them red-handed.'

I said: 'You've just stopped the Orient doubling their attendance. Anyone prepared to climb over a wall for that deserves a medal, not a nicking. You charge 'em, not me.'

Last seen, the kids were scarpering up the street, away from the ground. Sorry, Orient!

It was on one of these weekends that I got the lucky break which would give my whole career a lift. She was petite, Asian, with long dark hair and soulful eyes that would have fooled anyone. Her name was Kuljit, and her one big mistake spun the wheel of fortune for both of us. Sometimes the fickle finger of fate can work in your favour after all.

Saturday afternoon, and a sports shop in Leytonstone High Street had fallen foul of a couple of con merchants who had bought several hundred pounds worth of designer sportswear, paying with a duff credit card. I visited the shop and told the proprietor I'd do what I could. Scams like this are two a penny. I'd give him the courtesy phone call, and that would be that. But the following Monday morning he was on the blower again, and there was no doubt about his excitement as he spoke in a low, urgent voice. 'DC MacLaughlin? You won't believe this. They're back.'

'Who's back?'

'They are! The people who fleeced me on Saturday.'

'What?' I couldn't believe anyone would be that stupid.

'It's true. They're here now. Same bloke, same girl. They've asked me if I'll take a cheque.'

'Delay them as long as you can. I'll get a police car over right away.'

Thirty minutes later two faces were sitting in the charge-room as I walked in, one male, one female, both looking sheepish. The bloke was black, early thirties and cocky with it. The girl was something else, in her twenties, flashing a couple of gold teeth at me when she smiled. She turned out to be Afghan. Her English was perfect, with an East End accent.

Over the next hour I gave them the verbal third degree. Charlie Boy's attitude was, 'You got me, charge me or let me go.' I charged him. The woman, when I took her into a separate room, was prepared to talk.

She was a 'baby mother', a Caribbean term used for women who go through the degrading experience of being one of several girlfriends of a single West Indian. The charmer, not to mince words, is putting it about – and leaving a kid as a token behind each bedroom door. These studs measure life by the amount of sprogs they can sire, and have no shame. The tax payer picks up the bill. Kuljit had a couple of kids by two different dudes, and needed extra income to support them. She turned to crime.

The pair worked as a double act. They would visit City pubs in the Square Mile at lunchtime and wine bars in the evening, smartly dressed, masquerading as a couple. Their *modus operandi* was for Charlie Boy to drape his coat over a chair next to her, nick someone's handbag and slide it under the coat, then they'd openly leave together. Kuljit was the cover, keeping up the chat.

I can't say it too often. People just don't believe it's going to happen to them – until they see the empty seat where their bag was. Safely away, our friends would find somewhere quiet to search the bag, divvy the cash out between them, and Kuljit – who, I have to give it to her, was the best kiter I ever met – would hang on to the cheque books and credit cards.

Then they'd start spending. Those two could get through a dozen handbags in a day, using up the cheques as fast as possible. On average, they could count on an hour before the alarm went out, the finance house was alerted and the cheque was stopped or the credit card cancelled.

This bright pair had been on the road together for more than a year, so you'd think they'd know better than to go back to the same shop within two days and try the game on again. But designer sports clothes were good currency, and could be sold on for cash. It was sheer greed that had brought them back. They had also fallen foul of the old adage, 'proper preparation and planning prevent piss-poor performances.' 'We hit the same place twice. It was a complete cock-up,' Kuljit told me crossly. She was more angry with herself than with the Old Bill.

Her story came out. She had been brought up on one of the poorest estates in Hackney with six brothers and sisters. Her mother was an

Afghan immigrant who couldn't speak a word of English. 'Kuli' had become the breadwinner. Streetwise and crafty, though eventually not streetwise enough to save her from a couple of stretches inside for kiting, she'd developed a natural cunning that kept her alive when mixing with some very bad company indeed. She also developed an appetite for fraud.

From the outset, I felt there was something different about this girl. Nothing sexual, though she certainly had her share of sex appeal – she liked dark meat anyway. Maybe it was the gold teeth that put me off. But as we talked, I found the barriers unexpectedly crumbling. She poured out her life story – not as a sob story, purely as fact. And the names with it, some of them the most notorious villains within the Jamaican fraternity. The Yardie cult was growing by the day, with shootings as regular as a breakfast boiled egg.

The hot spots for the hitman parade were Stoke Newington, Brixton and Stonebridge Park near Wembley, but Hackney had its share and still does. Hearing the names gave me an idea. I sat back and folded my arms.

'What am I going to do with you, Kuljit?'

I was playing it cool.

'Duncan, give me a chance.'

We'd actually been laughing together, even as I was weighing up whether she'd be getting six months or a year. Some sixth sense told me: 'Stick with her!' Now she gave me a half smile, and a flash of gold.

'Why should I?'

'I can send something your way.'

I spoke deliberately. 'You know I can charge you right now. But for some reason I've got faith in you.' All the time that half smile, those sexy eyes – and those gold teeth. 'If I kick you out for six weeks while I make inquiries, that gives you time to show me what you can do.'

'What are you asking for – drugs? Guns?'

She was talking about men, not just the merchandise. It meant I'd get bodies *and* the goods.

'Both, but I'll settle for either right now. You've got six weeks.'

It didn't take that long. Within a month we were paying her reward money, £200 in cash in the regulation brown paper envelope. A sawn-off shotgun had been found behind plasterboard in a house off Mare Street, and its owner had been picked up along with it. He was a big fish, a quartermaster. We're not talking IRA; this was a Yardie who would rent it out to fellow blacks when they needed some hardware for friendly persuasion on a personal debt or a bank robbery. The usual deal is to rent out a gun for, say, £250 – and if it is used the quartermaster will say: 'I never want to see that piece again!' And charge them £500.

Kuljit came up with the goods, and earned herself paydirt for taking out not just the weapon but the villain with it. More importantly for both of us, she became part of my harem, the most prized informant I would ever have. That girl was solid gold – and I'm not talking about her teeth.

I can still see the gleam in her eye as she counted out the money in a dingy back booth in a pub off the Lea Bridge Road. With us to see fair play was Dave Morgan, my DCI, recently of the Drugs Squad and one of the best men you could ever find. He had been my DS at King's Cross. In pay-outs of this kind from the 'grass fund' you had to have someone of senior rank to supervise it. Only Dave would ever know Kuljit's identity.

We watched her finish her drink and get up – Coca Cola, she never touched alcohol. She took in the whole pub with a quick glance round the edge of the booth and then, with a final gold flash, she walked out alone, leaving Dave and me in the shadows. All three of us knew that if anyone spotted her and realised what she was doing, she'd be dead meat tomorrow.

'What do you think, Guv?'

'Duncan,' he said soberly. 'Look after that girl. Where you're going, she could be worth a mint.'

'Going? Where am I going, Dave?'

'You're off to my old team on the Central Drugs Squad at the Yard. Congratulations, Mac. That'll cost you a drink. And by the way, you failed your promotion exam.' Typical Dave, droll as always.

'Dave,' I said, looking him squarely in the eye and grinning the broadest grin of my life, 'I don't give a fuck. It's the present I wanted. Christmas has come early.'

TWENTY-EIGHT

THE DRUG SQUAD

May 1989. The Central Drugs Squad occupied half of the sixteenth and part of the fourteenth floor at New Scotland Yard, with a view of Westminster Abbey and Big Ben from the windows. Founded in 1963 by Sir Joseph Simpson, then the Commissioner, it consisted of six teams, labelled A to F, and was one of several squads that made up the International and Organised Crime Branch, headed by Commander Roy Penrose.

E and F were comparatively recent units set up in the past two years to counter the sharp increase in drug-related crimes. A seventh team, known as Operation Lucy, was based across the river by Vauxhall Bridge, and was created specifically to combat the growing menace of the Yardies, the ruthless Jamaican influx bringing unprecedented violence to the streets. The drugs genie was out of the bottle, and at night there were virtual no-go areas as the warring factions turned parts of London into a battleground.

The six principal teams were made up of one detective inspector, four detective sergeants and eight detective constables, six teams of thirteen men apiece totalling seventy-eight in all. Above them the Squad was run by DCS Derek Todd, a fantastic guy, and his deputy, Detective Superintendent Tom Glendinning, both Scots, plus two detective chief inspectors in between. When Tom retired, incidentally, he went on to become head of British Airways security. Both men were strong characters, but humorous with it, and I had the most enormous respect for them. Their attitude was friendly and man to man. If I should walk into The Tank and find either of them there, it was guaranteed they'd buy me a beer – and it was none of that 'senior management' hierarchy, but Christian names from them and a 'Guv' or a 'Boss' from me.

On my first day I arrived prompt at 9 a.m. at the Yard, suited and booted, and took the lift to the sixteenth floor to introduce myself to the guv'nor. 'Come in and sit down, Duncan. Welcome to the Drugs Squad.' DCS Derek Todd stood up in his office to greet me and I recognised him immediately from his regular appearances on TV. Not on a celebrity chat show or the likes of *Who Wants to be a Millionaire*, but on the news programmes whenever there'd been an important drug bust. A distinguished figure in his early-fifties, DCS Todd stood 5ft 10in. tall, stockily built, and I could well imagine his earlier, if brief, career as a professional footballer playing for Carlisle. Sharp-eyed viewers may have noticed a wreath of grey smoke curling up behind his head whenever he was interviewed. A habitual smoker, he invariably had a fag in his hand, and would hastily hide it behind his back as the cameras homed in. The man was strictly non-politically correct, and I warmed to him immediately as we shook hands. He had a sense of humour, and sometimes he needed it.

For instance, one Christmas tradition was a Yuletide dinner for the whole of the Drugs Squad, where we would raise money for the RUC Widows and Orphans Fund. The highlight was an auction where a particularly ghastly tie was auctioned to the highest bidder, who could then stipulate which poor sod would have to wear it every day for the next month. The tie itself was a pale blue Christmas number with snowmen, Santas and elves skiing all over it, and it would be handed back and kept in a safe for next year.

Guess who emerged the victors? Got it in one – we did. And who was the fall guy? Why, our boss of course – and you may have seen DCS Derek Todd soberly answering questions about 'significant seizures' to an eager TV reporter a month later with elves and snowmen clinging to his neckwear. The RUC got £100 in their fund, and we got a laugh. I told you the boss was sporting. But even Toddy's limits had been slightly stretched the previous year when the 'prize' was a John McEnroe-type headband, which someone had picked up as a freebie from McDonald's. It was red and yellow, with lights that flashed on and off intermittently. The Chief Super got it again, and his punishment was to wear it every Monday morning when Commander Roy Penrose, held his weekly briefings for heads of SO1 departments.

'I just wish the boss had ordered me to take the bloody thing off,' Derek Todd complained later. 'Instead he said: "It's for a good cause. Keep it on!" So I had to.' These meetings were known as 'Monday morning prayers', but somehow Toddy's went unanswered. Could it be that the chief had been through it when he was in command of the Drugs Squad himself?

'You come highly recommended,' Derek Todd told me without preamble. 'You'll be joining E team.' I felt a jolt of excitement. E team were the best of the best, the most successful drug busters in the country. They had been built up by my mate Dave Morgan, last seen sharing a pint with me in my old manor, who had been promoted from DI with the drugs squad to DCI in charge of CID at Leyton. And unbeknown to me Dave had actually held me back from that elite posting until I could join his old team. Now I'd heard it first-hand from the big man himself, and I felt a surge of gratitude.

'Dave Morgan's replacement won't be here for a couple of weeks, so you'll be meeting Simon Johnson, who's holding the fort.' I'd met Simon before, a detective sergeant and an ex-Royal Marine. But instead of a short-back-and-sides he sported long blond hair down below his shoulders and a droopy moustache. In his own words he was 'scruffy as fuck' – and a chain smoker to boot. But he held that team together like glue, and would turn out to be the best sergeant I ever worked with.

'One more thing,' the chief pointed at a cabinet against one wall, filled with books and police manuals. 'In the cupboard below you'll find a couple of bottles of Scotch. It's unlocked. If you boys come back late at night and The Tank's closed, feel free to help yourselves. One condition – I expect it to be replaced.'

'Thank you, sir. I'll remember that.' *Fuck me*, I said to myself. A senior officer who can treat his troops like adults. I've arrived!

The main office was an eye-opener. The room was big enough to take sixty detectives, all with their own desks. Opposite the windows with the imposing Abbey view, a line of glass cabinets ran the length of the room. It was stacked full of paraphernalia – the police word for drug artefacts that often comes up in a trial. Curved opium pipes, cigarette holders for spliffs, dark brown slabs of cannabis itself – all labelled 'Paki Black', 'Moroccan', 'Afghanistan' and other sources – Thai sticks, syringes, snorting tubes and spoons, hashish, leaves, plants, sheets of LSD tabs, uppers, downers, barbiturates, even jars of cannabis oil (a very rare commodity, which you drip in a line on to an ordinary cigarette), all of it seized by SO1(4) and returned after the trial that followed. I stared in fascination at this bizarre museum of misery – or ecstasy, depending on where you're coming from.

There were a couple of dozen men and women sitting or standing around the room, and I thought for one moment I might have stepped into the Unemployment Exchange. Skinheads, pony-tails, earrings, jeans, leather jacket, sandals and a Hell's Angel with tattoos mingled together like drop-outs. I immediately identified E Team by Simon's unkempt figure and the wreath of blue smoke around his shoulder-length hair. He spotted me and strode over with a huge grin, while the cigarette stayed in his mouth. Come to think of it, I never saw him without a fag-end hanging from his lip. How did the guy eat, for God's sake!

'Duncan! Welcome aboard! We heard you were coming. Meet the gang. Your desk is over by the window.' This would be my home for the foreseeable future.

I recognised some of the faces. They were busy beavering away bagging exhibits, making notes, filing them into drawers. Simon filled me in. 'Yesterday we took out a team of Yugoslav heroin importers. Aerosol containers. We watched the meeters and greeters at Heathrow, and let them run. Then we hit them at the drop in Kensington.' He grinned. 'They never thought they'd be rumbled using that M.O. Aerosol containers! But we had a good source.'

I was puzzled. Importations are down to the Customs and Excise.

'What The Church don't know doesn't fucking hurt them,' Simon said crisply.

'Church? What's religion got to do with it?' I'd never heard the expression.

'Cuzzies. We call them The Church. "C and E" – close enough to Church of England.'

'Oh . . . Customs . . .'

'There's something you should know, Mac. That's a dirty word in this office.'

I couldn't be sure whether he was joking, but as the weeks went by I realised the depth of the political rivalry between the two factions. In fact it refers to the Investigation Department (ID) of Customs, not the boys in blue who open your case at Heathrow.

The Church's remit is to seize drugs, not people. If they get the courier, that's a bonus. And if they get the Mr Big at the end of the line, that's like winning the lottery. From our point of view, we wanted Mr Big, which meant letting the drugs run, follow them to their destination and take out the people along the chain all the way to the top. The courier would always come back.

I was introduced to Chris, Steve, Pete – and Maureen. The rest were out and about. One was out and about as far as America. This was the big time! Chris, a short stocky little man with a beard and glasses tapped me on the elbow and waved a piece of paper at me. 'I deal with all the team equipment. Sign here, here and here.' He put the sheet away, reached into a drawer and produced a 'covert' radio and harness, the radio being flat enough to fit under a T-shirt and not be detected provided you wore it in your armpit. There was also an *A–Z*, and a laminated sheet filled with a mumbo-jumbo list of letters and numbers. 'This is your surveillance code sheet. We work with SO11 surveillance teams on a daily basis. They only communicate in this language. He tapped the sheet. 'If you want to keep up, learn it!'

He handed me the *A–Z*, together with a transparent clear plastic grid filled with blocks little more than a centimetre square. 'What's this for?'

'It's an overlay for the *A–Z*. All the SO11 map books are printed with this special grid on them. Must have cost a fortune. But you can pinpoint a street almost to the nearest foot.'

A half-smile came over his sombre features. He made Mr Grumpy seem happy. 'Quite honestly you might as well rip out page 48 and throw the rest away. Most of our drug bust ops end up there.'

'What's on page 48?'

'Stoke Newington,' said Mr Grumpy.

I might have known.

I spent my first evening with my new team in The Tank. Let me explain. The Tank was the drinking den on the ground floor of the Yard situated directly behind the Eternal Flame, which flickers in the entrance by a memorial book of fallen officers killed in action. Every day a new page is turned.

The Tank was a no-frills watering hole with a linoleum floor, no carpet and the cheapest furniture you could pick up from a Sunday flea market. The pictures on the wall could have come from a car boot sale. Fishing boats in a harbour, mountains and lakes, all totally naff and nothing that referred to the great Metropolis or law enforcement whatsoever. There were also several holes in the ceiling, rumoured to be the result of accidental discharges from coppers who had forgotten to put the safety catch on their weapons.

The great thing about The Tank was that you could say whatever you wanted, and it didn't matter if you were overheard. It kept to normal pub hours, but unlike The Feathers next door or The Old Star on the corner, there were no outsiders or journalists earwigging for the latest gossip. The place was basically a large box, so ill-lit that when you walked out into the reception area, you blinked at the light.

The bar ran along one wall, staffed by smiling Asians and West Indians. Directly opposite was the Wailing Wall, with a waist-high ledge for glasses and a clientele that seemed to consist mainly of men in smart suits with loud ties and public school accents.

'Why the Wailing Wall?' I asked.

'God knows,' Simon responded. 'But Special Branch hog it every night. You'll get used to their little ways. They share our floor and the three above us. But don't be surprised if you're in the lift with them and they don't want to press the button to show you where they're going. They're full of shit.'

Sure enough, I could hardly make out the Wailing Wall for suits and pipe smoke. SB is officer material, with more than its share of graduates and ex-military types. It is also the butt of the Met's notoriously coarse humour – 'Like other people take the piss out of the Irish, we take the piss out of the SB!' explained Pete, with undisguised relish. It goes beyond rivalry. In fact the friction that exists between the Special Branch and the average copper is legendary. We see them as aloof and self-important. They see us as a bunch of ruffians. True, we didn't always dress for dinner!

I had my own run-in with them some time later. One morning the phone rang. It was reception downstairs. 'There's a young black guy down here would like to speak to a Drugs Squad detective.'

'I'll be down in five minutes.'

Waiting for me was Eddie Murphy, or someone who could have been his double. Young and handsome, he was twenty-two, and spoke good English clipped with a slight African accent. He was from Sudan, he said, and had just arrived in Britain from Khartoum. He wanted asylum – but then so do a lot of people.

He came straight to the point. 'I'd like to give you information about two kilos of cocaine in return for political asylum.'

'That makes a change from money,' I said.

'Listen to me, sir,' he said, politely but urgently. 'I'm a very important man. I work for the Sudanese Government, and I have much information I would like to impart.'

'Oh yes?' I said. 'Such as?'

With complete seriousness, he said: 'I am an assassin for my government. Right now I am able to tell you which British government workers in Africa have been nominated for execution, and those others who are at present under surveillance.'

We meet our share of nutters in this job, and it takes all sorts. 'Really? And exactly how do you go about your business?'

'I either strangle them with piano wire, or I poison them.'

He saw my expression. I was actually trying to stop myself laughing out loud.

'If you don't believe me, sir, I'll give you the name of your MI6 operative at the British Consulate. Also a list of the gentlemen under consideration to be killed.'

I sighed. You have to humour them, but this was pushing it a bit far. 'All right. Tell me.'

He spelled out half-a-dozen names and positions in the diplomatic corps.

'Thank you. Give me an hour. And here,' I fished in my pocket, 'take this fiver and get yourself something to eat. There's a McDonald's over the road.'

He trotted off obediently, and I went upstairs and made a call to the Foreign and Commonwealth Office. 'I'm sorry if I'm wasting your time,' I told a woman on the African Desk. 'I've got Walter Mitty in here. He's been spinning me a cock-and-bull yarn about the Sudan. But I've got to check it out. If I give you some names, will you confirm them for me and ring me back? That way you'll know that I'm the genuine article.'

Within twenty minutes she rang me back. 'The names check out. And I think I know what you've been discussing. Murder, for a start? And blackmail?'

'On the button. He's talking assassination. But I don't know about blackmail – yet.'

Her voice had risen a fraction. 'I don't know who your Walter is, but he obviously knows what's going on. We'd like to know too.'

He was waiting for me.

'This way, please!' I escorted him through a door to one of half-a-dozen interview rooms, not bugged, where we could talk in private. And the incredible story spilled out.

Walter gave it to me chapter and verse, a whole range of Brits at the Consulate who were targets for potential assassination. But he'd had enough. Call it conscience. More likely he felt that he had become merely a cog in a killing machine, soon to be dispensable, and wanted out before the sword fell. He also mentioned honey traps, the classic sexual entrapment pioneered by the KGB, with female staff particularly vulnerable. Other names were even more pertinent – Sudanese 'operational teams' with names like Midhat, Nazar, Maarouf, Wael-adel, all of them infiltrated into Britain as sleepers and even now waiting for the call to commit political killings. Since these would take place on the streets of London, it was time to sit up and take notice.

'Forget the two kilos,' I said. 'There are some people I want you to meet.' The people were SB, a detective inspector and his sergeant. The meet took place at the Royal Court Tavern next to the famous theatre in Sloane Square. Neutral territory. Walter was understandably nervous about having too many coppers around him, especially in his line of business, and for all he knew the basement of the big house was a torture chamber. Actually it's an underground garage, and the only squealing comes from the tyres. Over cider for him and beers for us, the lunchtime debriefings began.

I'd registered him on the Informant Profile forms we now had to submit as Nigel Mansell, Formula One ace and soon to become world champion. Walter didn't know it, but he deserved it. Champion, alias for champion grass! I sat in for four days on the trot, nothing too intense but they were probing all the time. I began to feel like his guardian angel as he turned to me repeatedly for guidance.

On the fifth day my phone rang. 'We want to bring him in.' Now he was SB's baby. Fair enough, it was what I expected and more their line of business anyway. I walked up the two flights to the eighteenth floor and knocked on the end door. A detective chief inspector looked up.

'Ah, Duncan!' He was affability itself. 'We'd like to thank you. Not just on our behalf – but the Ambassador conveys his thanks from Khartoum. Personally. You may not realise it, but at least one life has been saved already by your information.'

I was flattered, but I had to be realistic. 'Any thanks should go to Nigel.' The DCI knew his alias. 'While I'm here, boss, amongst all that paperwork are some of my notes. I need them to finish off my report.'

His expression changed. 'I'm sorry,' he said abruptly. 'All that information is confidential.'

'But . . .' I thought he was joking. 'But . . . I wrote it!'

'You still can't have access to it. As I say, it's confidential.'

It dawned on me that he might not be joking after all. 'You're having a fucking laugh, Guv'nor. Every bit of paperwork in that pile is written by me. Is this some kind of SB joke?'

'No joke,' he said tersely. 'This man is now SB property, and you have no authority to contact him again. There is no more to say.'

'Yes, there is,' I made for the door. 'You lot are a waste of fucking space.' And I walked out. You will gather that I was more than slightly miffed, and at times like this you have to speak your mind or explode.

It must have been all of a year later that I was catching a tube in Holborn Underground Station. A figure rose over the escalator, and we saw each other at the same time. 'Duncan!' Nigel had changed. He was now a dapper young City type, with a pinstriped suit, loud tie, briefcase and the obligatory mobile phone in one hand. He pumped my hand.

'How's business?' I was both surprised and genuinely pleased to see him. 'Bumped anyone off recently?'

His smile faded. 'They wouldn't let me call you,' he said. 'I work for your government now. They've given me a nice flat in Lavender Hill. Life is good.'

'You've got my number,' I said, without asking for his. 'Call me any time.' We shook hands again, and the image of piano wire popped fleetingly into my mind.

I'm still waiting.

TWENTY-NINE

OPERATION APPLEJACK

My first week as part of SO1 gave me one useful pointer: always expect the unexpected. Order can turn into chaos with one phone call. It began at nine in the morning, when I had just walked in. 'Duncan!' Simon beckoned me over. 'There's a job on. One of the teams downstairs needs some spare bods. Maureen, Bill, Dave and Steve are going along. I've volunteered your services. Briefing in ten minutes. Okay?'

'No problem.' I was itching for action anyway.

On the fourteenth floor, a detective inspector with A Team went through the details. Twenty of us sat around, making notes. 'It's a quick in and out, ladies and gents. Four ounces of coke. There's a meeting at Heathrow in two hours. The Church don't know and don't need to. Two black guys flying down from the north will be meeting a third India. It's a quick buy, cash transaction. Once the deal's gone down, we'll move in and scoop up the bodies. We're calling it Applejack. That's it. Any questions?'

'India' in this context has nothing to do with the sub-continent. It's our surveillance term for a target: 'I' for 'individual', deriving from the phonetic 'I for India'. An informant had given the tip-off. I was assigned to wait at my desk as part of the reserve team should we be required, which seemed unlikely. It looked like I was in for a quiet day after all.

On the face of it, Operation Applejack seemed straightforward enough. All teams begin their ops with their own first letter, and we get to choose the names ourselves. There's no mystique about it. Every couple of weeks we'd be asked to jot a few names down on a sheet of paper, and mostly they got used. E Team had been involved with Eagle, Earplug, even Elephant, just like hurricanes on the weather map but without doing so much damage.

Half the team were despatched to Heathrow for a quick arrest. They had descriptions of the pair of carriers, and the flight number. When the trade was made it would be a quick 'Step this way, sir!' and into the van outside. Four ounces of coke, you're looking at four golf ball sizes of the white stuff, not huge potatoes but worth picking up.

The first we knew that all was not well was a call to E team from the control room. 'The footies (police speak for a surveillance operator on foot) have radioed in. The two suspects weren't met, and now they're on the tube into London. A Team following. Your orders are to stay put.' Bill was our senior officer, a detective sergeant, so he would call the shots for our little group standing by.

An hour later the scenario became more confused. The pair of likely lads had gone by tube and taxi to – guess where? P48 on the *A–Z*, otherwise known as Cokey Stokey. The control room monitored the messages. 'They've entered a Turkish sweat shop, and we've got an address.' Then, 'They're out again, and they've got a blue carrier bag . . . They're into a taxi, heading back to the tube . . . Destination probably Heathrow . . . But just in case,' a pause, 'E team go to Euston Station on the off-chance that they catch a train home.'

We broke a lot of rules getting there, dumped the cars in nearby streets and made it to the station concourse just as our earpieces broke into life. 'Anyone getting this?' It was one of the footies from A Team. 'Indias one and two are at Euston, on the concourse, buying tickets.' That's when we saw them, two West Indians, turning away from the kiosk. One was carrying a blue carrier bag.

'Christ! That's them!' We fell in behind them, separately, doing our best to look like mid-afternoon commuters, and trailed them through the gates and on to Platform 10. We watched as they climbed aboard a 125 InterCity express.

'What do we do?' I asked. We hadn't got tickets, and we'd have to be careful about flashing our warrant cards around on the train. Surveillance teams are always taught to behave as much like the public as possible. Merge in. Be a face in the crowd, but not a face anyone notices. Buy tickets.

It was too late for that now. 'Get on the train, and play it by ear.' Bill, the senior man, took charge. 'I'll call CO.' He disappeared behind a pillar to talk urgently into his radio. 'E Team are on the train, and we've got them boxed and coxed.'

The pair were travelling standard fare, one facing the engine, the other with his back to it. We split up and took turns from the far ends of their carriage, making sure we didn't make any sudden movement or linger too long in their vision. Bill intercepted the ticket inspector and flashed his warrant card without giving any reason. 'There are five of us on this train. They'll make themselves known to you. Just don't tell anyone. By the way, where's this train going?'

'Manchester Piccadilly,' said the official. 'Three hours.'

'Christ!' said Steve. 'It was going to be Heathrow and we end up in fucking Manchester!'

'We're out of our ground,' said Bill. 'We'll get GMP (Greater Manchester Police).' He located a pay-phone at the end of First Class, dialled a number and spoke rapidly. Then, after a quick glance to make sure the Indias were still in place, he was back.

'Manchester are going to fly a couple of guys down in their helicopter, get them on to the train at Stafford, and they'll take over. We sit tight here as back-up. There'll be a reception committee at the terminal.'

Sure enough, we made contact on the next leg. We left Maureen and Pete to watch from their vantage points, and actually wandered past the targets on the way to the buffet, looking anywhere but making eye contact. But I noticed how one of them kept the blue bag firmly on the floor between his knees.

Two burly men in bomber jackets and jeans were waiting, with heavy Mancunian accents. They had another surprise for us on this day of surprises. 'You know what? These guys have been down to the Smoke to pick up some smack,' said the first.

Bill looked startled. 'We were told it was four ounces of Charlie.'

'More like a kilo of smack,' said the second. Meaning heroin, a class A drug, and worth a quarter of a million quid on the street and a long spell in jail if you're caught with it. His craggy face broke into a grin. 'Thanks for everything, guys. Now you can sit back and watch the fun.'

All we'd done was catch a train and babysit the bad boys, but it's always nice to be appreciated. The fun began about ten seconds from the moment the pair got down from the train at the terminal and set off along the platform with that easy loping stride of West Indians without a care in the world. They were laughing and joking as they passed the open door where we waited, just in case anyone needed any help. So we had a front-row view when they were taken out.

There must have been a dozen plain-clothes cops, some armed with pickaxe handles, who jumped them. They came swarming out from behind luggage trolleys, crates, pillars, everywhere. I learned later that the Assistant Chief Constable of Manchester was on the platform to watch the arrest, if you can call it that. It was more like one huge mêlée as the targets tried to make a run for it, and ran into a wall of fists and pickaxe handles. Then there was simply a mass of bodies on the platform, squirming and shouting, before handcuffs were snapped tight and the prisoners were hauled to their feet and led away.

The first man on the train crooked a finger at us. 'Hey, over here. Come and see this!' He was bending over the blue carrier bag. Inside was a brown paper parcel, which someone had cut open just enough to get a view of the contents. Peering over his shoulder I saw a wedge of brown powder. 'Bingo! Say hullo to a quarter of a million quid!'

That night we found ourselves the local heroes. We went out on the lash, as we say, and coppers being coppers we celebrated Manchester's biggest-ever heroin seizure in style. As the beer flowed in their nick's version of The Tank, one of them nudged me and said: 'We might have some more work for you.'

'What's that, then?'

'We've got an op. on the go that's very confidential and involves some big names.'

I had to tell him: 'I'm new to all this. But we're open to anything. Who are they?'

'This is for your ears only.' And he gave me three names. I gaped in disbelief. Two international footballers and one well-known Olympic athlete. If you've read the memoirs of Ron Atkinson, *Big Ron, a Different Ball Game*, published in 1998, you'll find a clue on p98, where Ron says:

> There is a well-known England international, with a long Premiership career behind him, reputed to be the biggest dealer in football. He cornered the drug market and, apparently, whatever substance you wanted, he would very quickly have it available.

What Big Ron failed to reveal was that there were in fact two soccer stars, and he had been manager of both of them. He was taken apart in the press for saying it when the book came out, with accusations of sensationalism and trying to promote sales.

But as far as the GMP Drugs Squad are concerned, they were the ones who got away.

THIRTY

INVASION OF THE BODY PACKERS

Two weeks later, the E Team's new boss arrived. DI Peter North actually bore a marked resemblance to the actor Peter Wyngarde of *Department S* fame, all the way down to the droopy Mexican moustache that adorned his upper lip. Northy, I can safely say without any fear of contradiction, was the most accomplished and professional DI I ever had the privilege of working under. It was no coincidence that the best man had been chosen to lead the best team.

He was widely acknowledged to be one of the top undercover operators in the whole country, and was a senior lecturer on the Home Office undercover course for aspiring recruits. I often wonder how many villains are sitting in their cells today unaware that it was the charming Mr Smith (or whatever other alias he was using) with the Pancho moustache who had infiltrated their gang and put them there.

I liked him from the moment I set eyes on him. I'd only been a fortnight into the job, and he gave me a friendly grin and said: 'Well, we're both the new boys here. It's up to us to make a name for ourselves!' That would be his attitude all the way through, which he disguised behind a relaxed air and a quiet voice. Strolling around our corner with hands in his pockets for an informal chat, he kept things calm.

On his first morning he set out the ground rules. 'The bottom line is this. When it comes to Class B, cannabis, amphets and the like, I'm not interested unless it's a couple of hundred kilos or more. I'm not wasting this team's reputation or time on chasing piddling amounts.' A couple of hundred kilos is roughly ninety-one bags of sugar in anybody's kitchen, and several years in the clink, but Northy had set his sights higher. 'If we must take on hash, let's do it in tons! But if it's powder, I want every grain of it.' Powder, of course, meaning cocaine and heroin; Class A.

As I got to know him, I learned something every day. Indentations, for starters. 'You do not write on anything, and I mean *anything*, that might leave an impression underneath it. I don't care if it's a love letter to your girlfriend – indentations have given us grief that we can do without.' Today's modern ESDA (Electrostatic Detection Apparatus) testing has certainly played its part in high-profile cases, among them the Guildford Five and Winston Silcott's trial in the PC Blakelock killing.

'I told you I'd look after you.' My lady with the golden teeth was on the blower. By now I had rechristened Kuljit and established her in the informants' system as Eddie Cheever, the American Formula One driver, who no doubt would have been flattered at this signal honour. 'How soon can we meet?'

'What's it all about?' I hadn't seen or heard from her since Leyton.

'How about a couple of mules bringing in two kilos of coke from America? I'm going to be the meeter and greeter.'

That was enough to light a fire under my feet. Mules are drug couriers, and come into two categories. 'Body packers' carry it about their person, 'stuffers and swallowers' carry it within their person, if you get my meaning.

The 'meeter and greeter' is waiting at the arrivals, helps them with their luggage and chaperones them to a safe house where the stuffers get rid of the double-thick condoms while the swallowers wait to let things happen naturally. Customs and Excise have a special cell at international airports where they can detain the guest until nature takes its course. It has minimal furniture – just a bed and a bog, with a special filter system attached to the loo so that the poor Cussie who draws the short straw can fish around and pull out the condom and its contents. The known record as far as I am aware is nineteen days' waiting time while The Church stood by for action. The mules know the risk they take – it's a horrible and painful death when a condom splits and the Charlie or smack leaks out.

The Church is supposed to be aware of illicit importations, and if we do a joint op. with them they do the prosecuting afterwards. The mules get pulled, and no one suspects we had a hand in it.

Northy was impressed with Kuljit when I took him to meet her in a Hackney pub. His jungle instincts made him cautious, but Kuljit gave us chapter and verse. 'They're flying in from New York tomorrow, and each is carrying one key (kilo) of coke. My job is to babysit them for a couple of days then send them home with their dosh.'

'Stuffing or swallowing?'

Kuljit had heard all the street language, and didn't need a translator.

'Neither. The gear's packed on them.' She gave us names, descriptions and flight details.

Northy nodded in satisfaction. 'Good enough. I like what I've heard. We'll have Customs do a routine pull in the Green Channel. But you'll still have to go because there may be a third eye. Just lean on the barrier as if you're expecting them and act naturally.'

Kuljit shrugged. She knew it was for her own safety.

I took her to Heathrow at dawn next day as the first vapour trails from far-flung places were filling the sky. I stayed in the car, remembering Northy's words at the previous night's briefing. 'This girl's good. She's done it before, and she knows what she's talking about. Take care of her. But I'm sorry you'll have to miss the fun. You stay out of sight.'

One of Northy's golden rules was that the informant handler never, ever, gets involved in either the arrest or the kudos that follows it. That way he can't be forced to compromise his source in court when the defence counsel play 'hunt the (informant) handler'.

It went like a dream. You may have noticed an anonymous structure in the baggage hall at big airports, slightly raised and with a commanding view of the whole arrival zone. The only unusual factor about it is that the windows are darkened. We call this the Wendy House, and you can be sure of one thing: behind the window a vigilant Customs official is watching.

The two women came through together and headed for the Green Channel – nothing to declare. 'Would you step this way please, ladies!' And in small rooms behind the partitions the contraband was found: half a kilo strapped to each hip. Other popular hiding places are the inner thigh, under the armpit, tucked in the groin and even sewn into the skin. Equally imaginative is impregnating the clothing with cocaine solution, a method favoured by Colombian smugglers.

The pair ended up in Isleworth Crown Court, pleaded guilty – and still got a seven-year stretch. The message to all concerned was, 'We don't like people bringing nasty substances in from foreign fields'. As for Kuljit, she got £1,200 for each kilo from the reward fund, and I got another pat on the back.

Best of all came the pint I was bought that night by Detective Superintendent Tom Glendinning, no less, and the words that came with it. 'I like what I see, Duncan. Less than a month with us, and you've produced more goods than some of the deadwood around here give us in three years.' Two keys of coke is no small pickings.

'I've got a lot more where that came from,' Kuljit confided when we went for a drink to celebrate her winnings. 'I can tell you something now, Duncan: I've got a sideline.'

'Yeah? Such as?'

'I go to New York and body pack other mules. For a fee. A large fee . . .'

Christ! No wonder she could afford a brand new soft top sports car every year. 'I once packed eighteen kilos of coke on a woman. A big black mama! Well, that's what she looked like afterwards, swaggering through at Heathrow. And she got away with it.'

I did some swift mental arithmetic. If you knew what you were doing, cut the stuff properly and had the nerve to sell it through all the way down to street level, you could net a quarter of a million pounds sterling per kilo. At eighteen kilos, that mama was worth marrying – or mugging.

Eventually Kuljit would become my link with the DEA, America's Drugs Enforcement Administration (known unsportingly by us Brits as 'Don't Expect Anything'). My lady with the golden smile was responsible for several 'significant seizures' in New York, swelling her bank balance equally significantly with green backs, and my reputation into the bargain.

THIRTY-ONE

FORMULA ONE

Getting to New Scotland Yard from a nick was like the difference between a Sunday kickabout on Hackney Marshes and playing for your country at Wembley. I'd been a detective several years and in my enthusiasm I thought I knew the job inside out, and that it would be a piece of piss.

How wrong can you be? This was a different world, a world where anything could be obtained if you knew where to go. This was a world of bugs, lumps [tracking devices], phone taps, both landline and mobile, both legal and illegal. Once at the Yard you could snap your fingers and get anything, from simple black netting for surveillance purposes from the Special Events department to a Jaguar aircraft for aerial photos of a suspect amphetamine factory in a bleak Welsh valley. The Cold War was over, and half the time they were drumming their fingers waiting for someone to shout 'Scramble!' and give them a bit of action. An American Drugs Enforcement Administration [DEA] satellite could be requested to track a shipment of coke from South America, or a Royal Navy diesel submarine summoned to trail a fishing boat up the English Channel. An undercover detective laden with half a million in flash money in a briefcase – so-called because the villain on an undercover buy only sees a flash of it – would simply have obtained it from a vault at the Yard. The SAS at Hereford taught the Met lock picking and, as would be expected, there were none finer to teach an undercover buyer what to look for when purchasing a consignment of illegal weapons.

I've been involved in all of the above, and more. But you can't win 'em all, and sometimes you have to settle for what you can get. Such as the time I found myself on the motor-racing circuit tracking Grand Prix cars suspected of smuggling drugs around the world.

'What do you know about Formula One?' The question came from DI North one day as I sat at my desk.

I thought for a minute. Then: 'Cars go round and round, Guv!'

'In my office!'

I went in.

'Shut the door.'

I did so.

'Now, Mac, what I'm going to tell you is highly confidential, and originates from pillow talk. An ex-copper is shagging the ex-wife of a Formula One mechanic. After they've done the business and are having a smoke and a chat, she reveals to him that her former hubbie, who served six years for distributing cocaine in this country, is still connected with the sport, and is using his contacts to bring coke into Britain. He's the front man for some very senior people at the highest level in motor racing. I want you to put a stop to it.'

That switched the green lights on for Operation Equipment, and with it my growing interest in Formula One, which finally became a passion, a sport which in the coming years would lure me to the other side of the world to watch.

I started my research into the circus the usual way – with the ringmaster. In this case there were two of them, Bernie Ecclestone, president of FOCA (Formula One Constructors Association) and Max Mosley, chief of the FISA Manufacturers Commission. Neither man could have a shit without me knowing about it. Other names followed. Operation Equipment began in 1989, and was so big it was still going on when I left the Force nine years later.

The *Sunday Times* blew the whistle on the scam with a front-page splash story headlined 'FORMULA ONE LINKED TO COCAINE SMUGGLING'. The team I led uncovered evidence that traffickers were bringing the drugs into Europe from South America, stashing the stuff in car parts and particularly in vehicles mangled after a crash. Who's going to look inside a wreck?

While the pot was bubbling, Ecclestone called me up out of the blue one evening at home. Somehow he had found my mobile number. 'I understand you're the detetective who has been investigating me.'

'Yes,' I said. 'That's me.'

'What's it all about?'

'I'm sorry, but I'm not at liberty to discuss a confidential operation with you.'

'I want it to be known that I've never condoned drugs. I have two daughters. If I thought that anyone in my sport was involved in drugs they'd be out, finished.'

And that was that. We never spoke again, and eventually the inquiry went on the back burner.

The tentacles of the investigation stretched world-wide. Police in Japan had evidence to suggest that one major team were laundering money for the Japanese crime syndicate, the Yakuza. But at the end, I was left with a nasty taste and not much else. Most frustrating of all was the fact that we just didn't have the money or resources to tackle power and wealth at that level. A fortune was spent on this operation, days and nights of surveillance, beavering away. At the end of it all our reward was a heap of publicity and a breath of scandal.

I'm still waiting to see if the chequered flag is ever lowered to signal the end of the case. But I'm not holding my breath.

THIRTY-TWO

BROWN PAPER PARCEL

I had a quick rummage through my pockets before leaving the building, took out my wallet, warrant card and car keys, unfastened the inscribed Rolex and dropped the lot in my desk, locking the drawer. The last thing I wanted if things went pear-shaped was any form of ID whatsoever that would give away what I did for a living.

Satisfied that I was clean, I made my way to the Post Office across the road from the Yard, where I purchased a medium-sized Jiffy envelope and stamps, taking care to use the sponge in water rather than my tongue. No way was my DNA going to be found on the back of the Queen's head. I'd address it later. Gripping the envelope with a piece of Post Office literature to avoid leaving prints, I slid it between the pages of the *Evening Standard* and walked the few yards to St James's Park Underground station. I'd have worn gloves, except that they might have caused a few comments in high summer.

By that time, 1991, a Home Office diktat had decided in their dubious wisdom that the Central Drugs Squad should be merged with the Regional Crime Squad, despite the fact that ninety per cent of all drugs seized in the UK have at some stage passed through London. The date of that decision, incidentally, was 1 April.

Purchasing a ticket to Kensington High Street, I headed off westbound on the District Line tube, hopping off one stop early at Earl's Court. No one seemed to be following me, or if they were they were damned good. A quick call from a public box to a mews house just off Kensington High Street ensured that the coast was clear. The last leg was a ten-minute stroll, with frequent stops to look in shop windows and double-check I wasn't being tailed.

As I climbed the steps to the front door I could hardly have foreseen that this was the start of a trail which would end with my wandering around the streets of London and Antwerp for two days, with a £6 million Rubens wrapped in brown paper under my arm . . .

Mario Andretti answered the door himself on the first ring. Not the racing driver Mario Andretti, but the alias by which he was known to anyone asking questions at the Yard. I'd given it to him myself, and although he was British the name suited him. He was in his thirties, dark and swarthy, with a five o'clock shadow that never left his cheekbones. In the real world Mario was a part-time mini-cab driver and a full-time drugs dealer.

By now my roll-call of informants had grown into a small empire, and I had run out of World Cup soccer aces. I preferred motor racing anyway. I had taken to handing out to all my new grasses the pseudonyms of top Formula One racing drivers, as if dispensing a New Year Honours list. This was directly contrary to police regulations, which stipulate that no informants' alias should bear any resemblance to real persons, past or present. But I couldn't resist it, and so far no one upstairs had bawled me out. Names like Eddie Irvine, Oliver Gavin, Damon Hill, Pedro Lamy and Eddie Cheever went on the A-team, and I can tell you now that three of them were women! My boys and girls took a different track to that of their famous counterparts. Professional criminals each one, they were sources of information to be bullied, cajoled, praised and bollocked as the occasion demanded.

'Come in, come in!' Shifty as ever, Mario cast a swift look up and down the street, then urged me inside. He led the way upstairs to a big lounge with a high ceiling, which left plenty of space to absorb the sweet-smelling smoke that had drifted up regularly ever since he had moved in three years ago. A couple of hangers-on were there, two young women in their twenties, sprawled out on the leather sofa with their arms wrapped round each other, smiling seraphically – and dead to the world. One I recognised as a TV weather girl, and I raised an eyebrow at Mario as we picked our way past them. But now wasn't the time to ask for an autograph, even if she'd been capable of writing her own name, or for me to inquire if there'd be a depression in the Thames area tomorrow.

'Coke heads,' said Mario, with an offhand shrug. He eyed me sharply. 'You never saw them, right?'

'Never saw who?'

'Exactly.'

Then: 'Come through, my friend. I've got something for you.' He led the way into the kitchen, where I exchanged a nod with his girlfriend Tara, a beautiful Irish wench with the kind of exquisite facial bone structure that must have been been passed down the family for generations. She was seated at a scrubbed wooden table, engrossed in the ingredients before her. I'd met her on several occasions in the past and was confident that she had no idea of my profession, or her smile wouldn't have been quite so warm. I was just a guy whose meetings with her boyfriend were very soon followed by an injection of cash into the family coffers. She was weighing out a pile of what must have been at least two kilos of cocaine on a set of electric scales, one kilo being about the size of a two-pound packet of sugar, and she was cutting it into two parts of coke to one part of Mannite.

Now Mannite, if you haven't come across it in your local pharmacy, is an Italian baby laxative. It also happens to be a particularly effective adulterating agent with which to cut coke. Not only does it have the flaky appearance and antiseptic taste of cocaine, but it also dissolves within a few degrees of coke's melting point of 112 degrees Fahrenheit. What's more, it is invisible the instant it is dropped into water, and totally undetectable. The one area where it fails the test is when you rub it on your gums above your front teeth, my own personal way of checking a score. Your gums go numb. There is another area that afficionados of this drug tend to rub – the end of their vital organ, allegedly giving themselves the most enormous erection. And no, this one I've never tried.

Tara toyed with the scales. In no time at all two kilos of cocaine would be converted into three, thereby increasing the profits of the family business by an extra £30,000 or so. It happens all over town. I wonder how many cokeheads are aware that they're sniffing a laxative up their sad little noses?

'Okay, Mario. What have you got?'

I had first met Mario three years previously, when I had been part of a pre-dawn team that kicked in the door of a West London property which had featured prominently within a Home Office 'authorised facility' – a telephone tap. The Central Drugs Squad knew it wasn't a huge den of iniquity, but from little seeds big trees grow and it was worth a bust.

I found Mario cowering alone in his bedroom. He had good reason to be frightened. In the room were four ounces of cocaine hydrochloride and £3,000 in cash. He was in the shit, and he knew it. The law would interpret the possession of such a quantity of drugs as being evidence of intent to supply. That meant he was a pusher, and that in turn meant a long spell in the slammer.

Within seconds Mario was pleading with me. Could we do a deal?

I kicked the door shut. 'Let's hear what you have to offer.'

'Keep the Charlie and the cash. It's yours.'

'Thanks,' I said. 'But it's names and seizures I'm interested in. You scratch my back, I'll scratch yours.'

Within a minute I was scribbling in my notebook. Names, addresses, car details and numbers. I knew some of them already, and it was the genuine article. Mario was moving in the right circles. I had seconds to make a decision.

'Okay, you've got it. I've found half an ounce of Charlie and a couple of hundred quid. That could be for your personal use.' An ounce is roughly the size of a golf-ball, so it was hardly a mountain of the stuff. 'But you double-cross me, and I'll come back with the dogs – and keep coming back. You savvy?'

Mario savvied. Several months later he appeared at an inner London Crown Court, pleaded guilty and miraculously (or so he thought) went down for only nine months. Since the time had been served on remand with all the benefits provided – family visits, your own clothes, a less harsh regime if you haven't been convicted – he walked free from the dock.

True to my word, I had looked after him. Mario's information led to a major quantity of smack (heroin) being seized in the Midlands. Now it was payback time on my part. Unknown to anyone else, a 'text' – a simple letter compiled by myself and signed by London's most senior detective – had been sent to the sentencing judge. The document basically requested that consideration be given to treating the person before him leniently. Texts aren't guaranteed to work. This one did. Mario was out of custody and into the 'system'. From now on he was one of my boys.

As an informer, he was protected from the criminal fraternity, the judiciary and the police. As an active criminal, he was constantly at risk of having his cover blown. You never knew whose name would emerge into daylight when the stones were being turned over during an investigation. Mario was of no use to me if he ended up inside, and even less use if he ended up dead.

I had gone out of my way to protect him, just as I had done with all my new-found 'contacts'. The names had to be registered on a central computer at the big house, on a highly confidential database accessed only through the Criminal Intelligence Branch. But nobody's perfect, mistakes get made; nothing and no one is infallible. In the words of the father who promised his son he would catch him if he fell backwards, then let him crash to the ground: 'First lesson in life, my boy. You don't trust no one!'

So for the purposes of registration I created completely new identities for my informers. Men became women. Black became white. Old became young. A whole new cast of characters took the stage, each with its own fictional appearance, background and occupation. I was scriptwriter, producer and director.

'I've got you flagged as well,' I would tell each of them, once they were firmed up to my team and on the computer. 'Just an extra precaution.' Anything to reassure a snout when he or she starts to twitch.

'Flagging' is a procedure whereby an officer can pinpoint the system, a person, an address, a phone number, a car registration, the name of a boat – just about anything – and effectively throw an invisible net around his subject. The alert automatically sounds the instant any other department develops an interest in it and attempts to hack in. The idea is to prevent any unexpected search or arrest upsetting an ongoing investigation, but I adapted it as the fail-safe switch for my informers. Other organisations world-wide have a similar early-warning system – LAPD, with whom I worked in Los Angeles, call theirs the 'War Room'.

Now, in the flat off Kensington High Street, I repeated the question. 'What is it? Is it the Yids?'

He shook his head. 'They're a non-starter. They know they're being watched.'

That didn't surprise me. Mario had been supplying information about an Israeli coke team operating out of the St John's Wood area, barely a cricket ball's throw from Lord's. We had made a couple of moves, attempting a surveillance, but these guys were good. Their compulsory military training probably helped, and every member of the gang was self-disciplined and surveillance-aware. I knew how they knew we were on to them. Israelis are among the most professional criminals I ever came across. The previous week one of our team had fallen for the oldest trick in the book, a ploy the IRA Provos often used. It was a simple anti-surveillance ruse. The suspect makes a call from a telephone kiosk. He hangs up the receiver, and as he leaves throws a ball of screwed-up paper to the floor. From a safe distance a 'third eye' is watching, whose job is simply to observe if some dickhead retrieves the bait.

It had happened to us with the Israelis. One of our lads, a newcomer still wet behind the ears, had returned to the sixteenth floor triumphantly brandishing the creased piece of paper with a number on it. The number turned out to be London Zoo. 'What are they sending us – boys to do a man's job?' I groaned to Simon, as the crestfallen detective realised someone had made the proverbial monkey out of him.

So, no luck with the Israelis. 'Okay. We'll let them run, and take another look later on.' They might just put a foot wrong some time, but we wouldn't hold our breath. 'So – what else?'

There must be something special for him to drag me all this way across town. And there was.

'What do you know about art? As in masterpieces?'

'Not a lot. Actually, nothing.'

He poured me a beer. 'Well, sit back and listen to this.'

Some of it I knew. In 1986, a team of Dublin gangsters had raided the palatial County Wicklow mansion of Sir Alfred Beit, scion of the South African diamond dynasty, and made off with the cream of the millionaire's art collection. Among them were masterpieces by Vermeer, Gainsborough, Goya and Rubens.

'What's all this got to do with me?' I asked. This had all happened seven years ago. The notorious folk hero Martin Cahill had been linked to it.

'Well,' said Mario carefully, 'I might just know how to point you in the right direction so that you stumble over one that is still missing, a picture by Rubens, entitled *The Dominican Monk*. Very valuable. My contact can't get rid of it, and its asking price is down to £25,000. It's worth six million. That's all I can tell you right now, but are you interested?'

'I'm interested,' I said. 'Very interested.'

'Then let's celebrate,' he said.

We both knew that this meant a sack of gold for Mario in reward money from our fighting fund for tipsters, and a big boost for my own career prospects. We raised a few glasses, and when I finally dragged myself off into the night I remembered something. 'Oh, one last thing. Do you have a soap of puff going spare? There's a party coming up at the weekend. The host asked if I could help liven it up.'

'Sure, Duncan. No problem.' Mario produced a block of cannabis from a side cupboard, and I held the Jiffy bag open for him between the pages of the evening paper.

'Thanks, chum. I'll be in touch.'

I dropped the letter in the post box on the corner. That was my good deed for the week, and my host would be a happy man in the morning.

The operation was code-named Delete, and it went as smooth as silk. Mario tipped me off about where we could find the fence who was harbouring the painting. He lived on an unassuming housing estate in Borehamwood, near the BBC studios where they make *Eastenders*. I led the six-strong raiding party, five at the front, one round the back to cut off an escape.

I rang the bell, and a portly middle-aged man answered the door. 'Excuse me, sir. I've got a ticket to search your premises. I'm looking for a painting.' I flashed my ID card as well as the search warrant, since I had a beard and long hair and looked more like an out-of-work musician than a police officer. 'Can you help us?'

'Sorry, I can't help you.' His eyes shifted.

'Come now – are we going to wreck the place, or are you going to show me where it is?'

'All right.' He was an old lag, and knew the score. He jerked a thumb inside. 'They're in the lounge.'

'They?' This was a bonus. And so they were, the Rubens and a Palamidiz, a Dutch painter whose painting had also been part of the Beit collection. They were both carelessly wrapped in brown paper and propped behind a sofa. 'Come on, Sonny Jim. I'm taking you in.'

The Rubens measured around three feet by two. I'd imagined it would be a rolled-up canvas but in fact they were both painted on wood panels, nailed on struts at the back. I looked into the eyes of the bearded monk, and the eyes looked back at me. More than that, they followed me wherever I moved. I'm no art connoisseur, especially of sixteenth-century Flemish painters, but I knew I was holding something special.

The fence was later charged with dishonestly handling stolen goods, and sent away to a place where the only art he would find would be in the pages of a prison library book. Before that, the prosecution lawyers needed to verify the Rubens before going to court. They'd have looked a bit silly if it had been a fake. We also needed to inspect it for fingerprints.

Which is how I found myself the following day back in the Met forensic laboratory in Lambeth, armed with a pair of goggles and being ushered into the windowless garage normally used for examining car bombs. Right now it was empty apart from the Rubens propped on a chair in the centre, bathed in an ultra-violet glow, with a lot of space around it.

'Put these on please, Mr MacLaughlin.' I was handed a pair of transparent medical rubber gloves. There were three of us: myself, a Yard boffin and the fingerprint man, and it was like watching Star Wars as the print man slowly passed a laser beam over the painting, inch by meticulous inch.

'Look here!' Suddenly he stiffened, pointing at the lower right-hand corner of the painting, where the monk's habit touched the frame. 'We've got one!' He peered closer, then registered disappointment. 'No, nothing new. In fact –' he took another look. 'This must have been done at the time of the painting. It's embedded in the oil. See here . . .'

And there, under the ultra-violet light, a print stood out in stark relief on the monk's habit, in the bottom right-hand corner. No member of the public would ever see it. I was staring at Rubens' own thumbprint. Today the painting hangs in the Irish National Gallery in Merrion Square, Dublin.

Still they weren't satisfied back at the Yard. 'We've got to have this painting verified by an expert – and that means a trip to Belgium for you, Duncan,' said my immediate boss, a detective chief inspector.

Fine by me. It took two weeks of paperwork to get a *Commission Rogatoire*, the authority to take the painting out of the country and be given police cooperation in Belgium when I got it there. I needed a pass for myself and a guard – preferably armed, if I was going to be toting a priceless work of art around with me.

Whatever its monetary value, my new-found friend the monk was still irreplaceable. Interpol helped smooth the path and all in all it looked like a doddle.

How wrong can you be!

My destination was Antwerp, and the Museum of Fine Art where a certain Dr Paul Huvenne, the world's leading authority on Rubens, would be waiting to shake my hand, and hopefully verify the painting. Dr Huvenne had an impressive CV, including a post as head of the Rubenshuis Museum and other taks like organising exhibitions such as 'Antwerp Masters of the Hermitage'.

I knocked on the door of the DCI's office to tell him the good news and get him to sign the form. He looked at the docket. 'One too many. You're on your own on this one,' he said curtly. 'We don't have the funds and we don't have the manpower.'

'Guv'nor, I've got to get from here to Brussels, and then to Antwerp, and I'll have a £6 million painting with me. I should be carrying, let alone have a guard.'

'No way. Get the locals to give you a police escort from Brussels. And I want you back the same day.'

I got on the blower to Brussels. 'I'm on my own. Can someone help me out?'

'Sorry,' said a Flemish voice. 'We'll look after you when you reach Antwerp. You have to get there on your own.'

Back to the DCI. He was unmoved. 'Get it insured, and make your way over on your own. Go direct to Antwerp if you can.'

A quick call to a City insurance company, and I was knocking on his door again. 'They want over a hundred grand as a premium for forty-eight hours of insurance.'

'What! Well, fuck the insurance. Just get there any way you can.' He flapped his arms like a headless chicken. 'I don't want to see you again. Out! Oh – and don't lose it!'

Sometimes there's no point in arguing. Two of us could have flown British Midland to Brussels for £60 each, but alone I wasn't going to risk it. Instead I found a flight into Antwerp's small airport direct from London's own City Airport by the Thames, for £400. Oh well, that's the Met accountancy for you.

The flight was at 7.30 a.m, too early for the Yard safe to be unlocked. There was only one thing for it – I took the painting home by tube, still wrapped in its brown paper and tucked under my arm as if cemented there by concrete. I slept with it under my bed. Bev was not amused. 'What on earth have you brought that thing home for?' It might have been a viral infection. 'What happens if the house burns down in the night?' I was never a match for feminine logic.

Antwerp. The painting stayed on my lap for the short flight. At the tiny airport a pair of glum Poirots in plain clothes met me off the plane, and drove me direct to the Museum. The monk's reproachful eyes followed me as I unwrapped him from his undignified mantle.

'Ah, Sir Alfred must be very relieved.' The professor was fiftyish and looked more like a typical family GP than a world-renowned art expert. In his office he studied the painting from all angles, finally pointing to a crest scored into the wood. 'Ah, this seal is from the school of Rubens!'

The good doctor busied himself with a pile of documents charting the painting's history from auction houses across the years to the Beit museum. Finally he straightened up with a triumphant smile. 'Yes, I can verify that this is indeed the real thing! Congratulations.'

My away-day to Brussels had proved fruitful, if expensive. But there was no comeback from the guv'nor when he saw my expenses sheet, which included a nice celebratory lunch in Antwerp.

Well, if I'd been mugged and lost the Rubens, he'd have been in the shit too, wouldn't he?

THIRTY-THREE

'ANYONE GOT ANY CLINGFILM?'

April 1991. Volunteers were being sought for rural training. With my usual habit of putting my name down for anything that sounded exciting without thinking the consequences through, I stuck my name on the list. Rural training included CROP, which stands for Covert Rural Observation Position. This is not to be confused with rural surveillance, the course I was later to undergo. CROP simply involves working from a 'static' hole in the ground as taught to Special Branch and C11 (later SO11) by the army, though naturally this is a vital part of the job.

Rural surveillance is more. A lot more. The course covers basic planning of a mission, reconnaissance, stalking, map reading, something called 'pivot peripheral' and other in-depth training. Pivot peripheral refers to the limits of the area we put under surveillance in a kidnap or blackmail case where one man, usually a member of the police carrying the money, is running from phone box to phone box to answer the blackmailer's call, the way Clint Eastwood did in *Dirty Harry*. You are even taught how to 'decompromise' yourself from an awkward situation if someone trips over you hiding in the bushes. 'You're not a gung-ho Special Forces soldier, even if you are behind enemy lines in a manner of speaking,' our instructor impressed upon us at our first session. 'So don't think you can quietly terminate the threat. Meaning that you talk yourself out of it rather than cut his throat.'

Detective Superintendant Tom Glendinning, second in command of the Drugs Squad and a man for whom I would have walked on water if asked, had put the idea into my head. In The Tank one night, he beckoned me over from the bar. 'What do you know about CROP work, Duncan?' he asked.

'Something the Branch and C11 play at, boss.'

'It's more than that. It's the cloak without the dagger. The Reegie are into it in a big way, and The Church are even getting in on the act. I can see long-term advantages for this Squad if we have guys trained in it.'

Glendinning was a forward-thinker, and had big plans for his branch. He was immensely proud to be on the Drugs Squad, and had confided to me over a pint on an earlier occasion that he saw his job as being like that of the Manchester United manager, the legendary Alex Ferguson. At that time Ferguson's task was to rebuild United, breaking Liverpool's monopoly on English soccer. Likewise, Tom wanted to rebuild the Central Drugs Squad, which had never been able to shake off its tarnished image after some unhappy corruption trials in the '70s. In addition, the Drugs Squad had been living for too long in the shadow of its more glamorous cousin, the Flying Squad.

'You're the guv'nor,' I told him. 'Get me on the course and I'll give it a go.'

'You like clingfilm, then?' he said, with a chuckle. It was an old joke. On a live op. site you always left the surrounding area sterile. If only the makers of clingfilm knew how useful their product was for dumping into when nature beckoned. 'Well, you'd better get used to it. Have another pint.'

Two weeks later I took a job car and headed north. At that time surveillance had become a big issue, sparked off by the death of DC John Fordham at the hands of Kenneth Noye while on undercover surveillance inside the grounds of Noye's mansion in West Kingsdown, Kent, in 1984. Overnight, criminals as well as the general public became aware of one of our major hush-hush practices, much to the annoyance of the Yard all the way up to the Home Office. The result was that selection and training of officers took on a whole new importance.

The army undertook our training. Special Branch attended Stirling Lines, Hereford, renowned headquarters of the SAS. C11 went to Ashford in Kent, regimental depot of the Intelligence Corps. I found myself in the heart of Derbyshire, passing through the gates of the Regional Crime Squad National Training Centre in the Peak District. Together with fifty carrot crunchers from the provinces, I was to undergo a four-day pre-selection course, starting with fitness tests.

I felt good. To increase my stamina, and much to the annoyance of my wife, I had been getting up before dawn each morning for the past month and running five miles across the Chingford heathland and into the fringes of Epping Forest prior to a two-hour drive to the Yard. It was just another nail in the coffin of my marriage, though at that time I was unaware of it and so, in all probability, was Bev. Even harder was abstaining from fast food, call it junk food if you like, kebabs and the curries which form a large part of a detective's staple diet. But the reward was worth it – leaner, meaner and keener, that was DC MacLaughlin as he parked the squad car in a space outside the main building and reported for duty.

I was pleased to find the familiar faces of other Met RCS detectives, throwing their kit onto neighbouring bunks. The rest were out-of-townies. But it seemed we had one problem in common: none of us had actually monitored our fitness levels since those far-off days. What kind of condition were we really in?

The small Met contingent made its first mistake by taking a stroll into the nearest village in search of the local pub. There we sat, hunched over pints of Guinness, apprehensively going over our prospects for the next four days. Back at camp, we were still voicing our forebodings when someone produced a bottle of whisky and handed it round.

Next morning it is safe to say we were not in the best shape to face the world, and particularly whatever delights they were going to throw at us. We gathered in the gymnasium for a briefing, which seemed somehow different from others I remembered from the past. Maybe my memory was going.

First stop: a running test. No problem in that region for Duncan, with his long legs and outsize lungs from the five-mile early-morning canters back home. But instead of a running track, we were led out to a square of tarmac the size of two tennis courts. On either side a white line had been painted, with a police cone at each end. 'At last they've found something useful to do with them,' I muttered out of the side of my mouth.

'Quiet, there!' It was just like the old days. I felt a frisson of déjà vu. The PTI, in tracksuit and trainers, stood with a clipboard in his hand. 'Now listen to these sounds carefully while I explain what you're going to do.'

We were to line up in groups of twelve on one of the white lines, facing each other across the intervening square. The idea was to sprint across the court to the opposite line alternately, like a relay race, and get to the other side before a high-pitched *ping* sounded from an electronic box nearby. The times between the *pings* would gradually decrease.

'This, gentlemen, is the updated version of running around a track against the clock,' announced the PTI. 'You may be interested to learn that all police training establishments now use this test, as do the fire service, the military and even the FA at the England soccer camps.'

Ready? *Go!* On the yell I dashed off, covering the space like a greyhound, expecting the *ping* at any moment and going so fast that I crashed into the wire mesh fence beyond as the other recruit took off. But it seemed an eternity before the bell sounded. 'If the FA use this to test fitness, no wonder a fat bastard like Gazza makes the squad,' I said to my companions on the line.

My smugness was misplaced. As the *ping* became faster, my legs started to give. Six minutes later, I was a rag doll. Only one guy remained running by then, and one *ping* later he was out too. The PTI made notes on his clipboard, then ordered us back to the gym. Today I gather they've introduced this exercise into schools – poor little sods!

Next we were weighed and measured, and an alarming device like a pair of pliers was attached to pinch our skin, with the apparent purpose of obtaining 'body mass index readings'. Then came 'tests to calibrate suppleness', which involved a lot of bending and stretching, before the next hurdle. Physical exercises: standing jumps, a full minute of squat thrusts, another minute of press-ups, and finally sixty seconds of pull-ups on a bar, with no rest in between. Just thinking about it makes me tired, even now. There were several PTIs walking around observing us, writing busily.

A succession of other exercises culminated in strength of grip, basically squeezing on a contraption like the hand grip on a pistol. One of the PTI's watched me, jotted something on the pad, then called me over.

'Very strange,' he said, frowning. 'These readings are inconsistent, and not what we expect. The grip on your right hand is nowhere near your left.' He paused. Then: 'But the good news is that your left wrist is the strongest of all the students here today.' I could only put this anomaly down to the fall I'd had on the soccer pitch at King's Cross when I'd broken my wrist, actually both of them, all of nine years ago.

'What's this test for, anyway?' I asked.

'You might find yourself scrambling along a cliff face or hanging on to a tree,' he said. 'We need to know you can support your body weight.'

It made sense.

'And one other thing –'

'What's that?'

'It lets the students know if they've got the strength to dangle from a window sill when the girlfriend's old man comes home unexpectedly.'

That made even more sense.

Now came a brief lecture on rural clothing. Everything depends on the weather, and since you're not going to be moving a muscle for long spells, you don't want to get cramp or freeze to death when the temperature drops after midnight. So warm clothing is essential: thermal underwear, woollen pullover, balaclava, gloves, boots, camouflage Gore-tex outer gear, an empty lemonade bottle with a screw top for urinating into and a roll of clingfilm in case things get unbearable.

On warm nights in the height of summer, you don't want to sweat. If you've got rivulets of perspiration running into your eyes you won't be much use trying to focus through the binoculars. It all has to fit into your bergen (military rucksack), along with a Green Maggot (sleeping bag) if you're on double surveillance with a partner and can get the chance for a spot of kip. As for food, you never eat a lot. I always made do with a couple of Mars Bars and a bottle of water.

Next day came the dogs. Or rather, the dogs came at *us*. RAF police dogs, snarling and barking and tugging at the end of their chains as if they were auditioning for *The Hound of the Baskervilles*. The drama began with our lining up in a field, all of us with one arm encased in thick padding. The PTI blew a whistle – and one by one we were off, haring across the field as if the devil himself was on our heels. In fact it was an Alsatian, and he was looking for something to bite on.

The first hint you have is a sound like a galloping horse approaching fast behind you, together with a hungry panting that does not bode well. Then it's like being hit by an Exocet. You are knocked off your feet, slammed into the ground and find yourself chewing grass and frantically waving your padded arm in the air for Fido to fasten his teeth into. It's a small sacrifice, because there are other parts of your anatomy you most certainly don't want nuzzled.

I felt a slicing pain in my hand and realised the padding had slipped in all the excitement, and the creature had drawn blood from the base of my thumb. The scar is still there to this day. 'Here!' A shout from the handler and the dog reluctantly withdrew. I couldn't help noticing they always wagged their tails after bringing down a victim, another goal to the home side.

Another test involving the dogs: you are ordered to stand with your back to a farm gate, while the handler holds the dog back on a thick leash, so that the beast's snarling muzzle and bared teeth are literally no more than three inches from your groin area. At least I survived that one without speaking in a high voice afterwards. And the scar on my thumb – well, it's a reminder.

A visit to the pub by the Met contingent helped dull the pain in my hand, and I finally got to bed at 1 a.m., ready for a good seven hours' kip.

Two hours later I was dragged from a deep sleep by the sound of thunderous explosions, which my spinning head finally identified as the training staff going up and down the corridor outside banging noisily on our doors.

'Up! Get up!' came the shouts. 'Get yourselves dressed and kitted up. Outside in fifteen minutes.'

I focused my bleary eyes on my watch. Three a.m! Bastards!

'What the fuck am I doing here?' I said out loud. Somewhere in the real world down south in London there was a nice desk waiting for me.

Outside under the night sky we assembled in line, clutching our rucksacks which were all we had with us. Two coaches pulled up out of the darkness. 'All right, all aboard. Keep your eyes closed, and your heads down.' Inside the coach an instructor walked down the centre aisle, distributing blindfolds. 'Put these on!'

Half an hour later the coach pulled up. We fumbled our way off, still blindfolded, and lined up outside. 'All right, now turn left and place a hand on the shoulder of the man in front of you. Now – move!'

We shuffled off into the unknown, and I had a sudden picture of a group of World War One soldiers, blinded from the trenches by a gas attack, the way I'd seen them on old black and white newsreels. I could feel a breeze on my face, and caught occasional night sounds. Otherwise there was deathly silence, apart from the scraping of our boots on the road. Every fifty paces or so the cortège stopped, and whispered instructions could be heard from the front. Then the line moved forward again.

After ten minutes of this we were finally halted and ordered to remove our blindfolds. We were on the edge of a field, and I could make out the silhouettes of trees and shrubbery rising like a black wall by the light of a quarter moon which appeared fleetingly behind scudding clouds. The whole thing had an unreal air about it, like playing soldiers in a war game.

'This is your hide.' One of the instructors materialised at my elbow. He gestured at a copse of holly I could dimly make out not far off, which looked to be about seven feet high.

'Get in and make yourself as comfortable as you can. It's your home for the foreseeable future. Now listen carefully: keep your eyes peeled, something might happen. We'll be checking. If your position becomes painfully apparent or you're caught sleeping, you've failed the course.'

For Christ's sake, how long was the foreseeable future? Well, hang on, it couldn't be more than two days before the course ended. But forty-eight hours stuck in a bush suddenly seemed an awful long time. Especially a holly bush.

Now, where had I packed that clingfilm?

I clambered into the thicket in the semi-darkness, snagging my combat jacket on branches and scraping my face on spiky leaves. Christmas was coming early this year, and there was nothing festive about it. I dragged my bergen in after me, and prepared for a long, lonely session. Home sweet home! And now came the moment of truth. The foliage came down like a shroud as I scratched around, trying to make a space without disturbing the cover. I pulled out a rough blanket from the kit bag and laid it out on the damp earth, with a sheet of waterproofing to keep out the moisture. But nothing that rustled. The only light I had was an infrared torch to use when I logged anything in my notebook.

Luckily it wasn't too cold. But as any camper knows, there's always a chill in the air in the hours before dawn that stings your cheeks like tiny pinpricks if you're out in the open. I rubbed them vigorously with my gloved hands to get the circulation going and settled down, listening to the sounds of the other blokes creeping into their own foxholes wherever they might be, and doing much the same as me. I unwrapped a piece of chewing gum for something to do, sighed deeply and tried not to think too much about the insect life that was probably on the move all round me. This was their territory, after all, and I was the interloper. I settled deeper into my thoughts. If I couldn't commune with nature, I had to become a part of it.

Then I just sat there.

I knew roughly what lay ahead: hours of boredom and discomfort, interrupted by a few vital seconds of intense concentration. '*Something might happen.*' But what? Normally on a surveillance you know the target, and have a good idea what you're looking for. This time the good idea was a big fat zero. What the hell was I doing there?

Our instructors had impressed on us that if we got through this course we would be the best of the best. They liked to quote a story about a team who were on surveillance at an LSD factory near the Welsh border. 'They were hunkered down so close to the suspect's farmhouse they could see a kink in the bugger's penis when he undressed for bed with his girlfriend!' That's the condition known as Peyronie's Disease, which distorts man's best friend. 'At least it gave them something to talk about. Mainly how much pleasure she got out of it.'

Daylight slowly filtered across the sky, muzzy at first and then lightening into a grey dawn streaked with sunlight to the east. Now I could at least determine the direction I was facing, roughly south. In front of me was a large field, broken by clumps of thicket and beyond, woodland. It was a good shooting wood, I thought instinctively, noting the beeches, oaks and ash trees with thick undergrowth which would be teeming with unseen wildlife. I thought it might be MOD property, but later learned that it was rented out from a farmer for a couple of days.

At least it was out of season, so we wouldn't get in the way of a load of buckshot unless some joker loosed off on the prowl for foxes or rabbits. Pheasants, partridge and grouse are safe between 31 January and the glorious 12 of August, which means the watchers in the woods hiding out on surveillance manoeuvres are safe too. At least, I hoped so. Except, of course, there's the lowly wood pigeon, for whom it's always open season.

For something to do, I tried to second-guess the objective. To my left was shrubbery, which bordered two sides of the field. Parting the ivy cautiously, I found a low dry-stone wall immediately behind me. Good. That would help keep out the wind. Further along was the gate where we must have entered.

An hour later, a lone figure emerged from the bushes away to my right and wandered unheedingly across the field in the direction where the coaches had dropped us off. I focused the binoculars, and was about to log the event in my notepad when I recognised him as a fellow rookie. That was quick. Obviously the guy had decided he couldn't hack it, and was taking the easy route home. One down, fifty to go. He wouldn't be the last. By the afternoon we had lost twenty. Some just rose from their concealment and walked away from their makeshift homes, unable to tolerate the solitude or the discomfort. Others had been caught sleeping, and were ordered off by the instructors.

They had tried to catch me out, twice, but I was wide-awake and ready for it. There'd been the sound of a boot rustling in the grass, and a whisper: 'Who's in there?'

'MacLaughlin, boss!'

'Good man. Carry on.'

I carried on sitting.

By late afternoon I had established a pattern, inching my aching limbs silently into a crouch every fifteen minutes to prevent cramp. Even looking at my watch gave me something to do. I made up little games with wood lice and spiders, catching them with my plastic mug before letting them run free, challenging myself not to make any sharp movement that might be detected by the stalkers trying to catch us out.

Suddenly – a stirring from the undergrowth on the edge of the wood. Two figures emerged and made their way quite openly to an area dead ahead of me that was covered in gorse. Kneeling down, they began to excavate a pile of rocks, pulled out something wrapped in a cloth and replaced the stones. Then they walked purposefully in my direction, passing in front of me on the way to the gate. One of them was holding an AK47, the Russian-designed assault rifle infamously known as the 'widow maker' and favoured by so-called freedom fighters of every persuasion. It's a weapon that is lethal at close range but actually somewhat erratic from a distance. The other was carrying a duffel bag. They were chatting animatedly and loudly in Irish accents, which even to my ear sounded phoney. Where had they found these failures from Central casting? Or maybe they'd been away from the Emerald Isle too long.

'Have ye got the Semtex then, Murphy?'

Their voices carried clearly on the light breeze.

'Sure Oi have, Seamus. D'ere's a whole heap of it in here. Bejesus, we'll blow them Brits roight out of the water.'

'Are we usin' a submarine, then?'

Their laughter faded out of the gate and into the distance.

I scribbled the words 'Possible IRA cache' and 'Semtex' down in my log. Throughout the day and into the night candidates appeared from the bushes to trail off to the coach and after that to the journey home. Others were led away by the training staff, having dozed off at their posts. I kept awake thanks to the holly, which was ready to give me a sharp poke if I slumped one way or another, but some of the officers stayed suspiciously bright-eyed and bushy-tailed throughout the whole exercise. These, I learned later, were having their second attempt at passing the test – and they'd come prepared. 'Amphet, mate,' one of the old lags confided to me, safe back in the billet. 'Take enough of that stuff and you'll stay awake for days.'

Amphetamine sulphate. Had I know what we were in for, I'd have blagged a supply off one of my informants. As it was, the holly did the trick, even though afterwards I looked as if I'd come off worst trying to separate a pair of squabbling alley cats.

In the early hours the two pseudo-Paddies returned. I tracked them by their voices – again, they were making no effort to be discreet. The weapon sounded as though it was being stripped and replaced in its rocky grave. I made a note in my log, and another as they gloated loudly about their night's work. Then they tramped off noisily into the night. Somehow I couldn't see it happening quite like this in the hills around Armagh, but it enlivened the time.

Precisely thirty-two hours after our arrival, I suddenly leaped out of my skin. A hand had quietly come over the wall behind and rested on my shoulder. 'All right, lad. Time's up! Well done.' The chief instructor gave me a broad grin. 'Back to the coach.'

On the way back, I sat next to my mate Paul Finnigan, who had also lasted to the bitter end. 'You coped with the isolation, then?' I inquired.

'No problem,' said the Mad Irishman. 'I just passed the time away trying to think of every woman I've ever made love to.'

'What did you do with the other thirty-one hours and fifty-nine minutes?' I joked.

One more test remained. Claustrophobia.

THIRTY-FOUR

POTHOLE

The circular metal disc looked like any other manhole cover, the kind you see on any street in any town. But underneath, out in that remote mist-shrouded field in Derbyshire far from prying eyes, lurked a terror zone. This was the final test, the one we all dreaded most.

Imagine a series of tunnels that had been conceived for the military, and for the Special Forces in particular. The SAS, SBS and other more secret operatives had all been through something similar, no doubt, when training for special missions.

'Call it the final frontier – not space, but lack of it!' the sergeant dressed in DPM (Disruptive Pattern Marking) clobber told us, as we lined up in front of him. On the coach he had told us his name was Frank, and that was all we needed to know. Apart from the fact that he had built the bloody thing. It was a March morning, light fog was rising from the field like wraiths of wool, and at any other time it would be a day to look forward to. Not today.

This was CT time – T for test, C for claustrophobia.

The ten of us eyed the skipper with respect. Standing there in the middle of nowhere, up in the wilds of the Peak District, the other thought that occurred to me was whether this was such a good idea after all.

Back at camp the night before, they'd tried to psyche us out. It was all part of the mind warfare. 'Think of Room 101 in George Orwell's *1984*. Your worst nightmare,' one of the instructors had told us encouragingly over a beer in the bar.

None of us slept easy that night. When they roused us from our beds before dawn to give us a hearty breakfast before putting us into a coach, for once there was no laughing in the ranks. No laddish jokes. Just a dour silence as ten condemned men (I told you they'd psyched us out) threaded through the country lanes and on to a vast muddy slice of MOD territory twenty-five minutes away.

'Right, now listen up! Let me tell you what you're in for.' Sgt Frank stood in front of us, tall and lean and tough as teak. He'd spent six months creating an underground Hampton Court Maze, under the direction of the top brass who dealt in these covert matters. In the short time the selection course had been running it had achieved its own reputation as word filtered back through the ranks.

Sgt Frank – I never knew his full name, and never saw him again – fixed us with a stare as chilly as the dawn air. 'Down below here you'll be crawling through a series of horizontal and vertical tunnels. It's pitch dark. You're all alone.

'There's an object somewhere in there. Your job is to find it, identify it and come back and tell me about it. One thing. There's something wrong with it. Something . . . different.' He was building the tension like Hitchcock. 'That'll prove to me that you really got there, so you won't be inventing anything, will you?'

We shook our heads in unison. 'No, Sarge!'

'Good. Remember, no one's forcing you to go down. You've all volunteered. If you get through, you're in. Five stars. If you lose your bottle – sorry, son, you're out. There's the exit. Goodbye.'

Sgt Frank beckoned me over. 'All right, sunshine! You're first. Turn out your pockets.' He was looking for matches, and anyone stupid enough to try to conceal a pencil torch in his clothing. I was wearing a bog-standard military combat jacket, together with matching DPM trousers, nothing fancy, and nothing bulky that might get snagged on a bit of protruding rock.

'Ready?'

I nodded back at him. As ready as I'd ever be.

'Okay – down you go.' The lid made an ominous grating sound as he lifted it back on its hinges.

'We'll be listening for your knock, then we'll let you out. Don't bother to shout or scream down there – we can't hear you. Got it?'

'Er – got it, Sarge!' *What if I get stuck?* I kept the thought to myself, knowing that everyone else was thinking the same thing anyway.

'Good luck.'

My first glimpse was a rusty iron ladder leading down into blackness. Gingerly I lowered myself over the rim, boots fumbling for the rungs. A dank smell of stale air wafted up from below, coupled with another odour that I couldn't immediately identify.

I looked up at Sgt Frank as he lowered the manhole cover on me. My last sight of him was a tight-lipped smile before the lid clanged shut and the light was blotted out.

The definition of claustrophobia is 'a pathological fear of confined spaces'. Scholars probably know it comes from the Latin *claustrum*, or *cloister plus phobia*. Not being a scholar I didn't know or, right now, care too much.

I just hung there like a fly on a wall, gathering my wits and nerve. Inky blackness. No sound, no movement. Nothing. Just total darkness, so solid you could almost touch it. And the sound of my own laboured breathing.

Calm down.

And then I knew. Somewhere in that maze of tunnels beneath me a dead creature was waiting. Suddenly I could identify the smell – a sweet, pungent aroma. I'd smelled it before. The kind you get from a rotting corpse.

I took a deep breath, wished I hadn't, and started slowly down the ladder, lowering myself rung by rung into the narrow shaft. If I moved my shoulders two inches to one side or the other I felt the brick walls closing in on me. I tried not to think about it, or I'd start shouting.

'One rung . . . two . . . six . . . ten . . .' I counted aloud, my voice sounding dead in that airless place. My elbows brushed the walls. Christ, it was narrow!

Finally, twelve rungs down, solid ground. I crouched in the pitch darkness, trying to work out my whereabouts, fumbling for walls. It was a small area, just enough to turn round in – and yes, there was a hollow space here . . . and here . . . and here. Three tunnels. One would lead to the chamber where something nasty awaited me.

First tunnel. I set off on hands and knees, knowing the odds were that I'd probably have to come back anyway. But before I did, I put a handkerchief in the entrance. That way I could identify the tunnel next time round. Clever, eh, Sarge? Would anyone else think of it? The tunnel walls were circular, which meant I could move reasonably freely, touching slimy brick on either side. The ground beneath was damp, and my knees sloshed through icy puddles of water.

Up above, it was spring. Birds singing. Flowers about to blossom. Down there it was winter, pitch black, and I was in a muck sweat of tension and uncertainty. *Christ, what am I doing? Don't let it get to you, Duncan.* I moved my right hand in front of me, making circular motions like a blind man who has lost his white stick and has no idea what's in front of him.

Ten feet in, and my outstretched hand hit solid wall. A cul de sac. OK. They'd made a tiny space, so I wouldn't have to crawl backwards. I turned myself in a tight ball like a hedgehog. The walls and roof came in on me, scraping my back and constricting my movement. But I made it, and retraced my path. My fingers touched cloth. The handkerchief, my point of reference. Good news. One down, two to go.

Next tunnel was on the right. I'd decided to go clockwise. This one was a couple of yards longer – with the same result. Dead end. I shrugged myself round again in a tight U-turn – and stuck!

Jesus Christ! My neck was tight against one wall, my whole body pressed like a foetus with my knees suddenly jammed against the other side. Steady, lad! I pushed a wave of rising panic away into the dimmest recesses of my mind, willing myself to stay in control. I'm 6ft and 12 stone, and thank God I'm not fat or I'd never have made it. The macabre thought actually swam in that they might have to cut my legs off with a chainsaw, and I pushed that demon hastily away before it took me over.

The slime on the walls saved my sanity. I could move my neck an inch, then another – then suddenly my body was uncoiling and I was facing the way I'd come. I stayed on my hands and knees for a long moment, chest heaving. The sound of my panting filled the blackness.

Back again into the central area, and this time I knew it was the final run. Ten feet in – and without warning my questing hand plunged into space. The gap in the ground was big enough to fall through. *Bingo*!

Another shaft. And a ladder. *Going down! Household goods, sports equipment, ladies underwear*! Anything for a laugh. But by now I was lost and totally disorientated, trapped like a rat in a sewer – and having to descend even further into the hostile earth. This time I knew that there was something waiting for me in the darkness below. One rung . . . two . . . three . . . here we go again! And now the stench of decaying flesh overwhelmed me like the perfume of the dead. Fighting the temptation to press the panic button, I gritted my teeth. *Remember what the surge said, my son. You volunteered for this. No one forced you. You're trying to prove something to yourself, so don't give in. Or one day you'll have to come back and do it all over again.*

A long way down this time, fifteen rungs and all of twenty feet. Soft ground under my boots. A single tunnel leading away. Something ahead. I was crawling again, and talking of rats in sewers, the stupid thought comes into my head: *what if it's a rat lying there waiting for me*? Holy shit, we're back into *1984*, where Winston Smith has his face forced into a rat's cage, *his* worst nightmare, waiting for it to be ripped out. We all have our Achilles heel, and I can tell you now that my own Room 101 is – yes, rats. If I put my fumbling hand on a rat, even a dead one, I'm gone!

It wasn't a rat. Just six feet in, the thing took me by surprise. My outstretched hand, circling defensively, touched matted hair, sodden wool. I felt a cold nose, an ear. The head was quite small. *A sheep's head*! But there was something missing.

The body!

The jokers upstairs had beheaded it. This mess in the blackness was all that was left.

I fumbled on. My brain was working overtime. Was this the trick? It was no good going back and saying, 'The body's missing.' They'd say 'We know that.' There had to be something else.

It was the left eye. My fingers went into the socket to prove it. Nothing there! Jesus, what kind of warped mind thought this one up?

Now I crawled backwards, the space too tight to turn in. And I wasn't going to risk getting stuck again. I must be more than thirty feet under ground. There were no angles, at least, and the floor was straight and level. My sleeve snagged on a piece of rock at one point, but I got back to the foot of the ladder and went up it like a monkey up a rope, feeling my sticky fingers on the rungs.

Back along that last alley. Up the ladder. Banging on the manhole cover, shouting my lungs out. '*Open up! Open up!*'

And then a grating sound, a chink of light, and blessed fresh air with daylight streaming in.

I emerged from the tomb into that glorious glare, blinking. The March air tasted as good as any air I'd ever breathed. The sweat was pouring out of me, and the smell of rotting sheep's head clung to me. Sgt Frank was waiting, and he grabbed my arm and heaved me up on to dry land. The others looked at me with a mixture of curiosity, apprehension and – dare I say it? – respect.

I'd been under almost half an hour.

Sgt Frank took my elbow and led me to one side. 'All right, son. What was it? Say it quietly.'

'A sheep's head, Sarge!'

'And?'

'One eye was missing.'

'Well done, my son.' He made a mark on a clipboard. 'Now get back on the coach, and have a kip. You're not to talk to a single soul until they've had their go. Understand?'

Through the coach windows I watched the others. Some lost it, taking one look at the black pit below the manhole cover and bottling out. No one blamed them. How could you? I felt more sorry for them than anything else – after all, the lads had got that far, only to fall at the last fence. It was tough, but as the man said, it separates the top guns from the toy pistols.

That night, celebrating in the Mess back at camp, Sgt Frank bought me a pint. 'Well done, son, you deserve this. You're one course away from becoming part of the elite. Get through that and you'll find yourself in some very interesting places. Like one guy I know who was actually buried in a roundabout in the middle of a main road to keep surveillance on a suspect IRA ring . . .'

'That's interesting? You've got to be kidding!'

'I'm not. He was there for two days, and nobody knew. Wait and see what they'll dream up for you. Anyone who survives what you've been through and comes out of it smiling leads a pretty exciting life. Maybe you'll even get to meet the stag guy.'

'The stag guy, Frank?'

'Coolest I ever met. A month ago. Sometimes it's a sheep, other times it's a goat down there. This time I used a stag's head, antlers and all, with an eye missing. One guy came back, and he'd identified the stag correctly.

'I asked him: "Which eye was missing?" He said: "Both of them!" and put out his hand. He was holding the other eye in his palm. So I had to give him top marks, didn't I?'

THIRTY-FIVE

KENNETH NOYE

'Kenneth Noye is a naughty boy!' I hummed the litany under my breath as I lay in the long grass facing a four-star hotel near Brand's Hatch, Kent. Below me, the car park was full of the kind of cars you see belonging to salesmen and company directors working off expense accounts, and enjoying a good business lunch on the firm.

My own lunch had consisted of a tin of cold, job-issue Irish stew and a small bottle of water. By piercing the double-layered can, it was possible to cause an internal chemical reaction between the inner and outer skin of the tin, which in turn heated the contents. Not today though. I was far too near the hotel. The last thing I needed was anyone coming to investigate the smell of such culinary delights. But that was okay, though I could have done with a decent steak and a good red wine on this chill winter's day. I had to keep a clear head and a keen eye, for the villain who would soon be Britain's most-wanted man was down there in the hotel, and right now was odds on sitting in the nude as he conducted his own bizarre business meeting – in the hotel sauna.

Kenneth Noye. Not just your ordinary run-of-the-mill villain. He was a master criminal with a wealth of form and a certain style, as well as a vicious temper that had already claimed one of our own, DC John Fordham, and would claim another in a road-rage murder on a bridge above the M25.

At this point Kenny was doing a sixteen. The man nicknamed 'Goldfinger' had gone down for a long stretch for laundering proceeds from the Brinks-Mat gold robbery, the 1983 armoured car job when £26 million of gold bullion changed hands. Now, after several years inside, he was allowed out for three days a week. The idea of the rehab was that he should wander around, meet his mates and get used to the outside world to 'become reinstated into society', to use the official duff jargon. Dream on! It simply gave Kenny the chance to plot further mischief, if he was so inclined, and plan his coming-out party.

My job was to keep a watch on him, and report back on what he did and on the people he met. We were more interested in another drama in which he had taken centre stage, and for which many of us felt he had yet to pay the price. Two undercover cops from C11, DC John Fordham and DC Neil Murphy, had penetrated the grounds of Noye's rambling mansion in West Kingsdown, Kent, with the unlikely name of Hollywood Cottage, by clambering over a barbed-wire fence and creeping through the trees towards the house.

The estate, which police suspected of being the nerve centre for the distribution of the bullion, comprised twenty acres of lawns and trees, protected by electronic gates and a menacing trio of Rottweilers. Our boys were unarmed, in balaclavas and camouflage fatigues, and they were there to set up a radio link for a C11 team camped outside. C11, otherwise known as the 'ghost squad', was a surveillance and intelligence unit set up in the early '60s, by now a fifty-strong force of hand-picked men and women whose job was to spy on top underworld figures. They use the most sophisticated equipment, and are even known to carry special yeast tablets and sprays to put off inquisitive dogs.

John was one of the good guys. He had once remained standing up to his neck in cold water for two days, repeat two days, during a stake-out, and the joke among the unit was that he'd spoken contralto for a week afterwards. That night the jokes stopped being funny.

The Rottweilers sniffed him out and backed him up against a tree while Neil took off, then stood by as their master came running up to see what the noise was all about. John never got a chance to use either yeast tablets or a spray on the ferocious animals. Those beasts, named after the German town of Rottweil, are known as 'the butcher's dog' because of their liking for red meat anyway.

Noye stuck a knife into him eleven times, before pointing a shotgun at the dying officer and threatening to pull the trigger. The back-up party crashed in and arrested Noye.

Ken claimed self-defence, and walked free. But he couldn't beat the rap on the Brinks-Mat charge, and was jailed for sixteen years. That was the background and scenario when I came in on the act.

We wanted him badly. I wasn't C11, who had disappeared into obscurity on this particular number. I was SO9, Regional Crime Squad. It was a delicate operation, and I was assigned to assist another rural, Dave, whose team were devoting all their efforts on Noye. We memorised Ordnance Survey maps and aerial photos that had been specially taken for us before we moved in on the target.

A distant roar drifted across the fields from Brand's Hatch, tin-top cars practising for a forthcoming race meeting as I hunkered down into the shallow grave I had dug out of the damp earth. We had chosen the place carefully, ever since I'd studied the Noye dossier a week ago. It told me that on his days out he would head straight for this big hotel amid the leafy fringes of a North Downs village for meetings with other faces in his kind of game. They weren't there to play bridge or indulge in a knitting session in front of the fire, that's for sure.

Both Dave and I were in camouflage, with mud and dark cream smeared on our faces. The car park was surrounded by an embankment on three sides, and there were woods above it. So we'd have no way of being silhouetted against the sky. We had chosen a spot below the tree line where I felt confident we merged in with the foliage as far as we possibly could. Unless someone actually trod on us they'd have no idea anyone was hiding there – or so I hoped. This is what the Ghost Squad is all about. Knowing the quarry, and what he could do, it was the last thing I wanted . . . and might well be the last thing I ever did.

Our position looked straight down on the front entrance. We went in before daylight, after being dropped off half a mile away in a field behind the woods and working our way down through the trees to set up our post. Most times on surveillance you use binoculars. This time we carried telescopes – green 'scopes for night vision, drawn from SO11(2), the technical wing of Criminal Intelligence Branch. In the whole of my career I never used or even saw a 'scope like you see in the movies. Has no one told those Hollywood big shots that green is better for night vision? The routine was familiar. Unpack our black bergens with the 'scopes and cameras. Make sure the lenses are draped in black netting so there'll be no sudden reflection of sunlight that might bounce off the hotel's upper windows. Have the radio ready. Scoff and water bottles to hand. The trench we'd hollowed out was under a thick bush where we could lie flat, facing the hotel. Then we dragged netting over our bodies and our dark woollen hats. And waited . . .

We lasted a few weeks before we were spotted.

Our instructions were basic: check every vehicle coming and going, however seemingly innocent, note the numbers and radio them back to base so they could be checked with DVLA in Swansea.

'Alpha Mike! Alpha Mike! We have a Foxtrot November X-ray Bravo Whiskey One. Alpha Zulu Charlie Quebec two up. It's an Alpha

Uniform in Charlie Quebec. Charlie Oscar. Oscar Sierra and November Sierra doors opening. Alpha Tango. Bravo Oscar. Bravo Papa. One moment, it's India one and Papa India three. Alpha November towards the Charlie Quebec entrance and an in, in, in. Loss of eyeball, loss of Alpha Tango.' Translation: 'Standby. Standby. A black BMW 700 series approaching hotel. Two up. It's a stop, stop, in the hotel car park. Offside, nearside doors opening. I have control. Target out, passenger out. One moment, it's target one and possibly target three. Off, off, towards the hotel entrance. In, in, in and I've lost sight, I've lost control.'

During those weeks I spied Noye's stocky figure several times. He would roll up in a big car – big, but nothing ostentatious and not always the same – and spend a few seconds standing in the entrance, taking in the fresh air and getting the prison odour out of his lungs before sauntering through the front door into the hotel. In that time he also casually took in all the other parked cars, and let his eye casually wander up the slope to the woods. There were moments when his hard gaze seemed to be locked on mine, staring straight into the 'scope, and those were the moments when I kept very, very still. If a wasp had stung me, I wouldn't have moved a muscle.

His companions were on the whole burly men in sharp suits. Sometimes a face brought back a twinge of memory, without my being able to put a name to it, in which case I would mention the fact once the coast was clear for transmitting. Our prime concern was secrecy.

This time there was no question of phone taps or bugging rooms. Our team knew through a prison insider that Noye and the 'faces' would get stripped off, and hold their board meetings in the hotel sauna with just a towel to cover their blushes – for just that reason. That way they could be sure no one was taped or wired, the same way the Crime Squad had the Scaly conference back in Islington. It works both sides of the fence.

'So that's what they mean by old sweats,' my colleague Dave muttered when he first heard the tip-off. But in truth Kenny and his mates were totally paranoid about being grassed up, even though any traitor discovered in the camp knew he'd end up in concrete, which kind of kept the volunteers down. Gangsters are like that. Nervous. And careful. An undercover friend of mine in SO10 (Covert Operations Group) once contacted a Miami big shot as part of a drug-busting operation. Mr Big finally agreed to see him after a lot of persuasion, but insisted on choosing the spot for the meet. Where? 'The beach off South Miami. And bring your costume.'

After the initial niceties were over, the drug dealer told my chum to strip off and accompany him out into the surf where they could talk. 'It's a nice day for a swim.' They left their clothes with a bodyguard on the beach, and marched out into the water.

Cautious Mr Big was also concerned about directional mikes and phone tapping. They know the equipment we've got these days can perform sonic miracles, and pick up a gnat's whisper half a mile away. Fifty yards out to sea amid the noise of the surf is as safe as you'll ever get, 'wherever the mike might be hidden', as my undercover friend told me later with a wry grin.

You can't be too careful. Whatever the upshot of their little seaside get-together, that particular mobster was never arrested.

'Anything moving?' Incoming calls would go straight into an earpiece. Noye had the instincts of a jungle cat. The Regional Crime Squad couldn't afford a repeat performance of the Fordham disaster, so there was no question of a mobile phone that might go off by accident and blow the whole thing wide open. So earpiece and radio it was.

'No change.' In code, November Charlie, I told the faceless inquirer that Noye had arrived with two other men, and they were all inside. Anybody else could have been one of three dozen men who had driven up or parked and entered the hotel. No faces that I could identify had swum out of the past.

We'd passed on the numbers, and HQ had them sussed within ten minutes, though what Intelligence did with the information I never found out. Presumably it was useful, or they wouldn't have kept us there.

We saw the boys in and we saw them out. Kenny would appear on the steps and wait for his car to slide up alongside. Usually he was by himself, unless he had arrived openly with any companions. Now they all left individually, with no hint of recognition or acknowledgment, so the 'members of the board' could have been anyone.

Dave and I waited until the dust from their wheels had long settled and darkness was upon us before we moved. Then we ducked back through the woods and trotted off to the waiting car, rubbing our stiffened joints and glad of the exercise.

After four weeks it all ended abruptly. The targets had come and gone, or so we thought, leaving without any noisy farewells. Noye had been picked up as usual, and his Merc 500 disappeared in the direction of Wandsworth where he would continue his stay as Her Majesty's guest.

Suddenly, as darkness began to shroud the car park and lights sprang on in the hotel, came an urgent voice in my ear. 'Nine Charlie Sierra rural units, out, out, out!' snapped the voice, without bothering to waste time on security. 'They know you're in there. Get out, quick! *Move*!'

Christ Almighty! I hissed at Dave: 'We've been spotted!'

But there was no movement. Nothing to tell us who had seen us, or who might even now be watching as we stuffed our gear into our bergens and hurriedly beat a retreat from our hideout back into the welcoming umbrella of the woods. That made it even more spooky, because your imagination starts jumping. We moved at a crouch through the trees, silently but speedily retracing our steps by instinct. Shadows reached out and withdrew as we scurried along a track, and a sudden image came to me of PC John Fordham sprawled on the ground with eleven stab wounds in him and three Rottweilers being held back. I pushed it away, knowing how the night can play tricks with your eyesight and your nerves.

On the far side of the wood we knelt for an entire minute, still as statues, straining for the crack of a twig behind us.

Nothing. Satisfied at last, we trotted back across the field to the car.

'What was all that about?' I snapped into the radio.

The disembodied voice said flatly: 'Later!'

And later they did tell us. Back at the Yard, a senior officer at the debriefing said simply: 'It came up on a facility [telephone tap]. They knew they were being watched, don't ask me how. But we can't risk them having a stroll round the park and finding you. So you won't be going back.'

'Thank Christ for that,' I muttered to Dave beside me. 'Maybe now I can get a decent lunch at last.'

Kenneth Noye, branded an 'evil gangland boss', would kill again. He was convicted of stabbing a young man named Stephen Cameron to death in the much-publicised 'road-rage' M25 murder in 1999. Noye fled to Spain after the killing, and was arrested in a restaurant near Cadiz. He started the millennium with a life sentence in top security Whitemoor Jail, Cambridgeshire.

THIRTY-SIX

MICHAEL SAMS

Flat on my face in the ditch, wrapped in my Green Maggot sleeping bag where I had spent the last twenty-two hours, I saw him coming at last, just a will-o'-the-wisp of movement against the pitch black wedge of the woods on the hillside opposite my vantage point. But it was human, and it was moving. I strained my eyes through the darkness and the leaves covering me, peering through an infra-green optic at the slope, keeping my chin near the ground to block any warm vapour from my breath hitting the cold night air and giving away my position.

A whisper in my ear-piece from the radio confirmed it. 'Stand by! Stand by! Movement on the hill. He's coming down.'

Carefully easing my hand back, I loosened the .38 Smith and Wesson in its shoulder holster. I found myself grinning. Someone was about to be in for the surprise of his evil chicken-shit life.

The kidnap and murder of Julie Dart had shocked the nation. Its aftermath in the fog-shrouded fields and byroads of West Yorkshire could have come straight from the script of the first *Dirty Harry* movie. Except that instead of Clint Eastwood as a seasoned detective running himself into the ground racing from phone box to phone box, it was left to an inexperienced estate agent named Kevin Watts to follow the paper trail of messages left by a cold-blooded kidnapper who already had blood on his hands and was prepared to spill more. I was part of the chase, lost in the fog in a hunt that turned into a shambles which would have been *Keystone Cops* – laughable but for two things. A teenager had been bludgeoned to death with a hammer, while another terrified girl was manacled inside a wooden box waiting for her own death sentence to be carried out by a one-legged psycho with a grudge.

Yes, it was as bizarre as that. Before I became involved, the drama had been running for six long baffling months. The story began on Tuesday, 9 July 1991 at the White Swan pub in Chapeltown, Leeds, to be exact. The place was its usual noisy self when the landlord called 'Time!' and sent the customers on their way. Among the regulars who gathered outside on the street were a group of prostitutes who plied their trade in the area that had once been the best-known red light district in Britain. That was a decade earlier, when it was the haunt of the Yorkshire Ripper, otherwise Peter Sutcliffe, who was now safely behind bars forever.

Julie Dart was a pert teenager who stood apart from the other women that night. Aged eighteen, she looked a little unsure of herself as she took up her position on the pavement, and waited. She was petite and blonde, and looked out of place among the more experienced 'toms' strung out along the roadside. Spencer Place was supposed to be safe again, or as safe as it ever could be for women who sell sex to strangers, but people who remembered her later said she looked nervous and apprehensive.

In fact Julie was a laboratory assistant who was engaged to be married, and had never been involved in prostitution in her life before that night. But she had money worries and owed a large debt to a friend, and she had been talked into trying her luck in Chapeltown. It was not a bright decision, and proved to be a fatal one.

A red Mini Metro pulled up beside her and the passenger window was wound down. Julie had a brief conversation with the driver, then got in, and the car pulled away. She was never seen alive again.

This would be the first stage in a cat-and-mouse game that unfolded as the warm summer days went by – days of frustration for the police and agony for Julie's mother Lynn and her fiancé Dominic Murray. On 12 July a letter arrived at her mother's home, shakily written in Julie's own hand, saying that she had been kidnapped and urging the family to contact the police immediately. This was the first clue to the fact that we were dealing with someone who did not follow the usual kidnappers's pattern – 'keep quiet, or else'.

Later that same day a second letter arrived at the local police station, typed on two sheets of paper. If Julie Dart was to be seen alive again, a ransom of £140,000 was to be paid – by the police. Again, this was unusual. It was as if whoever it might be was playing games with the hunters, taunting us.

The letter gave specific instructions. Following them scrupulously, on the evening of 16 July a WPC sat by a phone in the waiting-room at Birmingham New Street station with a bag containing the ransom money in used £50, £20 and £10 notes. The phone rang on the stroke of seven, as arranged. But no one was on the line, and there were no more calls.

How could anyone know that Julie had already been dead a week?

When the awful truth came out, it was the stuff of nightmare. After she was picked up outside the White Swan, Julie had been threatened with a knife, blindfolded and forced to strip naked. The kidnapper drove her sixty miles to Newark, Nottinghamshire, to a ramshackle workshop he rented in an isolated yard which backed on to the River Trent. The walls were soundproofed over to muffle any cries for help. He had welded metal sheets over the windows and, even more chilling, had constructed a box out of timber and hardboard as a primitive cell for a potential prisoner he had yet to find. Measuring eight feet by four, the box had air holes drilled in the top and a heavy chain bolted to the floor, to which the killer manacled his victim by her ankle.

He had even wired up a burglar alarm linked to the phone in his own house half a mile away. That night it rang in the early hours – and the kidnapper raced back to find that the desperate girl had broken out of her cell by smashing the walls, only to be held fast by the chain on her ankle. Now she had seen his face. She had to die. The bastard attacked her from behind with a hammer, pulled a length of cord across her throat and dumped the body in a plastic wheely bin in the workshop.

All this was going on, and we hadn't a clue. By now the Regional Crime Squad were on the case, and they had realised it was something out of the ordinary. Blackmail and extortion were not new to us, but this one had a feel about it that made us all instinctively uneasy.

It was on Friday, 19 July that they found her body. A farmer in Lincolnshire came across a bundle dumped in long grass in a corner of a field. Inside was the naked body of Julie Dart. In that moment a kidnapping became a murder hunt. Behind the headlines, we were all aware what it meant: the ransom negotiations had been going on for days, with the kidnapper knowing full well that his victim was dead. What kind of maniac were we dealing with?

Over the next weeks, five more blackmail letters arrived at Leeds police station, where the Incident Room was working flat out. He still wanted money, callously apologising for the death of Julie but repeating his demands, and even arrogantly declaring that so far he had been unable to find a new hostage. But he was looking.

Instead he came out with other threats. He had planted a firebomb somewhere. He would sabotage a main-line train. Finally, he had found a prostitute, and taken her. In desperation, the Reegie placed an advertisement in the personal columns of *The Sun* newspaper: 'For Julie's sake, let's try again.' As Christmas approached, still nothing. No street walker was reported missing, and we decided the threats had to be a wind-up or a hoax. But we were still edgy, and couldn't take chances with any lead, however slender.

Then came a seeming breakthrough in the catch-me-if-you-can game, which is the point where I came in. It seemed that other blackmail threats had been made to Tesco supermarkets, with the grim message of 'pay up or the food gets it', targeted at innocent shoppers. I was on standby for Operation Orient, the name given to the Julie Dart murder hunt, ready to assist any Force that had a lead in the case which had dominated the headlines throughout that cold winter. Five months had elapsed since Julie's body had been found.

'He's demanding £78,000!' Jose DeFreitas was team leader, a Reegie veteran whose expertise in surveillance was unmatched. A deceptively suave, handsome detective of Portuguese descent, he would have made a good gigolo. He had also been in more tricky situations out in the field than my youngest daughter trying to take her first steps.

Jose made the announcement on a wet January morning in an anonymous office close to the Yard, a place with no recorded address, where two of us sat with him wearing sombre expressions, making notes, and realising we were now straight in at the deep end. 'The bastard has come out of the woodwork at last, and given us a drop: it's a field near the M25 at Box Hill. Tomorrow.'

Box Hill, Surrey. My old stamping ground with Banham's Boys. I knew that area like a map printed on the cheeks of my arse. Last time we'd been playing games with logs of wood. This time it was for real, and if it was Julie's killer, then God help him! 'How do we know it's him?' I asked. 'He's tried it on with British Rail. But why supermarkets?'

'We don't,' said Jose flatly. 'But his planning is good, and he has all the other hallmarks of the Dart nutter.'

'I'm ready when you are,' I said, and stood up. 'When do we go?'

'Right now. We'll start getting the gear together. Is your pink card up to date, Mac?'

I nodded. 'Yes, of course. But why the need to carry?'

'If this is the psycho blackmailer who did that girl, then he may be armed.'

The pink card was my authority to draw a weapon from the armourer. We would all be carrying .38 Smith & Wessons. The Colt .45 Magnum beloved of action detectives like friend Clint may be all right for Dirty

Harry, and its stopping power was unarguable, but in a confined space the Smith & Wesson was more adaptable.

I stood by the window, staring out at the rain sleeting down over Victoria. The outline of Big Ben was just a misty outline in the distance by the Thames. The day reflected our mood. Surely there couldn't be two nutters with the same *modus operandi* out there?

Julie's killer had proved his threats were not to be taken lightly – unknown to the public he had threatened to derail an Inter-City express somewhere in the North of England unless we handed over £150,000.

The demand came in a note tied to a large piece of stone and left dangling over a railway bridge at Stoke on Trent. It had crashed through the train-driver's window and he was lucky not to have been seriously hurt. Another ransom demand had been left on a bridge near the M1. Food blackmail seemed a long way from trains and bridges but, like I say, we couldn't take chances.

I turned away from the window. 'Who else is on the team?'

'Just you, me and Lips.' Jose indicated the other man in the room, and that was good enough for me. 'Lips' Lansdown was in his late thirties. What little hair he had left was prematurely grey and complemented his ruddy complexion. His nickname originated from his colossal mouth, a pair of smackers which Mick Jagger would have been proud to own. Though no oil painting, he had an annoying habit of pulling the most attractive women, with models his speciality. I couldn't have wished for a better partner to watch my shoulderblades out in the field. Lips was one tough cookie, a top rural bod. Unusually for a detective, he didn't drink. He had given up the booze for good a few years ago, after waking up one morning in the third floor CID office at his local nick to discover tyre marks on the wall and his motorbike parked behind his desk.

I gave him the thumbs up. 'Good, mate!' He returned the grin. We had worked together on several live ops, and each knew the other's reputation. All three of us were Regional Crime Squad detectives who undertook rural surveillance as part of our duties, but we were all DCs attached to different teams. It was the luck of the draw that had brought us together. Though we were on the same level of the pecking order, I liked to think I had an edge because I had made rural surveillance a speciality.

Jose added as an afterthought: 'Oh, and Finnigan too. He'll be with us.'

'Shit,' I thought, 'Not the Mad Irishman!'

'That's him,' said Jose, and this time he was wearing the grin. Without meaning to, I'd voiced my reaction aloud. 'We'll be operating in pairs. Paul will be with you.'

DC Paul Finnigan was a good buddy, and the insults we traded were part of what had kept us together over the years. He was a wiry copper whose one failing was his seeming inability to put his hand in his pocket when it came to buying his round. In short, he was a tightwad, and I'd told him so to his face, many times.

'Do you know, Paul, I've never seen you buy anyone a drink. In fact I've never seen you buy yourself a drink.' It never worked. Shameless was his middle name, but he had such a gift of the gab that he could talk for Ireland.

I spent the rest of the day making preparations. Jose would take care of firearms and ammunition. Paul would join us later that day for the full briefing. Meantime I packed my bergen: gillie suit, DPM clothing, Green Maggot, face paint (which I'd mix with mud to stop moon glare reflecting off my skin), and the all-important roll of clingfilm, just in case nature called. Batteries for the radios – plenty of them, for as many a copper has discovered, batteries don't like the cold and have a habit of dying on the job. Usually, sod's law dictates, it's at a crucial moment in the operation.

Encryptic radios are a must on any surveillance. Comparatively new at that time, they receive literally scores of frequencies, pinging from one frequency to the other to prevent any unwanted listener from tuning in. I threw in a roll of black insulating tape, which I'd use to prevent my earpiece dropping out. Earpieces are tiny listening devices that look like a little pink sea shell and fit snugly into the ear. They are practically invisible to the eye, even in broad daylight. You can't buy these little beauties in any shop, and they're treasured like gold dust. Home Office regulations stipulate that they're not to be shared, for reasons of hygiene. But the Yard hadn't enough money to equip its specialist units as we would have wished, so they turned a blind eye when the devices were passed around and other people's cerumen (wax, okay?) went from one eardrum to the next.

Laying out the precious miniatures on a cloth, a picture came back to me of the first time I handled one of these things. It was day one of my career in the Drugs Squad. When the others heard I was going to pick up my earpiece from Denmark Hill, the Met's technical lab, they gathered round my desk like a bunch of conspirators. Chris, the team's quartermaster, did the talking: 'Listen, Mac. When you get to the main room, you'll find a cupboard on your right, just behind the door. Second drawer from the top will be just above your head. It's full of earpieces, and we don't normally get a chance to get ourselves a few extras. If you're left alone, just reach in and grab a handful. Okay?' 'Well . . . Okay.' I was dubious, but as the new boy in the class I felt I had to go along with it. 'Second from the top?'

'Right. You'll earn yourself a heap of brownie points, I promise you.'

It worked like a dream. The boffin had to go into the next office to pick up some paperwork. With one eye on the half-open door I pulled at the drawer, put a hand in, felt a box full of tiny shells and scooped up a fistful – just as the door swung open again. I just made it, stuffing the contents into my pocket and retaining an inordinate interest in a picture of Fleet Street in the '30s on the wall.

I returned in triumph. The team hastened round. 'Have you got them?'

'Sure I got 'em.' And I dealt a hand of shells on to the blotter.

'You bloody fool!' Chris was not quite so cordial as before. 'Look at them! They're black!'

They were, too, like a scattering of chocolate drops on the desk. 'What's wrong with that?'

'They're for black coppers, idiot, that's what's wrong! We have white ones. White ones for white men, black ones for black men. Get it? These will stand out a mile if you're trying to pass yourself off in a crowd. They'll lynch you.'

'Oh. Sorry. Er – perhaps I should take them back ?'

'No you shouldn't. There are enough black cops around. We'll trade them on for something *we* want. Next time, try and get it right!'

Sometimes there's nothing you can think of to say. But I'd learned something useful. Earpieces make good bartering currency.

Back in the office, I was almost through. I laid out my gillie suit – gillie as in stalking. Except that this one was made of hessian and covered in military tank string, through which I would later weave twigs and foliage. I folded everything neatly, went over it once more, and stored it in my bergen. That night I stayed in the office, inside the cocoon of my Green Maggot on the floor under a desk. I passed out like a light and dreamed of nothing at all.

The briefing took place at Kenton police station in the early hours of the following morning, one of the Met's outer bastions in north-west London, but within easy reach of the orbital M25 which would get us down to Box Hill inside an hour.

Paul joined us. Perched on the edge of my desk, he lit one cigarette after another. 'Could be the Dart killer, then?' He blew smoke over me without thinking.

'For Christ's sake, Paul, can't you put that thing out?' I had the mother and father of all headaches, and I looked the way I felt. Like s-h-One-t. Finnigan looked as bad as I did. Unshaven, teeth yellow, hair unwashed. That's surveillance for you – never wash your face or hair, or clean your teeth when a Rural Op is looming. It's not just sounds that carry in the stillness of a night vigil. The target might well smell toothpaste, aftershave, soap or shampoo on the hillside.

'You're just sodding well liverish, Duncan. Anyway, the smoke smells better than you do.' He dropped his cigarette into the dregs of his coffee and lit up another. Jose and Lips were poring over an Ordnance Survey map spread out on the table. Moving his fingertip around the area, Jose explained that we would be relieving two SO11 Rurals who were already on surveillance at the ransom-drop location. Our job was to cover the plot (location) for the next twenty-four hours, when Chummy would make his move. Jose warned us that we would probably recognise the courier with the money, one of ours masquerading as a Tesco employee.

I felt the familiar tingle of excitement at the nape of my neck, something I could never get used to but that always happened at the start of a big job. We synchronised watches and climbed into our combat fatigues. Then we had a final run-through of our kit, checking and rechecking each item. I would take a bottle of water and a supply of Mars Bars to keep me going, minimal rations.

Jose suddenly looked up. 'Where's your earpiece, Paul?'

Paul hesitated. 'Lost it,' he muttered.

'Bloody hell,' I burst out. 'I suppose your pink card has lapsed, too.'

He leaned over, blowing smoke in my face, and this time it was deliberate. 'As a matter of fact, yes.'

'Then what the fuck are you going to do if he's carrying a shooter?' I blazed. Paul would be in a ditch with me. 'What's the bloody point of you coming?' We glared at each other like two bull terriers straining at the leash.

"Okay, shut it!' Jose barked. 'Just get tooled up – but not you, Irish!' He reached into a bag and pulled out the Smith & Wessons, pushing them across the table, pointedly ignoring Paul.

Finnigan blew more smoke, but at least this time he turned the other way.

The tension was getting to us.

I loaded six silver-jacketed bullets into the chamber, then thumbed six of the ten remaining spare rounds into a rapid loader, which is a simple device used for whacking fresh cartridges into the revolver in an instant. Finally I slid the gun into its leather shoulder holster under my combat jacket, feeling the comforting weight against my chest. In a separate harness under my right arm I had the flat radio, its power source and the leads that transmitted signals to my earpiece, now fixed snugly into my right ear. 'Ready to roll, chief!'

A nondescript red van with sliding doors was waiting in the yard outside. As we closed in on the plot the van wouldn't be stopping for any reason, certainly not a call of nature, in case the target was watching. More than one stakeout has been cancelled because some idiot had a curry the night before, and the others couldn't stand the stench in the van. Mother Nature wins again.

We moved off into the night, heading for the M25. The plan was that we'd split up into pairs, and cover the plot from two sides. Paul and I rubbed paint and dirt into our faces so that we became only silhouettes in the van.

'You didn't have a curry last night, did you, Paul?'

'Of course I did. Chicken vindaloo, the hottest I could get. And some neat chilli. You'll hear all about it soon enough.' At least he had his sense of humour back. The four of us laughed quietly, and settled down for the ride.

On any kind of mission there is very little chat. First, there's nothing to say. And second, nobody wants small talk at this time. We normally just sit and stare at nothing, alone with our thoughts, trying to stay calm. But suddenly I remembered something, and addressed Jose. 'By the way, have we got authority to carry?'

The others looked blankly at each other. Personally I didn't give a damn whether we had permission or not as long as I could feel the comforting weight against my chest. But we all knew that if it came to it at any future trial, it was an issue that defence counsel could play on and milk dry. Especially if we shot the target. No one had done anything about official permission.

There was a brief debate. The decision was unanimous. What the locals didn't know couldn't hurt them. The Surrey carrot-crunchers would remain in the dark.

The van turned left off the main A24, and started to climb. Outside, the night was crisp and cold. The moon was around somewhere, but now the sky was the darkest of blues, without a single cloud and every star visible, bright and sparkling in the firmament above us. It was a beautiful night – but brass-monkey time out there.

Everyone knew what to do when we reached the plot. We had been trained for precisely this kind of thing over and over again until we could do it with our eyes closed. The van would slow down, but not too much. Paul and I would roll out on the first drive past, hitting the ground like a parachute drop, then lie motionless on the spot until the van disappeared.

The rear lights were on, but the brake lights had been detached so that anyone watching in the distance would think the vehicle was moving normally. The interior light had also been removed so that it didn't go on when the door opened.

'Okay, get ready!' Up front in the driver's seat, the driver, a Reegie detective spoke in a low voice.

The van slowed to 20mph, the doors slid open on either side, and Paul and I were out, heads down, shoulders hunched, rolling and bouncing into the grass. The van scrunched off into the night, and the sound of the engine died away into utter, numbing silence. We gave it a full minute, then scrambled soundlessly away into the long grass. Crouched low, we made contact with the two shivering SO11 detectives dug into the hillside.

They were over the moon to be relieved, or would have been if there'd been a moon visible. Poorly equipped, they had somehow chosen a crap location that offered poor sighting of the total plot, but Finnigan and I had already chosen our vantage point. Now we lay concealed in gorse and bracken, taking stock of the scenery.

The drop was to be on the far side of a farm gate that opened from a country lane into a sloping meadow. The crest of the meadow was covered by woodland. The blackmailer had given detailed instructions that the bag containing specified bank notes should be dumped on the other side of the gate. We had picked our spot 200 metres from the drop, with a clear view all round, the only problem being that if we could see everything, anyone up there could see us if we moved. So . . . once the sun came up, we wouldn't move.

I heard the scrape of a match in the darkness.

'*Put that fucking thing out!*' I whacked the box out of Finnigan's hand. All that training and he was about to light up a bloody fag in the darkness.

He glowered at me, and managed: 'Don't do that again!' as he rubbed his knuckles. But he knew I was right, and this would be one shift where he had to forego his addiction to the dreaded weed.

By the time the first rays of the sun slanted through the field and began to melt the thick layer of frost, I was curled up in my Green Maggot, with Finnigan on first watch.

With the occasional but comforting chatter of the back-up Reegies coming through my earpiece, I drifted in and out of sleep. It wasn't the Hilton, but I couldn't complain, even if Room Service had packed up and gone home.

I wasn't sure exactly how many, but various Nine Charlie Sierra mobile units were utilising the frequency to confirm their positions. Back-up was saturation level. From whichever way the suspect intended to make his escape with the money, we would have him boxed in. Nobody was going to drive up, get out of their car, retrieve the cash and make off undetected. The occasional car that went by during the day was monitored with DVLA, followed by a Police National Computer (PNC) check in case the target was making a quick recce. We crossed our fingers that the computer might throw up a vehicle hired from somewhere in the North, the hunting ground of Julie Dart's killer. But by sunset there was still nothing. A couple of cars went by, and I closed my eyes each time in order to preserve my night vision. Then I bedded down to snatch more sleep.

'Wake up, Sleeping Beauty!' Paul shook my shoulder. It was an hour after dark, and we had been there around eighteen hours. The day had passed uneventfully as we took it in turns to watch, or get some kip. 'Something's happening.' Word had just come through that the ransom was on its way. The blackmailer had called again, this time confirming the drop beyond the gate.

Lying flat beside Paul, I felt the tension gnawing at my stomach. Suddenly minutes seemed like hours. The infra-optics bathed the gate and the field beyond in an eerie green light, making shadows play tricks and create dancing wraiths on the frosty earth.

A faint engine sound carried on the night air. Through the misty green curtain a nondescript family saloon, the kind a supermarket employee might own, appeared up the lane. It stopped by the gate. I watched the driver get out and open his near-side rear door. A bag was taken from the back seat, carried to the gate, and dropped over onto the grass. The undercover guy got back in the car and drove off. It was over in less than a minute. All unnecessary chatter on the radio now ceased.

The onus was on our four-man team not to screw up the collection. Paul and me in one field, Jose and Lips in another, about 500 metres away, with a sideways view of the sloping meadow, watching and listening.

Half an hour went by, very slowly. The silence lay on the hillside like a blanket, deadening everything. Even the radios had gone quiet.

Then the hoarse whisper from Lips in my ear. '*Stand by*! Movement on the hill.' A pause, then: 'There's some fucker coming down the hill and heading in the direction of the gate!' Radio etiquette on surveillance often goes into freefall in the heat of the moment. Adrenaline was pumping through us like a burst main, and as the tension grew our language grew worse with it.

I strained my eyes to pick up a movement, and thought I glimpsed him. But I couldn't be sure. 'Someone has to make a fucking decision quick!' I hissed at Paul.

Our job was to guide in the others. Nine Charlie Sierra units would attack on our instructions, as we quietly slunk off. Rurals did not get involved in actual arrests. Our job was to observe and report. But if this was the target the whole plan was going to shit. The back-ups were too far away, expecting the target to make his getaway by road where they could seal him off at all exits. It looked like he'd fooled us all because nobody had set up a watcher in the woods from where he was emerging.

'Come on, come on!' I growled into the radio. 'What the fuck's happening?'

'Stand by!' Lips again. Then, sharply: 'He's fucking well heading straight for the drop!'

'*Christ*!' Finnigan and I whispered in unison. It could still be a local farm worker taking a short cut, or simply someone enjoying the night air. This was unlikely, but not impossible. It could also be the killer of Julie Dart. We all knew the gamble: if we hit the wrong man we would have blown a first-class operation, and God knew what the blackmailer would do next.

I made the decision. 'We're moving in!' Paul and I scrambled out of our sleeping bags and stealthily made our way down the side of the hedge towards the road and the gate on the opposite side. Our boots rustled softly in the grass, but otherwise we made no sound. A hundred metres away, my earpiece came to violent life.

'He's at the cash!' Lips was screaming now. '*Attack! Attack!*'

Bollocks to secrecy now! The two of us legged it through the bracken like a pair of runaway steers, frantically looking for treacherous dips that could leave us with a sprained ankle and nothing to show for it. I had my gun out, taking care not to trip. A wire fence loomed up, and we took it together. Then we were in the road and into the lane with our boots ringing on the tarmac, and vaulting the gate.

I saw a shadowy figure bent, over the bag before he turned at the crunch of our steps. Then he was off up the hill like a stag.

Another voice yelled in my ear. 'He's doing a runner!'

I could see that. I ran past the bag and £78,000 and gave chase up the slope. He had a fifty-yard start on me, and was making for the inky-black woods at the top of the hill. After all those hours in the sleeping bag my legs weren't ready for a long sprint, but I kept going with the blood coursing through like lava, my chest heaving.

'Armed police! Stop!' It was more desperation than malice.

The bastard kept running.

'*Stop you fucker, or I'll fire!*' Now I was screaming. I didn't want to shoot him in the back, even though a rule from firearms training allowed such action. I needed to see a weapon first. A thought flashed through my mind, even then: this has to be the blackmailer. He's willing to maim or even kill harmless shoppers by poisoning the supermarket shelves. It could well be Julie's killer. If I wasted him it was only a matter of routine paperwork, followed by a spot of perjury at the Coroner's Court.

I had gained twenty yards, but the woods were growing darker and closer by the second. There was no sign of Paul. I gave it one more try.

'*Stop*! Armed police!'

And with that, amazingly, the chase was over.

The quarry suddenly threw himself on to the ground and lay there panting, face down, his lungs wheezing huge gulps of cold night air. Seconds later I was kneeling beside him, jabbing the blue-steel muzzle of the Smith & Wesson into his temple. I had to wait a few seconds to trust myself to speak. I heard the sound of muffled sobbing.

'Do exactly as I say, or I will shoot you. Do you understand?'

He attempted a nod, and whimpered something that I took to mean 'Yes'.

'Now take your hands out from under your body, very slowly, and place them where I can see them. Spread your arms! Slowly, I said – or you are history. Understand?'

Another nod. Suddenly he didn't look so dangerous. Medium height and build, late forties, thinning dark hair under a woollen ski hat, heavy jacket which had probably weighed him down in flight. I ran my hands over his body and found nothing more than a Swiss army knife. Behind me I heard heavy breathing, and Paul lumbered out of the night, his face dripping with sweat and – believe it or not – a fag hanging out of his mouth. He kicked the man's legs apart, and slapped on a set of plasticuffs. More heaving and blowing, and Lips had joined us after sprinting up the hill.

'You fucker!' he gasped. We marched our man down the hill to the lane, which by now was alive with flashing blue lights from a dozen police vehicles. Figures milled around beyond the gate, but stayed away from the actual ransom grip while a police photographer took happy snaps of the scene. As the blackmailer was led away by the Old Bill, someone showed me a long fishing line that had been found beside the bag.

'Now that is smart,' said Jose approvingly. 'You see what he planned to do? Tie the bag on to the hook, walk slowly back up the hill unwinding the line, then haul it in from the woods. If we came after him he could say he was Joe Public out for a stroll. But you caught him in the act, fellers, and luckily he panicked. But he's not the kidnapper.'

Jose had it right, all the way. The blackmailer was no killer. He turned out to be a local businessman with financial worries and a marriage that was going to the wall. There must be better scams than taking on Tesco, but the guy thought he was some kind of Professor Moriarty and would get away with it.

In fact he had been hiding all day in a hollow he had prepared up on the edge of the woods, scanning the countryside with a pair of binoculars and a full field of vision of the area below him. He would have spotted us if we had allowed ourselves to be tagged. The hunted and the hunters. Always take the high ground if you can. He planned to wind in his catch with a fishing rod we found in the lair, and had even gone to the trouble of weighing the equivalent amount of cash so that he could buy a fishing line with the appropriate breaking strain. Audacious beggar!

He got seven years. At the trial great emphasis was put on the way the Rurals had endured sub-zero temperatures and avoided detection. All four of us were awarded commendations for 'dedication and determination'. Another one for the wall of my loo.

The day after the capture, we celebrated back at the Yard, lifting well-earned pints in The Tank and telling each other what great guys we all were before heading home for a long, well-earned sleep.

Only one thing nagged uneasily at the back of our minds. We had reeled ourselves in a great catch, and saved Tescos a bundle. But there was a bigger fish out there somewhere. A hungry shark . . . and still cruising.

THIRTY-SEVEN

CHASE IN THE FOG

When it happened, as these things do, it came right out of the blue. On Wednesday, 22 January 1992, an estate agent named Stephanie Slater, working in the Birmingham office of Shipways, arranged to meet a client at a terraced house in Turnberry Road, Birmingham. The appointment was for 10.30 a.m.

Right on time, the attractive 25-year-old brunette arrived to find a middle-aged man who had given his name as Bob Southwell already waiting on the doorstep. She smiled a greeting and turned the key in the front door to let them both inside.

The call came at 12.20 pm the same day. A voice described as 'ice cold' by the receptionist who took it said bleakly: 'Stephanie Slater has been kidnapped. There will be a ransom demand in the post tomorrow. If you contact the police she'll die.'

Thus began one of the biggest manhunts of the last century, with more than one thousand officers – detectives and uniformed alike – mobilised. Shipways rang the local station. Early next morning I was on the road with Jose and Paul, heading up the M1 to West Midlands Police HQ in Brum. We had taken the dilapidated red van – looks are deceptive, she could do a ton when asked – with our bergens stowed away inside.

'It's a big one,' Jose had confirmed, replacing the car phone in its cradle. He had been getting an up-to-date report. 'The nutter's come out to play!'

He filled us in with more details. A total news blackout had been requested with newspapers, radio and television, all of whom had agreed to abide by it and in return were given daily briefings on the case. That was a relief.

We were to meet up with other Rurals ordered in from across the country, and divided into four teams of thirty officers apiece coded Yellow, Blue, Green and Red. Our mission was to work alongside the boys from the West Midlands and Yorkshire.

We had no way of knowing that even then Stephanie was being held captive in the same dingy workshop in Newark that had imprisoned Julie Dart. Once they were inside the house he was viewing in Birmingham, 'Mr Southwell' had pulled a knife on Stephanie, tied her hands and blindfolded her. Then he had forced her into his car and driven off. Now the poor girl was lying in a similar ramshackle prison, only this time constructed more strongly, at the total mercy of a sadistic killer, blindfolded, with her wrists and ankles manacled and her cuffs chained to a metal bar above her head.

Inside West Midlands HQ, it was bedlam. There were so many police arriving from everywhere that they couldn't accommodate us all. Frantic calls went out to local B & Bs, and matters weren't improved when we were informed we would have to pay out of our own pockets and claim it back later.

'No way, Jose,' I said, 'this doesn't sound right.'

Paul put it more succinctly. 'Bollocks to that. Just give us the cash.'

Jose phoned London, and received a terse reply. 'Put it on your credit cards.'

'We've fallen for that one before. No cash, no stay!' Jose was shouting down the line from the driver's seat. He was tearing a strip off someone, and no mistake. 'We're coming back. And you can explain to the bloody Commissioner why the Met contingent have just walked off the biggest case of the decade!'

That seemed to do the trick. Within hours, £400 in readies had arrived by motorbike courier, and we were ensconsed in a small B & B before heading off for a good curry at the cheapest Indian restaurant we could find. No five-star treatment on this one.

Things started moving fast. Kidnapping is a comparatively rare crime in Britain, and has rarely proved successful for the kidnapper – but all too often been fatal for the victim. The mind we were dealing with was particularly warped, callous enough to continue negotiating Julie Dart's release after he had killed her. Now the first ransom demand came through, and we knew that the nightmare scenario was being re-run.

The familiar typed letter addressed to Shipways was intercepted by police at Birmingham's main sorting office two days later. The price had gone up to £175,000, or the girl would die. There was a cassette with it, and Stephanie's faltering voice pleading: 'Please carry out these instructions. Providing you do, I will be released unharmed.' D-Day was a week later, with further instructions to come.

In the intervening hours I kept busy. I distributed thirty small luminous road markers to the Reegie rural teams, who themselves were billeted all over Birmingham. I had actually nicked the signs from road works in Kent on a quiet weekend, because I saw at once how useful they could be to the forces of law and order. That's my excuse, anyway. They were ingenious little things, temporary cat's eyes, that we would be able to use to guide in our pick-up trucks on a dark night's watch. They came highly commended. An instructor on one of our training courses had told us to pocket them whenever we spotted one.

I took an away-day to Hereford to borrow specialist kit from my friends in the SAS, mainly night sights and snow suits for the bitterly cold Pennines. Thanks to my contacts there, I had become the unofficial liaison officer between the Met rurals and the formidable army unit whose exploits are the stuff of legend and, occasionally, myth. The others hired more than a hundred vans and cars, doctoring them for their own use in the usual way, taking out interior lights, cutting brake light connections and dismantling seats.

The bugger out there was causing us a lot of grief and expense, but nothing to the agony felt by Stephanie's family and friends. We had to get him.

The initial police briefing in the conference room was full to overflowing, and for the first time I heard the kidnapper's voice. A second tape had arrived, with another plea from Stephanie to her father which ended poignantly: 'Look after the cat for me.' God knows how the family got through those endless hours, knowing that after what happened to Julie they couldn't assume their daughter would stay alive much longer.

But the kidnapper also called the estate agents, and spoke to her boss, Kevin Watts. This time a tape recorder logged the conversation.

'Have you got the money ready for tomorrow?' Cold, flat Yorkshire vowels. Watts stalled him as best he could, long enough for police to trace the call to a phone box on the A52 near Nottingham. They raced there, but the caller was long gone.

At the briefing, we listened hard. The carrot-crunchers had much more experience of a blackmailer's *modus operandi* than we had, particularly 'tiger kidnaps', where they snatch, for instance, a bank manager's wife and hold her until the distraught husband opens the vaults. We were told the stark facts: Stephanie's boss was to act as courier to deliver the ransom money. We wanted one of our own, but the kidnapper was adamant.

Kevin Watts was thirty-three and up for it. We would give him all the back-up we could, with a sophisticated throat radio mike to keep in constant touch, a bullet-proof vest and an electronic tracking bug hidden in the cash bag. But it took a lot of bottle to go out there alone, and possibly come face-to-face with a killer who had no conscience and no qualms. Publicly we praised his courage. Privately we just hoped he'd come through intact.

D-Day came, 29 January. It was one week to the day since the kidnap. The call to Shipways came through, as arranged, at 3.25 p.m. on the dot, thus meeting the psychological profile we had already built up of a methodical, meticulous mind that left nothing to chance. The worst kind, for the hunters.

Kevin took it in his office with the bag beside him, containing £175,000 in denominations of £50, £20 and £10, just as the kidnapper had stipulated, 7,750 notes in all. Kevin got his orders in the toneless Yorkshire voice that was now as familiar to us as our own, having been played over and over again until we'd recognise it in a football crowd. He was to go to Glossop railway station, ten miles south-east of Manchester, and wait by the phone box in the entrance. The line went dead.

It was a huge gamble. Kevin got into his Rover with the ransom on the back seat, and set off for Glossop. In the HQ Incident Room we moved too, scores of us surging out into the car park en masse to head off towards our various posts. The game, as Sherlock Holmes might have said, was afoot.

We had been assigned to Red Team. Kitted out in camouflage gear, and with our encryptic radios housed in shoulder holsters, we scrambled into our van with its sliding doors ready and oiled for a smooth exit. We should have been carrying, with a killer on the loose who could be armed with a set of nostrils for all we knew. But the top brass, safe and warm in their offices, had dictated otherwise, reasoning that our man had no history of using guns, so we had no need of them either. Instead we were armed with baseball bats and pickaxe handles, which wouldn't be much help from twenty feet away if it came to the crunch.

Our driver was a quiet West Midlands detective sergeant who had once shot dead a pregnant teenager in a siege and was still living with it. I had also discovered that a worrying number of detectives were comparatively new to the game, so the seasoned rurals had been split up across the massive dragnet to balance the inexperience of the rest.

Our starting point was outside a Birmingham shopping precinct where we parked to await instructions. Glossop was a hundred miles away, up the M6. None of us had any idea where we would end up – somewhere between Land's End and John o' Groats was a good guess, but it could be anywhere. Blackmailers usually send the courier on a wild goose chase before the actual drop – as in *Dirty Harry*, which was spot-on – and would probably be spying on one of the telephone kiosks to see if the police were waiting to pounce.

Our strategy was to have different teams tailing the courier, with a new surveillance crew taking over at each stop, and never travelling the same route twice. If a shadow van or a copper was spotted more than once it would jeopardise the whole operation.

'Christ, the weather!' Paul brought me out of my reverie, staring through the windows. A light mist was forming in the streets, turning the buildings fuzzy in the distance. 'Fog. That's all we need!'

'Head north!' The terse voice came through the radio on our frequency. 'Barnsley!' That meant a cross-country trip. The operation was two-pronged, coordinated by West Yorkshire's Assistant Chief Constable Tom Cook and his opposite number in the West Midlands, Phil Thomas. I could imagine them with road maps spread out on desks, the phone lines permanently open, as the killer's instructions came through.

Kevin Watts had taken the call at the station, as planned. The flat voice told him to look under the shelf in a second box, only 100 yards away. There he found a brown envelope with detailed instructions: 'Proceed to Barnsley.' There was a phone box on the A628, near a roundabout, with another message taped under the shelf. And a specific time to be there: 7.40 p.m. Kevin hit the accelerator, talking into the throat mike as he drove. It was dark and the fog was thickening by the minute.

For four hours the paper chase went on. At one point Kevin missed a turning, and found himself heading down a dual carriageway in the wrong direction. But it became clear to us that the denouement, if there was one, was taking us inexorably into the wild moorlands and peaks of the Pennines.

Suddenly Paul tensed, and held his hand to his ear.

The message had come through: '*Go! Go! Go!*'

The driver slammed his foot on the throttle, and the van took on a new lease of life. 'Oxspring!' I shouted. 'It's on the edge of Thurlstone moor!'

Two of us had the road map of the British Isles on our laps, straining to find the quickest route. The crisp tones of the officer in charge crackled through the van radio, directing routes to other units over their encryptics. The van swayed and roared through the night. Lamp-posts blurred past, washing buildings with yellow light as our own powerful beam danced off the fog ahead. The wipers were on double-speed, sending droplets spraying off the windscreen like glass bullets.

'It's a bloody pea-souper,' Paul muttered, wiping mist off the window with his glove. 'We'll fucking hit something.'

'Belt up!' said the driver, speaking from the front for the first time as we were thrown against the side of the van on a bend. 'Safety belt, of course.'

I felt my stomach churning. The area we were heading for was only a few miles from the field where Julie Dart was found. Paul must have read my thoughts. 'We're getting into the dead zone, fellers,' he said. 'This could be it.'

'Quiet!' I was struggling to catch other words in my earpiece. I was picking up Kevin's throat microphone direct. We couldn't be more than ten miles away now. I slammed his fist against the side of the van. 'Christ! His bloody mike's gone dead!'

'It's the damp weather. The equipment's up the spout,' Paul reasoned, which didn't help either the situation or the tempers in the van. We charged on through the fog, breaking every rule in the Highway Code, and the cacophony from the radio told us we were not alone.

Other units were being despatched here, there and everywhere as the officer in command struggled to make contact with Watts and the money. Chaos is probably too nice a word for it. The thick fog rolling across the moors had brought visibility down to a few feet. No one knew whether the killer was waiting in a car, or was even bold enough to be behind the shadow vehicles, following every move. We were the blind leading the blind, and somewhere out there was a terrified girl who was depending on us to save her life.

At that precise time, unbeknown to us, the killer was making his final preparations. Like a ghost in the thick fog, he picked his way along a disused railway track towards the bridge he had chosen for his purpose. He was leaning on a lightweight moped that fitted neatly into the back of his car, which he had left parked three miles away. And hobbling, because he only had one leg, with an artificial limb below his right knee. He knew exactly where he was, because he had picked the spot weeks earlier, and rehearsed the timing for what he had to do. No one else did.

Kevin was getting closer. A makeshift sign loomed up on the verge, and he almost missed it as his headlights swept past. 'Shipways', with an arrow to the right. Finally he found another message beside a red traffic cone and a black bag, stencilled on a piece of card, ordering him to transfer the money into the second bag, then go on foot with the bag to a phone box five hundred yards away, in the midst of the darkness and cloying fog. His hands trembling, he transmitted the news back to base, unaware that all that was coming through at the other end was a useless crackle of static.

In the mêlée and mist, units were everywhere. Sometimes we passed other cars going hellbent the other way. But now I raised a warning hand. 'Contact! *Contact*! 'The Incident Room had picked up the tracker signal from the moneybag. We roared along country lanes, hedgerows scraping the sides, and then someone's yell filled the van. 'Out, out, out!'

The van screeched to a halt, wheels skidding on gravel. Within seconds I was lying flat on my face in wet grass, clutching a pickaxe handle and realising I couldn't even see the end of it. I gulped huge lungfuls of poisonous fog into my throat, my heart pounding like a steam hammer.

Then I heard it, the sound of a train thundering past from close by. We were near a railway! Our man liked trains. It had to be Julie's killer.

'Bomb-burst! Bomb-burst!' Paul's shout came out of the fog, the invisible man telling us to go for it. We jumped up and fanned out, crouching and tense. Was I scared? Is the Pope a Catholic? A madman was nearby, possibly with a shotgun. Yes, I was scared. But I moved slowly forward, trying to make out shapes and movements. Then, a drone overhead. I cursed the stupidity of the police spotter plane. The kidnapper would realise no civilian pilot would risk flying in these conditions, and be warned off. Besides, no spotlight could penetrate that thick cloud beneath. I could only tell myself the plot had gone pear-shaped, and we had been forced to send up the Islander tracker aircraft in a last-ditch hope.

Shit, what a mess!

The man came out of the fog like a bullet. In a split second we were writhing on the ground, locked in combat the way it happens in Westerns when the good guy on horseback jumps the bad guy and knocks him off. Gasping, kicking and struggling, we rolled across the grass and onto hard tarmac and gravel. Then we came face to face.

'Bastard!'

'*Bastard*!'

It had to be Finnigan. We cursed each other until we ran out of expletives, then just sat there, panting. Paul reached into his jacket and lit up a fag, as Jose appeared holding an empty bag in one hand and a small gleaming metal object in another. The tracking device. No wonder the tracker plane had been flying in circles.

'He's swapped bags!' Jose stared at the useless grip, then flung it to the ground in disgust. 'This isn't our night.'

And it wasn't. Five hundred metres away, Kevin had come across a bridge. The phone box didn't exist. But a sign loomed at him out of the fog, with the word 'STOP' in big letters. And beneath it: 'On wall, wooden tray. Put bag on tray, then go.' Sure enough, balanced on top of the parapet was a tray with a rope hanging from it down into the darkness. Kevin did as instructed, and as he turned his back the killer below tugged on the rope. The tray and a bag with £175,000 in it crashed onto the sleepers in front of him.

The killer puttered away on his moped, with the bag stashed behind the saddle. He had even removed the front and rear light bulbs to avoid being seen. Behind him he left the forces of law and order in disarray, trying to work out what had gone wrong.

No, it wasn't our night.

They caught Michael Sams a month later. To the relief and surprise of everyone, he had released Stephanie Slater from her makeshift cell without even laying a hand on her, though no one could judge the depths of her mental torture. He even took her back home to release her outside her own front door.

While we were farting about in the fog and behaving like a bunch of Keystone cops, the resourceful loner had rolled back the sliding door to his workshop and told his hostage: 'I've got the money. You're going home.' He kept her blindfold while he drove her back in his Mini Metro to the street where she lived in Birmingham, so she never saw his face, not until the trial.

Once she was known to be safe, the news blackout was lifted and the media went to town. Two-inch headlines in the tabloids. Identikit artist impressions. It brought calls from the public flooding in, but the big breakthrough came when *Crimewatch* featured voice tapes of the kidnapper. A woman called Susan Oake saw it at her home in Keighley, West Yorkshire, and recognised the voice of her ex-husband, a loner with a high IQ who was also a railway fanatic. The jigsaw pieces slid neatly into place.

When the police raided his workshop, Sams greeted them with the words: 'I've been expecting you.'

Dark-haired and with piercing eyes, the engineer's grudge against society and life in general was exacerbated by his deformity. A cancerous tumour in his right leg had put paid to his passion of cross-country running. After the condition worsened following an accident, doctors were forced to amputate his leg below the knee.

Sentencing him to life imprisonment on four counts, the judge told him: 'You are an extremely dangerous and evil man.'

Yes, we were well shot of him.

THIRTY-EIGHT

THE YARDIES

By 1994, I'd had enough of the big house. Despite the undoubted prestige, power and perks of being part of New Scotland Yard, there was a down side as well. The place had become a conveyor belt of endless hours, lack of sleep and general discomfiture to my digestive system. Now it was time for a change of scenery.

I had also found the time to study for the next rung up the ladder, and had passed my sergeant's examination. There were still a few hurdles left in the shape of Board interviews, and these would take a few months to vault.

One of the prerequisites for promotion is day-to-day policing. If you want to get on as a detective, you have to be out there at the sharp end dealing with everyday matters like murder, rape, indecency, armed robbery and other cancers that afflict society. I managed to get myself assigned to Notting Hill, which sees its fair share of action, particularly during Carnival time. The way I saw it, and without any false modesty, the local nick wasn't getting a bad deal either. I brought five years of Yard experience with me, along with numerous Home Office courses I had completed such as firearms, surveillance, money laundering, advanced driving, and the pièce de résistance, a forty-five minute course on how to drive a Hackney cab!

The Yard has a fleet of black cabs at its disposal, kept for surveillance purposes, and a chosen few are obliged to take the driving test. Unlike your average cabbie who can spend up to three years 'doing the Knowledge', we earned our green badge inside forty minutes, driving around north London with an examiner making notes in the back.

The perk for this extra chore is that after a day's surveillance you can make yourself a few quid on the way home picking up a genuine fare – and hoping you know the street where they live. I can only guess at the number of Japanese tourists abandoned when their 'cabbie' has no idea where they wanted to go. 'Lanesborough Hotel, mate? Turn left at the zoo, and keep on walking!' It's happened. I'm sorry to say it, but I've done it myself.

The phone jangled by my bedside, interrupting my thoughts. Outside, the sound of a fountain splashing on the pool came into my twelfth-floor hotel room, and the sparkling Caribbean sea stretched all the way to the horizon. A heady mix of tropical scents and musky spices drifted on the hot, humid air.

It's a long way from Notting Hill to Jamaica, but that's where the drug trail had led me – and I wasn't complaining. This was a business hotel in the centre of Kingston, not a destination resort, and you were more likely to hear the odd gunshot in the distance than the happy squeal of kids around the pool.

Michael Schumacher's voice was on the line. 'You're back. Glad you made it safely.' Michael was one of my top informers. I had turned him in London, got him a reduced sentence for coke possession, and won his confidence over several visits to prison. He had been booted out of Britain as an undesirable, but he was grateful to me, and still coming up with the goods from 3,000 miles away across an ocean.

'I've got what you wanted.'

What I wanted was information on a Yardie who even now was sitting in a cell back in London awaiting trial, with every intention of getting off. He was a main man. I was equally determined he wouldn't.

The term 'Yardie' is not as sinister as most people take it to be. It simply derives from Back Yard, and like all Jamaicans with a criminal bent Michael (real name Herbie) had a street name too. Schumacher was strictly between him and me.

The information related to assets. The Drug Trafficking Offences Act requires that anyone charged with a drug offence that involves supplying has to be subjected to an investigation into his financial affairs. I had arrived in Jamaica to look into this, and my inquiries took me on a scenic tour of four other islands. It sure beat Notting Hill.

We arranged to meet at the hotel. His tall, slim figure threaded its way between the sun worshippers, air crew and business types, until he squatted beside me and produced a large manila envelope. 'It's all in here. Addresses, names, car details, where your friend banks. The lot.'

I slipped him $200. 'There's more to come, Herbie. There'll be a couple of grand in it, same as usual. The Yard will wire the High Commission.'

'Good, brother.' He pushed his knuckles against mine in the Jamaican salute. Then he paused. 'Hey now, take it easy. You know there's a contract out on you.' Then he turned and ambled off. By the end of the month his bank account would be increased by the amount an average Jamaican policeman earns in a year.

I knew all about the contract, and I had packed body armour in my luggage as a result of the tip-off, exchanging a few words with BA security on the way out to explain it. The vest was a white kevlar waistcoat which would fit under a baggy T-shirt, perfect for the tropics. The Yardie who was threatening the hit on me had done time in three HM prisons in Britain thanks to me, before being put on the big silver bird on a one-way ticket home. The word was out on the street, and I had to watch my back. I wasn't too worried, but I kept a careful eye over my shoulder every time I stepped out into the warm Jamaican sunshine.

Anyway, I had Wayne with me. Not John Wayne, though he fitted the bill. Wayne was my shadow and guardian angel, a Jamaican detective in his early twenties who had been assigned to protect me while I was a guest of their country. He opened doors and smoothed the way through officialdom. Wayne and the 9mm Browning tucked openly into his baggy trouser pocket made me feel safer. All I hoped was that he kept the safety catch on.

Together we spent several days slogging round land registers, bank vaults and lawyers' offices, examining documentation, searching for all the assets the 'main man' gained from drug money and other people's misery in the UK, laundering it back home in Jamaica.

It's a long haul from Notting Hill to Kingston, but it was my third trip and I was getting used to the place. Before my first time I'd had a warning from a customs officer on a three-year secondment to the island.

'Two pieces of advice for you, sir. When you arrive at the airport, make sure you only get a Jute cab. Any other, we'll never see you again.' Jute were the equivalent of New York's yellow cabs. 'Second, when you're driving, don't stop at any unofficial road blocks. You'll spot them at once. Drive straight through and don't worry if the people manning them don't jump in time.

'There are a lot of bad motherfuckers out here, and they don't care if they kill you or not. You could die from lead poisoning, and I don't mean the traffic. Otherwise it's a beautiful island. Enjoy it!'

I'm not James Bond, but I got the impression I might be starting to live dangerously – and this on the island where they made the first OO7 thriller, *Dr No*. But first I needed to find 'One a Day'. I had called from

London, and he had agreed to see me. He was a Jamaican detective, but not just any Jamaican detective. I had heard the name months before, in the seedy backwaters of Yardie culture south of the Thames where they spoke of it in hushed respect. His reputation made my job a little easier. I only had to mention the name, as a bargaining chip in any conversation ('Don't give me any grief, or when they deport you back home I'll make sure he's waiting for you!') to watch the defensive walls crumble and the information pour out like a dam bursting.

'One a Day', real name Robert, is a legend. A detective sergeant with twenty years service behind him. His name derives from the number of people he is said to kill, on average, a day 'He makes Harry Callaghan look like the local pastor,' Wayne informed me solemnly, like a guide reading from a tourist brochure. 'For a while he was taken off the street because he was wasting too many people, and seconded to Jamaica's Police Academy as an instructor. But the lawlessness that broke out had them begging for him to come back again.'

Robert had invited me down to his patch at Tivoli Gardens police station off the Spanish Town Road, in the heart of one of the most notorious areas of downtown Kingston and aptly situated next to May Pen, the island's biggest cemetery. We arrived in our rental car, me at the wheel and Wayne in the passenger seat (he liked to keep his gun hand clear) to be greeted by what looked like a scene from a Hollywood gangster movie.

Bodies hung out of car windows. Others lay sprawled in the gutter. Two men in colourful singlets were sitting blankly on the pavement, their backs to a wall. The colour was crimson. The ugly concrete walls of the police station looked like a Gruyere cheese, stained with blood. I counted seven corpses, including a child, and saw that blood was literally running in the gutters. A few people were gathering to stand and stare. It must have happened only minutes earlier.

'Welcome to Tivoli Gardens. You've just missed the fun.' One a Day stood 6ft 2in. tall, a large black man in his late 40s, with cropped dark hair and a 9mm Browning stashed in his waistband without the luxury of a holster. He extended a hand the size of a baseball glove before waving me to a chair under a wanted poster on the wall with a surly face on it, a name and a message scrawled in marker pen: 'If you see him, kill him!'

'You've been busy,' I said, nodding at the window. 'What the hell happened?'

'Oh, some spliffed-up rude boys mounted a GPMG [general purposes machine gun] on that building across the road, and decided to wake us up.' Christ! The GPMG is a big bastard, and fires 7.62 bullets fed on a belt through it. This a serious weapon, and it normally takes two to handle it properly.

'Anybody hit in here?'

'None of us, but there's a body count outside.'

'I know, I've seen it.'

Having been to a Kingston mortuary on an earlier visit to Jamaica, and counted sixty black bodies and one white person laid out in the same room, I wasn't as shocked as I might have been at the carnage. 'Did you get them?'

'No. I'll pick them up one day.' He would, too.

I had to ask him. 'Tell me, Robert. Do you really shoot one person a day?'

He chuckled. 'So they say, and I'm not denying it.' He winked. 'If you really want to know, it's about four a week.' Then his face hardened. 'They're a shit to society. Someone's got to flush them down the pan – and put a lid on it. I'm the person the Lord has sent.'

I wasn't about to get involved in a religious debate. Wayne and I left the enlightened one, and the battlefield, and headed for the public records office on the harbour front for a final check. On the way we ran into my worst fear. Jamicans drive on the left, like us, and I was at the wheel when I felt Wayne suddenly tense beside me.

He quietly slid his gun out from his belt and rested it between his thighs, keeping his hand on it like a cat who has just spied a mouse – or possibly right now it was the other way round. 'Keep driving!' he said tersely.

That's when I saw them.

We had taken a narrow side street close to the main Victoria Hospital. Ahead were seven or eight young men, probably in their early twenties, armed to the teeth with assault rifles and sub-machine guns. Oil drums had been placed on either side in a makeshift road block, with baulks of timber on top. I'll be honest with you: seeing those guns I was scared, as in shitless. These kids had no compunction about adding us to the daily body count. They were there to rob us, alive or dead.

'Don't stop. Just carry on driving, and when I give the word – go for it!' We were in a white Nissan – and Christ, it had to be an automatic! Why not a manual? I was trying to get away in an automatic car. All my police training came back – and meant nothing now. '*Third gear, third gear. That's the most important gear to get acceleration. Now slam it into four as you go for them!*' Instead I just kept trundling forward, around 25 mph, moving up to 30.

head down together and went at it like a bat out of hell.

I went through the barrier with my head pressed down on the steering wheel, and felt the car hit first wood, then flesh. There was a crunch of bone and sudden piercing screams.

One body I struck hurtled sideways to the left, another came up over the bonnet and rolled over the roof before vanishing, a third may have gone under the car. But we were away with a screech of tyres, just as they opened up on us. Imagine being inside a drum with a dozen people banging with bars on the outside, then the buzz of angry insects as bullets fly past. That's what it felt like.

After that we called it a day and headed to the Chelsea Jerk Centre, a small Kingston no-frills eatery. My hands were shaking, and I could hardly hold the bottle of Red Stripe, let alone drink it. Strangely, apart from blood and dents, we couldn't find a single bullet hole on the car.

'Just about. Who do we have to see to report it?'

'No one. Forget it. You don't get too much of this in London, then?' He sounded genuinely surprised.

'No, I bloody don't.'

'How many people have you killed, Duncan?'

'Until today, none. I've drawn my gun three times and pointed it at people, but never pulled the trigger. How about you?'

'I have no idea.' He shrugged, thought about it, then shrugged again. 'No, no idea.'

'How old are you?'

'Twenty-two.'

It figured. In Wayne's world of law and disorder very few young men reached their thirties.

'I've had enough excitement for one day. I'm going back to finish my packing and have a few more beers. All I need now is for a welcoming party to be waiting for me back at the hotel.'

Wayne gave me a sideways grin, and tapped the Brownie in his pocket. 'There won't be,' he said. 'I meant to tell you. That contract was lifted last night.'

I flew home at the end of a week that had seen seven bodies, one ambush and a contract killer put to bed. Just an average week in Jamaica, the side the tourists never see.

London was going to seem pretty quiet after this.

EPILOGUE

Things were changing radically in the Met, and not necessarily for the better. Morale was at an all-time low. In 1997 the CID and all specialist departments were to be returned to uniform under a decision by the Commissioner, Sir Paul Condon. This included Mounted Police, the Air Support Unit (helicopters), Underwater Search Unit, even the Black Rats; all felt the sword of Damocles hanging over them. This idiotic policy would in fact be rescinded by the new Commissioner following Condon's retirement, but by then it was too late for me. I had already resigned.

I had a few problems of my own. I had lost my wife and kids. I'd had a run-in with the top brass and I'd been tipped off that my days were numbered. I'd had more than twenty good years, but now it was time to call it a day.

I lay immersed in the bath, while the water went from hot to tepid to hot again, idly turning the taps with my toes. In the corner by the towel rack stood the spaghetti jar which I'd had for years and which was a map of my career, reflected in the various soaps that filled it, all from hotels I had stayed in during operations abroad. There were soaps of many colours, from Los Angeles, New York, Washington, Dublin, Amsterdam, the Caribbean – Antigua, St Lucia, Dutch St Maartin, Barbados, and most memorably of all, Jamaica.

What does an ex-cop do to earn a crust?

My mobile, ringing.

And a voice from the past, a voice I trusted and hadn't heard since its owner turned his back on Hereford and went freelance. 'Duncan? Is your passport up to date? I've got a team together and we've got a job on. Fancy coming out to play?'

'Let me check my diary, Cass.'

And the game goes on.